Series on
PROSPERING IN A GLOBAL ECONOMY

Foreign Participation in U.S. Research and Development

Asset or Liability?

Proctor P. Reid and Alan Schriesheim, *Editors*

Committee on
Foreign Participation in U.S. Research and Development

NATIONAL ACADEMY OF ENGINEERING

NATIONAL ACADEMY PRESS
Washington, D.C.   1996

NATIONAL ACADEMY PRESS • 2101 Constitution Avenue, NW • Washington, DC 20418

NOTICE: The National Academy of Engineering was established in 1964 under the charter of the National Academy of Sciences as a parallel organization of outstanding engineers. It is autonomous in its administration and in the selection of its members, sharing with the National Academy of Sciences the responsibility for advising the federal government. The National Academy of Engineering also sponsors engineering programs aimed at meeting national needs, encourages education and research, and recognizes the superior achievements of engineers. Dr. Harold Liebowitz is president of the National Academy of Engineering.

This publication has been reviewed by a group other than the authors according to procedures approved by a National Academy of Engineering report review process.

Partial funding for this effort was provided by the Carnegie Corporation of New York and the National Academy of Engineering Technology Agenda Program.

Library of Congress Cataloging-in-Publication Data

Foreign participation in U.S. research and development : asset or
    liability? / Committee on Foreign Participation in U.S. Research and
    Development, National Academy of Engineering/Proctor P. Reid and Alan Schriesheim, editors.
        p. cm. — (Series on prospering in a global economy)
    Includes bibliographical references and index.
    ISBN 0-309-05095-2 (alk. paper)
      1. Investments, Foreign—United States. 2. Research, Industrial—
United States. I. National Academy of Engineering. Committee on
Foreign Participation in U.S. Research and Development. II. Series.
HG4910.F68   1995
332.6'73'0973—dc20   96-11026
                                     CIP

Printed in the United States of America

Committee on Foreign Participation in U.S. Research and Development

ALAN SCHRIESHEIM, *Chairman,* Director and CEO, Argonne National Laboratory
PETER BEARDMORE, Director, Chemical and Physical Sciences Laboratory, Ford Motor Company
SAMUEL H. FULLER, Vice President of Research, Digital Equipment Corporation
JOHN E. GRAY, Vice Chairman, Atlantic Council of the United States
KARL E. MARTERSTECK, President, ArrayComm, Inc., San Jose, California
JOEL MOSES, Provost, Massachusetts Institute of Technology
THOMAS J. MURRIN, Dean, A. J. Palumbo School of Business Administration, Duquesne University
ROBERT M. NEREM , Parker H. Petit Professor for Engineering in Medicine, School of Mechanical Engineering, Georgia Institute of Technology
C. KUMAR N. PATEL, Vice Chancellor, Research, University of California, Los Angeles
EDWIN P. PRZYBYLOWICZ, Director, Chester F. Carlson Center for Imaging Science, Rochester Institute of Technology
MAXINE L. SAVITZ, General Manager, Ceramic Components, AlliedSignal Aerospace Company
CHANG-LIN TIEN, Chancellor and A. Martin Berlin Professor, University of California, Berkeley

NAE Staff

PROCTOR P. REID, Study Director, Senior Program Officer
PENELOPE J. GIBBS, Administrative Assistant

Preface

The past 2 decades have witnessed rapid growth in the involvement of foreign nationals in U.S.-based research and development. By establishing or acquiring R&D performing companies in the United States, foreign companies have come to account for a significant share of privately funded U.S. R&D. Similarly, foreign firms, individual researchers, and students have become increasingly engaged in the publicly funded R&D activities of U.S. research universities and federal laboratories.

These developments have elicited a mixed response from U.S. policymakers and the American public. Concerned that unrestrained foreign access to U.S.-based R&D assets may weaken the nation's technology base, increase U.S. dependence on foreign sources of technology, undermine U.S. military strength, or shift jobs and profits away from the United States, some observers have called for public- and private-policy actions to slow or reverse the trend. Meanwhile, others extol the benefits of deepening foreign involvement in the nation's technology base to the nation's economy and military power, and urge policy actions designed to facilitate, or at least not impede, the internationalization of publicly and privately funded R&D.

Thus far, public debate regarding the nature and consequences of growing foreign participation in U.S. R&D has been highly polarized, driven largely by anecdotal reports and highly generalized arguments concerning the pros and cons of free international flows of trade, investment, and technology. The following consensus report, prepared by a committee of members of the National Academy of Engineering, seeks to improve public understanding of and policy responses to growing foreign R&D participation by documenting, measuring, and assessing the most important modes of foreign involvement in privately and publicly funded U.S. R&D activity. Based on its findings, the committee proposes specific actions to minimize the costs and maximize the benefits of this trend to U.S. citizens.

On behalf of the National Academy of Engineering, I would like to thank my fellow committee members for their considerable efforts related to the project. I also commend the NAE staff that supported the project for their professionalism and contributions to the study's success. Proctor P. Reid, Senior Program Officer with the NAE Program Office, directed and managed the project, helped elicit consensus among committee members, and drafted much of the report. Penelope J. Gibbs from the NAE Program Office provided critical administrative and logistical support for the project. Bruce R. Guile, director of the NAE Program Office, contributed valued intellectual stimulus to the project during its initial stages. Greg Pearson, the NAE's editor, was instrumental in preparing the report manuscript for final publication.

I would also like to extend the committee's thanks to all those from government, industry, and academia who contributed to the project. In particular, I want to express our appreciation to those who participated in the fact-finding roundtable held during the initial stages of the project (see Appendixes) and to others who briefed the committee.

Finally, I would like to express my appreciation to the Carnegie Corporation of New York for its generous support of this project and related elements of the National Academy of Engineering's multiyear program of symposia and committee studies on technology, trade, and economic growth.

Alan Schriesheim
Chairman

Contents

EXECUTIVE SUMMARY 1

1 INTRODUCTION 15
The New Wave of Foreign R&D Participation, 16
Calls for Public-Policy Action, 18
Foreign R&D Participation in Context, 19

2 THE CONTRIBUTION OF R&D TO U.S. ECONOMIC
DEVELOPMENT 29
Research and Development: A Simplified Taxonomy, 29
The Multiplicity of R&D Outputs, 30
The Political-Economic Logic of Publicly and Privately
Funded R&D, 31
R&D, Innovation, and National Economic Development, 32
How the Benefits of R&D Are Distributed at the National
and International Level, 34
Implications for the Assessment of Foreign Participation in
U.S. R&D, 35
Conclusion, 36

3 FOREIGN PARTICIPATION IN PRIVATELY FUNDED
U.S. R&D 39
The Causes of Growing Foreign Participation, 40
Foreign Direct Investment, 42

International Corporate Alliances, 56
Opportunities and Risks, 58
Summary, 81

4   FOREIGN PARTICIPATION IN PUBLICLY FUNDED
    U.S. R&D 90
    University-Based Research, 91
    Foreign Participation in U.S. Federal Laboratory R&D, 112
    Foreign Participation in Recent Federal Industrial
        Technology Initiatives, 116
    The Implications of Foreign Participation in Publicly Funded
        U.S. R&D, 118
    Summary, 129

5   FINDINGS AND RECOMMENDATIONS 140
    R&D and Economic Performance, 141
    Foreign Participation in Privately Funded U.S. R&D:
        Findings, 142
    Foreign Participation in Privately Funded U.S. R&D:
        Recommendations, 145
    Foreign Participation in Publicly Funded U.S. R&D:
        Findings, 147
    Foreign Participation in Publicly Funded U.S. R&D:
        Recommendations, 151
    Changing Perceptions and Their Implications, 156

REFERENCES 159

COMMITTEE AND STAFF BIOGRAPHIES 172

APPENDIXES
    Agenda 181
    Participants 183

INDEX 185

Foreign Participation in U.S. Research and Development

Asset or Liability?

Executive Summary

This report examines the recent growth of involvement by foreign nationals—companies and individuals—in U.S.-based research and development (R&D). It assesses the consequences of this trend for U.S. economic performance and national security, draws conclusions, and recommends specific public- and private-sector actions to minimize the potential liabilities and maximize the potential benefits of increasing foreign participation in the nation's R&D enterprise. Proceeding from a belief that foreign participation in publicly funded U.S. R&D is governed by a different political-economic logic than foreign involvement in privately funded U.S. R&D, the report evaluates separately these two integrally related halves of the trend.[1]

ASSESSING FOREIGN PARTICIPATION IN U.S. R&D

The recent growth of foreign participation in U.S.-based R&D should be viewed in the context of two broad trends in the international economy. The first is a move toward deeper integration of the world's major national innovation systems[2] through the activities of multinational companies and individual scientists and engineers. The second, its corollary, is a convergence of the industrial and technological capabilities of industrialized countries. The committee is convinced that these trends, which have fueled the recent growth of foreign participation in U.S. R&D, will continue apace into the next century.

Many U.S. trading partners have long had significant levels of foreign corporate involvement in their domestic R&D activities. Indeed, U.S.-owned multinational companies have been the leading foreign participants in many of these

1

countries' national innovation systems. By contrast, the United States has had relatively less foreign participation in its domestic R&D enterprise. To be sure, foreign companies, scientists, and engineers have been attracted to the United States for decades, drawn by the size, wealth, and sophistication of the U.S. domestic market, by the strength of the U.S. basic research enterprise, and by the United States' unrivaled capacity for spawning new industries and products. Only recently, however, have a growing number of America's trading partners acquired the technical and economic capabilities needed for their citizens (companies and individuals) to participate on a significant scale in the U.S. research system.

R&D AND ECONOMIC PERFORMANCE

To assess the consequences of foreign participation in the U.S. R&D enterprise, it is essential to understand both the nature of R&D activity and how it contributes to economic development.

First, R&D activity yields many valuable outputs, and the benefits associated with them accrue to many individuals other than those who perform the R&D or own the intellectual property.

Second, in spite of the global communications revolution and the expansion of multinational enterprises, effective transfer of knowledge and technology—both within and among institutions—continues to demand the intensive and ongoing face-to-face interaction of highly trained scientists and engineers.

Third, because of the many barriers that impede the transfer of knowledge and technology, R&D activities tend to cluster geographically, and a large share of the benefits of R&D appear to be highly localized.

Fourth, in order to draw effectively upon advanced technological capabilities and R&D outputs beyond its institutional boundaries, a company generally needs to be performing R&D at a level commensurate with that of the organizations whose R&D activities it hopes to exploit.

Finally, neither R&D capability nor technological wealth is in and of itself a reliable indicator of the economic or competitive strength of a company or a nation. Rather, economic and competitive strength are determined by how effectively technology is used and managed in combination with other factors of production and marketing, such as labor, capital, and managerial and organizational capabilities. Similarly, the economic or other societal returns a nation may gain from a particular R&D investment depend on whether its innovation system can foster widespread diffusion and effective use of the outputs generated. These factors are, in turn, influenced by the quality (skill level) of a nation's work force, by the size, wealth, and technological sophistication of its domestic market, and increasingly by the ability of firms within its borders to access markets and technology abroad.

What these observations suggest is that for foreign nationals, the task of appropriating the many valuable outputs of U.S.-based R&D activity is significantly more complex and difficult than is generally assumed. Therefore, foreign-owned firms that wish to effectively exploit advanced technology and knowledge generated in the United States must establish a significant, technologically sophisticated presence here to do so. Moreover, increases in foreign participants' level of technological sophistication and capacity to extract benefits from American technology bring concomitant increases in the potential for reciprocal transfers of knowledge and technology to the United States. Finally, these observations suggest that under most circumstances, any country, including the United States, should welcome R&D activity within its borders regardless of the nationality of the R&D performer. If a large share of the returns from R&D investments are captured by those proximate to the R&D activity, and these returns are indeed considered desirable, clearly it is better to have R&D performed within one's borders than beyond them.

FOREIGN PARTICIPATION IN PRIVATELY FUNDED U.S. R&D: FINDINGS

Foreign participation in privately funded U.S. R&D has increased in the last decade through both direct investment (predominantly the acquisition of U.S.-based companies)[3] and intercorporate technical alliances (Figure ES-1). No single

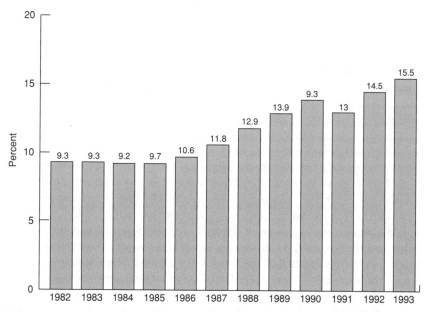

FIGURE ES-1 R&D spending by U.S. affiliates of foreign-owned firms as a percentage of all privately funded U.S. R&D, 1982-1993. SOURCE: National Science Board (1993); National Science Foundation (1995b); and U.S. Department of Commerce (1995).

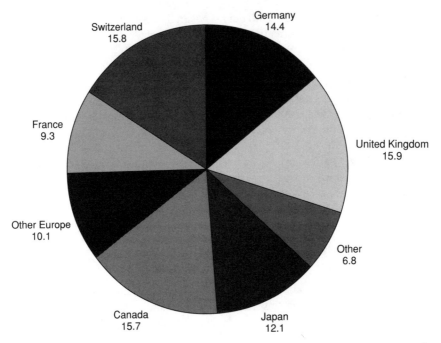

FIGURE ES-2 R&D spending by U.S. affiliates of foreign-owned firms, percent of total, by nationality of owner, 1992. SOURCE: U.S. Department of Commerce (1995).

country dominates the field of foreign investors in U.S. privately funded R&D. However, since the mid-1980s, the U.S. affiliates[4] of Japanese-owned companies have increased their share of R&D spending more rapidly than the affiliates of any other major investing country (Figure ES-2). Nearly two-thirds of all foreign-funded industrial R&D in the United States is concentrated in a small number of high-technology industries[5] (Figure ES-3).

For the most part, foreign parent companies have invested in U.S.-based high-technology in areas in which they have a strong export position or perceived competitive advantage. Foreigners become involved in American privately funded R&D for two basic reasons: to serve customers in this country better and to gain better access to American scientific and technological expertise. Most major foreign-owned R&D facilities are located near major U.S. centers of R&D activity, and most affiliate R&D performed in the United States appears designed to meet the immediate technical needs of U.S.-based production facilities. Comparative surveys of U.S.- and foreign-owned multinational companies suggest that the motives for engaging in R&D in foreign markets and the type of R&D activity vary by industry but are not significantly influenced by the nationality of the company.

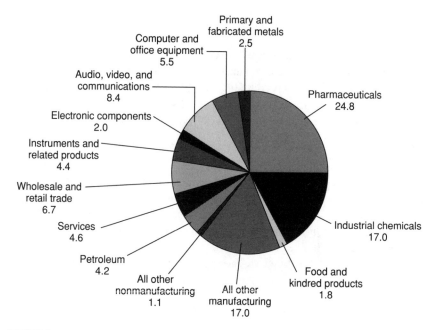

FIGURE ES-3 R&D spending by U.S. affiliates of foreign-owned firms, percent of total, by industry, 1992. SOURCE: U.S. Department of Commerce (1995).

Consequences for the United States

Growing foreign involvement in the nation's industrial R&D base brings with it costs and risks as well as benefits and opportunities for U.S. citizens.

The Quid Pro Quo

It is not possible to say definitively whether foreign companies take away more technology and associated economic value than they contribute to the United States through their participation in U.S. industrial R&D. Overall, however, with some variation among industries, the data suggest that the U.S. affiliates of foreign-owned firms import significantly more codified technology from their parent companies than they export to them or to unaffiliated firms abroad. In some cases, foreign acquisition of U.S. high-technology companies has undoubtedly resulted in lost opportunities and foregone wealth for U.S. citizens. The same may be said of situations in which foreign firms establish new high-tech facilities in the United States. Yet, in other cases, these two modes of foreign direct investment have created opportunity and wealth for Americans. On balance, the committee considers the growth of foreign direct investment in the United States and the proliferation of transnational corporate alliances to be positive trends—developments that enhance the productivity and wealth of the United States and its overseas trade and investment partners. Furthermore, the committee believes that foreign participation in privately funded U.S. R&D cannot be separated meaningfully from the larger trends in which it is embedded, particularly the internationalization of industrial production, in which the U.S. multinationals have played a leading role.

Asymmetries of Access

The difficulties U.S. companies have experienced trying to access markets and innovation systems abroad have had a profound effect on public perceptions and federal policies related to foreign participation in R&D. Direct investment is the most important way U.S. companies can gain access to privately funded R&D activities abroad. During the past decade, the policies of America's trade partners that govern such investment have come to resemble the more liberal policies of the United States. Nevertheless, barriers to access remain in some major economies.

Threats to National Security

Current U.S. security regulations and procedures appear to prevent most illegal transfers of militarily sensitive U.S. technology abroad by foreign-owned companies. However, they are less effective at addressing the medium- to long-term risks of delayed or denied access to militarily critical technologies posed by foreign direct investment, or mergers and acquisitions in general. The federal government lacks clearly defined, agreed-upon criteria to determine whether the technological capabilities of a company are militarily critical. This makes it very difficult to identify niche sectors where the risks of delayed or denied access may be particularly high. Furthermore, monitoring efforts and methodologies used to enforce U.S. antitrust laws may be inadequate to address the monopoly threat posed by mergers, acquisitions, and corporate alliances in niche defense markets, whether instigated by foreign- or U.S.-owned companies.

The Threat of Technological Monopolies

There is little evidence to suggest that growing foreign involvement in U.S. industrial R&D—through direct investment and alliances—has had a significant deleterious effect on the ability of U.S.-based companies to obtain key technologies, components, and subsystems required to make internationally competitive products. Many high-technology industries are already highly concentrated at the national and global levels. Hence, some of the many recent mergers, acquisitions, and alliances have probably fostered anticompetitive behavior in particular civilian high-technology industries. Here again, current enforcement of U.S. antitrust law may be inadequate to address attendant monopoly risks in particular industries. However, at present, there is no evidence to suggest that foreign firms are any more likely to engage in anticompetitive activity in the United States than their U.S.-owned counterparts.

FOREIGN PARTICIPATION IN PRIVATELY FUNDED U.S. R&D: RECOMMENDATIONS

The principal policy questions raised by foreign direct investment in U.S. industrial R&D cannot be separated from the nation's broader foreign economic policy agenda. The committee's first two recommendations recognize this linkage.

1. In the absence of clear threats to national security, Congress should avoid legislating restrictions on foreign participation in privately funded U.S. R&D.

The committee believes that discriminatory treatment of foreign-owned firms, except in situations where national security is threatened, imposes significant economic costs and risks on Americans. Such behavior discourages foreign direct investment in the United States and undermines longtime efforts by the United States to secure nondiscriminatory, or "national," treatment of its companies in foreign markets. The committee also cautions the federal government against invoking without good cause national security as a justification for restricting foreign participation in the nation's industrial R&D enterprise.

2. The federal government should continue to seek to open foreign markets to U.S. trade and investment through negotiation in bilateral and multilateral forums. The United States should hold itself and its trading partners accountable to existing international agreements and should redouble its efforts to negotiate more comprehensive, internationally enforceable rules on monopoly formation, foreign direct investment, technical standards, environmental regulations, and intellectual property rights. Above all, the United States should reaffirm its long-standing commitment to the principles of national treatment and transparency, or full disclosure of terms, in policies that influence international investment and trade flows.

Barriers to investment that result from structural- and policy-related differences among national economies remain a source of friction between the United States and some of its major trading partners. Negotiations to reduce these obstacles have been difficult and slow. Nevertheless, the committee believes that the United States' commitment to address these issues in international forums continues to serve the nation's best economic interests. Unilateral measures that contradict the principles of nondiscrimination and transparency are, in the opinion of the committee, likely to do more harm than good by discouraging more "good" foreign investment in the United States than "bad" and undercutting rather than strengthening the position of the United States in bilateral and multilateral negotiations. Therefore, the committee urges the federal government to resist pressures to force the pace of these negotiations with aggressive unilateral actions beyond those currently provided for in U.S. law.

FOREIGN PARTICIPATION IN PUBLICLY FUNDED U.S. R&D: FINDINGS

Foreign involvement in publicly funded U.S. R&D has also grown in recent years. Government surveys of the number of foreign graduate students, postdoctoral researchers, and other visiting researchers at U.S. universities and federal laboratories document a significant increase in the level of foreign participation since the mid-1970s (Figure ES-4). At the same time, meaningful data on the scope, growth, and nature of foreign institutions' involvement in publicly funded U.S. research is fragmentary, dated, and scarce. Available information suggests that foreign institutions account for a very small share (less than 2 percent) of all sponsored research at U.S. universities and federal laboratories and that investment is concentrated in a small number of U.S. institutions. As of the mid-1980s,

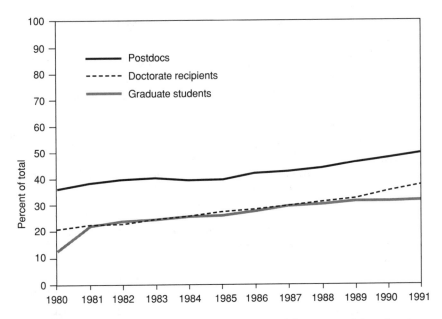

FIGURE ES-4   Foreign graduate students, postdocs, and doctorate recipients in science and engineering. SOURCE: National Science Foundation (1993a).

most foreign-sponsored research at U.S. universities was funded by not-for-profit institutions and was mostly in agriculture, medicine, and geology. There are no recent aggregate data on the current magnitude, disciplinary focus, and national shares of foreign-sponsored research at U.S. universities and federal laboratories. Nevertheless, recent survey data and anecdotal evidence indicate that Japanese companies are more diligent than their U.S. or European counterparts with regard to accessing, monitoring, and drawing upon the research capabilities of these institutions. Foreign participation has been minimal in recent federally supported industrial R&D initiatives, such as the Department of Commerce's Advanced Technology Program.

Consequences for the United States

As with privately funded U.S. R&D, the involvement of foreign firms and individuals in R&D sponsored by the federal government carries both risks and opportunities for the United States.

The Quid Pro Quo

The committee believes that the extensive presence of foreign graduate students, postdoctoral researchers, and other long-term foreign visiting researchers at U.S. universities and federal laboratories has, on balance, yielded significant benefits to the U.S. economy and its innovation system.

At the same time, although it could identify various costs and benefits of foreign institutional involvement in publicly supported U.S. research institutions, the committee was unable to determine their net economic impact. Its analysis found examples in which foreign-owned firms have profited, at times at the expense of U.S. firms and stakeholders. However, numerous cases also confirm that foreign firms have contributed both material support, technology, and intellectual resources to research universities and federal laboratories. Indeed, many if not most foreign-owned companies with extensive ties to U.S. publicly funded research institutions tend to have U.S.-based manufacturing and R&D operations. These operations employ Americans, buy from U.S. suppliers and equipment vendors, import and generate technology and know-how that is applied within the U.S. economy, and pay U.S. taxes.

Asymmetries of Access

Access by U.S. institutions and individuals to publicly funded R&D in other nations varies considerably. U.S. government, academic, and industrial researchers appear to have few problems accessing publicly funded research capabilities and activities within academic and government-operated laboratories abroad. Furthermore, access by U.S.-owned companies to government-funded industrial research consortia in Europe appears to be comparable to that extended foreign-owned firms in the United States. Japan, however, has restricted foreign participation in its publicly funded industrial R&D consortia to a greater extent than either the United States or the European Community.

International Burden-Sharing in Basic Research

The committee believes there needs to be a more equitable global distribution of support for basic research. International comparisons of R&D expenditures confirm that compared to the United States, most of America's advanced industrialized trading partners invest an equal if not larger share of their gross domestic product in basic research. Japan, however, despite recent efforts to expand its basic research capabilities, spends a smaller share of its gross domestic product in this area than the United States (and nearly half as much per capita).

FOREIGN PARTICIPATION IN PUBLICLY FUNDED U.S. R&D: RECOMMENDATIONS

Foreign participation in R&D funded by the U.S. government is regulated by a patchwork of confusing—and at times contradictory—bilateral intergovernmental agreements, eligibility requirements in recent federal R&D legislation, and agency directives. In the committee's judgment, leading U.S. research universities and federal laboratories have generally made good faith efforts to comply with federally mandated economic performance and reciprocity requirements. Nevertheless, the committee believes that these requirements may impede the ability of agencies to perform their primary missions as well as diminish the contribution of federal R&D programs to U.S. economic performance and competitiveness. Even worse, they may impose significant economic costs on the United States. Recommendations 3 through 5, directed at the federal government, are aimed at reducing the risks of these adverse outcomes and laying the foundation for more effective, mutually beneficial management of foreign participation in government-funded R&D in all industrialized countries.

Institutions that conduct R&D supported by the federal government should recognize that concerns about foreign involvement are more than a public relations problem. The actions of a limited number of American institutions have evoked legitimate concerns about the fairness and economic logic of certain types of foreign participation in publicly subsidized U.S. R&D activity. The committee urges universities and other performers of publicly funded research to address these concerns. Recommendations 6 through 8, directed at the performers of publicly funded U.S. R&D, outline steps these institutions might take to both become more credible and effective spokesmen for the costs and benefits of foreign participation and to make a larger, more constructive contribution to the public policy debate on this issue.

3. Federal agencies charged with administering public R&D resources should be empowered and encouraged to implement with greater flexibility the economic performance requirements embodied in recent federal R&D legislation. This should be done in a manner that is consistent with the core missions of the agencies involved, the realities of competitive corporate R&D practice, and the principles of national treatment and transparency.

Mission agencies now are being called upon to contribute more directly to U.S. economic growth and competitiveness through their R&D activities. To be successful, these agencies must become more adept at balancing this new charge with their core missions in a manner that is consistent with the opportunities and constraints of an increasingly interdependent world economy. This imperative demands strong interagency policy guidance. Such guidance should remind policymakers and the general public of the complex, highly case-specific calculus involved in the implementation of economic performance requirements. The need for flexibility, discretion, and decentralized decisionmaking in the implementation process should be emphasized.

4. Congress should strike reciprocity requirements from existing laws governing federal R&D spending and exclude them from future R&D legislation. Instead, the federal government should pursue more aggressively reciprocal access to publicly and privately funded R&D activities abroad through U.S. trade and antitrust laws, existing bilateral and multilateral trade and technology agreements, and the negotiation of more comprehensive bilateral and multilateral agreements.

The committee considers the potential benefits of reciprocity requirements to be small and more than offset by the costs and risks they entail. Such requirements contradict stated U.S. foreign economic policy objectives, undercut U.S. efforts to persuade other nations to move toward unconditional nondiscriminatory treatment, and encourage U.S. trading partners to introduce similar requirements. The lack of clear compliance standards makes these requirements very difficult to administer and exposes federal agencies and foreign companies alike to political and legal challenges. The committee believes that there are more promising unilateral, bilateral, and multilateral avenues for increasing U.S. access to both publicly and privately funded R&D in other nations. To strengthen the hand of U.S. negotiators at the international level as well as facilitate enforcement of existing international agreements concerning mutual access to government-funded R&D, an agency of the federal government should be tasked by Congress with monitoring and periodically reporting on U.S. access to government-sponsored R&D in other nations.

5. The federal government should continue to seek more equitable international sharing of the basic research burden through the negotiation of bilateral science and technology agreements, the development of government-to-

government international research consortia, and other mechanisms that foster international R&D collaboration.

The U.S. government should continue to encourage Japan and other nations to assume roles in the global basic research enterprise that are commensurate with their industrial, technological, economic, and diplomatic standing in the world. To facilitate this process, the U.S. government should expand its support of international public- and private-sector collaboration in areas of basic and precompetitive applied research. This can be done through bilateral science and technology agreements and through international research programs such as the Human Genome Project and the Intelligent Manufacturing Systems Initiative. Furthermore, the committee is convinced that the strength of the U.S. basic research system is closely linked to its openness. Efforts to restrict or artificially increase the cost of foreign access to U.S. basic research capabilities that might damage the U.S. research enterprise should be avoided.

6. The National Academies' Government-University-Industry Research Roundtable (GUIRR) should take the lead in promoting the exchange of information and "good practices" among the nation's leading research universities concerning their relations with foreign-owned firms, foreign governments, and other foreign institutions.

7. All institutions that perform federally funded R&D should have adequate procedures in place to manage effectively intellectual property resulting from publicly funded R&D. To assist U.S. universities and the federal government in this regard, the National Academies' Government-University-Industry Research Roundtable (GUIRR) should work with the Association of University Technology Managers (AUTM) and other appropriate organizations to develop and distribute good practices and general guidelines for the nation's academic research enterprise.

8. U.S. research universities and federal laboratories should expand efforts to establish quid pro quo with all foreign institutions that perform R&D. This might include increased exchange of scientific and engineering personnel.

CHANGING PERCEPTIONS AND THEIR IMPLICATIONS

It is the sense of the committee that many of the circumstances that have helped skew public discourse and policy in the United States toward a near-exclusive focus on the costs, risks, and asymmetries of foreign participation in the U.S. R&D enterprise over the last decade are changing. The widespread perception of the mid- to late 1980s that many American companies were less effective than their foreign competitors at harnessing the output of research generated in this country for commercial advantage is giving way to a more balanced view.

There is now a spirit of cautious optimism about the continuously improving technology management and competitive capabilities of many U.S. industries. Recent state, federal, and university initiatives—fostering R&D collaboration and more effective use and diffusion of technology and know-how relevant to industry—may have also contributed to a more positive view of the nation's industrial future.

At the same time, new concerns are emerging: the weak growth of industrial R&D in the United States, the contraction of basic and long-term applied research based in industry, and the implications of defense conversion for the nation's R&D system. It is uncertain how these concerns or the nascent optimism regarding U.S. competitiveness will influence how the public regards foreign participation in U.S. R&D. Regardless of how public perceptions evolve, in the committee's view, the conclusions and recommendations contained in this report will remain a useful guide to policy-making.

NOTES

1. Although some R&D activities in the United States are supported by a mix of public- and private-sector funding (both direct and indirect), the vast majority are financed predominantly through either public- or private-sector sources.

Privately funded R&D is directed at the generation, assimilation, and application of knowledge and technology to advance the economic interests of stakeholders in the company making the investment. In market economies, it is generally accepted that under most circumstances, private companies should be allowed to dispose of the products of their R&D investments as they see fit. In contrast, publicly funded R&D and its proprietary and nonproprietary outputs are viewed as public property to be used to advance specific U.S. national interests. For the most part, institutions that conduct or use the outputs of publicly funded R&D are subjected to greater public scrutiny than those that conduct or use the outputs of privately funded R&D.

Since only a small fraction of privately funded U.S. R&D is accounted for by private noncommercial/nonprofit organizations, the term "privately funded R&D" is used throughout the report as a synonym for company-funded R&D.

2. A national innovation system is defined by Patel and Pavitt (1994) as "the national institutions, their incentive structures and their competencies, that determine the rate and direction of technological learning (or the volume and composition of change-generating activities) in a country."

3. The U.S. government defines foreign direct investment as the ownership by a foreign person or business of 10 percent or more of the voting equity of a company located in the United States. A 10 percent or more equity interest is considered evidence of a long-term interest in, and a measure of influence over, the management of the company. New foreign direct investment can take two forms— the acquisition of an existing company or the establishment of a new company. (U.S. Department of Commerce, 1991)

4. A U.S. affiliate of a foreign-owned firm is a company located in the United States in which a foreign person or business has a "controlling" stake (i.e., 10 percent or more of the company's voting equity).

5. There are several legitimate methods for identifying high-technology industries. All rely on some calculation of R&D intensity (typically, R&D expenditures and/or numbers of technical people divided by industry value added or sales). This report draws on data gathered by the U.S. Department of Commerce and the Organization for Economic Cooperation and Development (OECD). The two organizations use different yet comparable definitions of high-technology industries.

The OECD classification of "high-intensity technology products" relies on directly applied R&D expenditures and includes those products with above-average R&D intensities. Direct R&D expenditures are those made by the firms in the product group. The OECD classifies the following industries as high tech: drugs and medicines (ISIC 3522); office machinery, computers (ISIC 3825); electrical machinery (ISIC 383 less 3832); electronic components (ISIC 3832); aerospace (ISIC 3845); and scientific instruments (ISIC 385).

The Department of Commerce definition of high-technology products (DOC-3 high-technology products) includes products that have significantly higher ratios of direct and indirect R&D expenditures to shipments than do other product groups. Direct R&D expenditures are those made by the firms in the product group. Indirect R&D describes the R&D content of input products. The DOC-3 industries include guided missiles and spacecraft (SIC 376); communication equipment and electronic components (SIC 365-367); aircraft and parts (SIC 372); office, computing, and accounting machines (SIC 357); ordnance and accessories (SIC 348); drugs and medicines (SIC 283); industrial inorganic chemicals (SIC 281); professional and scientific instruments (SIC 38 less 3825); engines, turbines, and parts (SIC 351); and plastic materials and synthetic resins, rubber, and fibers (SIC 282).

Comparisons of U.S. production data for high-intensity technology products, as reported to the OECD, with U.S. total shipment data for high-technology products—as reported to the Department of Commerce, according to DOC-3 definition—show that the OECD data represented 96 percent and 100 percent of the DOC-3 data in 1980 and 1986, respectively (National Science Board, 1989).

1

Introduction

The history of foreign involvement in the development of the U.S. economy and its technology base is as old as the Republic itself. A relative latecomer to industrialization, the United States rose swiftly to world industrial leadership during the latter half of the nineteenth and the early twentieth centuries by drawing heavily on technology, talent, and capital from abroad. The chemical industry, today one of the central pillars of the U.S. industrial research and development (R&D) enterprise, was built on technologies licensed from the leading German chemical manufacturers. First-generation immigrants such as Steinmetz, Tesla, Bell, and Berliner provided critical intellectual capital to the nascent electrical manufacturing and telephone industries. European investors financed the development of America's railroads and helped launch a number of major U.S. industries.

By the end of World War I, the United States had become the world's foremost industrial power. Nevertheless, the American economy continued to draw heavily on European science and technology through the end of World War II. The immigration of leading European scientists and engineers to the United States during and after the two world wars was instrumental in laying the foundation for postwar U.S. leadership in virtually all major areas of scientific and engineering research.

The 1950s and 1960s brought the consolidation of American leadership in the development and application of civilian and military technology, as well as a newfound preeminence in basic science and engineering research. During this period, the role of foreign participation in the U.S. domestic economy and R&D enterprise diminished. Europe and other parts of the industrialized and industrializing world continued to provide the U.S. economy with a modest stream of immigrant scientists and engineers, as well as graduate students in science and engineering. However, their numbers were dwarfed by an explosion in the supply of U.S.-born entrants into the system. U.S. multinational companies emerged as major forces in the transfer of technology and know-how from the United States to foreign economies. Yet, foreign direct investment[1] in U.S. manufacturing and foreign participation in U.S. industrial R&D remained insignificant.

This situation began to change in the 1970s, as technological and economic power became more evenly distributed among a growing number of industrialized countries and as markets became increasingly international. At the hands of an expanding population of U.S., European, and Asian multinational companies, the economies and innovation systems[2] of all industrialized nations, including the United States, became deeply interconnected.

THE NEW WAVE OF FOREIGN R&D PARTICIPATION

During the past decade, foreign participation in U.S. R&D has expanded rapidly. By both establishing and acquiring R&D-intensive businesses in the United States, foreign-owned companies have more than doubled their share of total privately funded U.S. R&D since 1980, accounting for over 14 percent in 1992. In the process, foreign companies and their U.S. subsidiaries have established extensive links with U.S. industrial, academic, and public-sector R&D performers through an array of alliances, joint ventures, personnel exchanges, and other collaborative arrangements. The same period has brought a significant expansion in the number of short-term and extended visits by foreign researchers to U.S. government laboratories, research universities, and other research facilities. U.S. research universities, in particular, have become increasingly dependent on foreign students, postdoctoral fellows, and faculty in most fields of scientific and engineering research and advanced education.

A Poorly Understood Phenomenon

The trend toward deepening foreign involvement in U.S. research and development has drawn a mixed response from the American R&D community, policymakers, and the general public. Those who regard the trend as a positive corollary to the expanding involvement of U.S.-owned companies in national markets and innovation systems abroad emphasize the mutual gains to the U.S. economy and the foreign individuals and companies involved. Foreign individuals and firms gain access to U.S. R&D organizations and the new knowledge, technology, and creative research methods they impart. In exchange, they contribute their own intellectual, organizational, and material resources—including knowledge, technology, and know-how—that strengthen the U.S. innovation system and enhance its contribution to U.S. economic development. From this perspective, foreign participation in U.S. R&D offers an increasingly important window on expanding industrial and technological competence abroad—an opportunity that many believe should be exploited more effectively by the U.S. public and private sectors (Florida, 1995; Graham, 1992; Graham and Krugman, 1991, 1995; Kenney and Florida, 1993b; Mowery and Teece, 1993; National Research Council, 1976). Yet, many Americans look upon the growth of foreign participation in U.S. R&D as a net economic liability for the country. From this perspective, foreign-owned firms and the nations in which they are based are poaching the returns on investment by U.S. citizens in the world's most open and productive research enterprise. Moreover, many believe foreign firms are taking unfair advantage of this openness to target technological capabilities of critical importance to U.S. economic security and development with the intention of controlling them and the future revenue streams they promise.

Further, many believe, in contrast to the situation in the United States, that U.S. access to foreign markets and R&D capabilities, particularly those of its foremost competitor, Japan, is considerably circumscribed. Indeed, some observers argue that barriers to U.S. exports and investment abroad have caused U.S. multinational companies to engage in the large-scale transfer of U.S. R&D assets and U.S.-generated technology to other countries. According to this view, foreign nations have erected structural or policy barriers that in effect "extort" U.S. technology and R&D assets in return for improved access to that country's markets. Given the perceived predatory behavior of many foreign firms and the lack of reciprocal market access, critics of foreign participation in U.S. R&D have called for private actions and public policies to stem or contain the tide (Glickman and Woodward, 1989; Spencer, 1991; Tolchin, 1993; U.S. Congress, House, 1989; U.S. Congress, Office of Technology Assessment, 1994).

Despite the intensity of debate surrounding this issue, neither experts nor the public has more than a limited understanding of the many different types of foreign participation in the nation's technology enterprise. Nor is there an appreciation for the forces driving such activity or its economic consequences. Indeed, the information necessary to understand the situation is hard to come by. There are data that document incompletely the R&D spending of U.S. affiliates of foreign firms, the number, size, and activities of their U.S.-based R&D facilities, and the extent and nature of foreign involvement in U.S. research universities and federal laboratories. To date, however, no systematic effort has been made to collect comprehensive data on foreign involvement in U.S.-based R&D activities, and only a few attempts have been made to develop more detailed, qualitative assessments of various modes of foreign R&D participation and their long-term costs and benefits to U.S. economic development.[3]

The lack of useful data, however, is only part of the problem. Many of the policy issues deriving from foreign participation in U.S. R&D are poorly defined. In part, this stems from the widespread confusion about the nature of R&D, how it contributes to technological innovation and national economic development in general, and how the multiple economically valuable outputs of R&D are transferred domestically and internationally. More confusion arises from the generally poor understanding of the profound differences in the structure, organization, strengths, and weaknesses of major national innovation systems, and of the implications these differences have for economic and technological relations between nations (Ergas, 1987; Imai, 1990; National Research Council, 1989a, b, 1990; Nelson, 1993). Further clouding the picture is the fact that many of the issues raised by foreign participation in U.S. research and development are deeply entangled—rightly or wrongly—with U.S. foreign economic policy and the future goals and organization of the U.S. research enterprise.

CALLS FOR PUBLIC-POLICY ACTION

As foreign involvement in U.S. research continues to expand, pressure for public-policy limits on such involvement is likely to intensify—with or without a thorough assessment of the costs and benefits to the United States. American research universities and nonprofit research institutes that are supported heavily by tax dollars have come under heavy criticism from members of Congress and the public for providing foreign-owned firms and their U.S. affiliates with access to academic research facilities, personnel, and research results through industrial liaison programs, technology licensing agreements, and contract research (U.S. Congress, House, 1989). Moreover, some within Congress and other parts of the public policy community argue that the U.S. government should rethink the procedures by which it monitors, evaluates, and regulates prospective foreign acquisitions of U.S. companies in "strategic" R&D-intensive sectors (Gaster, 1992; Glickman and Woodward, 1989; Spencer, 1991; Tolchin, 1993).

To date, federal attempts to regulate foreign participation in U.S. R&D in areas other than national security have focused on prospective foreign involvement in publicly funded[4] civilian R&D activities—chiefly university-based research and research conducted in federal laboratories and as part of government-sponsored collaborative R&D initiatives. Recent federal initiatives to provide limited direct support of precommercial industrial R&D (e.g., the Semiconductor Manufacturing Technology Consortium [SEMATECH], the National Science Foundation's Engineering Research Center program, the Advanced Technology Program [ATP] within the Department of Commerce, and the multiagency Technology Reinvestment Project [TRP]) have included restrictions on foreign-firm participation.[5]

Eligibility criteria for foreign participation in publicly funded U.S. R&D have been designed to ensure that most of the resulting intellectual property and associated economic value remain in the United States and that the home governments of foreign firms offer reciprocal access to similar publicly subsidized R&D initiatives.[6] Advocates of more aggressive management of foreign participation in U.S. publicly and privately funded R&D propose prohibiting foreign firms from licensing technology developed in U.S. government laboratories or publicly funded research universities or industrial consortia, more extensive screening of foreign direct investment, or requiring foreign firms to either exploit or license their technologies within the United States.

FOREIGN R&D PARTICIPATION IN CONTEXT

To appreciate the intensity as well as the nature of the public debate about the growth of foreign involvement in U.S.-based R&D activities, three changes in the global economic and technological environment must be considered.

First Among Equals in an Integrated Global Economy

The first major challenge to the U.S. innovation system derives from a shift, which has accelerated in recent decades, in the relative economic and technological strength of the United States compared with its trading partners. Twenty years ago, the preeminence and comparative self-sufficiency of the U.S. economy and national innovation system were taken for granted. Today, however, technological and economic power are much more evenly distributed among North America, the Pacific Rim, and the European Community. Moreover, the economies and innovation systems of all industrialized nations, including the United States, are now deeply interconnected (National Academy of Engineering, 1993).

Comparisons of national trends in R&D investment, patenting, scientific and engineering literature citations, high-technology production and trade,[7] and productivity growth all document a rapid increase in the ability of America's trading partners—above all Japan—to develop, absorb, and effectively exploit new knowledge and technology worldwide (Table 1.1). Likewise, the rapid expansion of international trade, foreign direct investment, and transnational corporate alliances during the past decade attests to the significant internationalization of industrial production and its associated advanced technical activities (Figure 1.1).

Overall, the internationalization of industrial R&D activity has lagged behind that of industrial production, marketing, and component sourcing. In some countries and industries, the internationalization of the entire value-added chain is proceeding more rapidly than in others. Foreign penetration of the U.S. economy and R&D enterprise has been particularly rapid in recent years, albeit starting from a relatively low base compared with foreign participation in the R&D systems of other nations. Today, foreign-controlled firms account for significantly larger shares of manufacturing output and employment in Germany, France, the United Kingdom, and Canada than they do in the United States (Table 1.2). As a share of total private R&D spending, R&D spending by foreign-owned affiliates in Europe and the United States is roughly equivalent. In Japan, by contrast, foreign penetration of the economy and industrial R&D base through foreign direct investment has remained insignificant compared with other industrialized countries (U.S. Congress, Office of Technology Assessment, 1994).

TABLE 1.1 Recent Shifts in the Balance of Technological Strength Among Industrial Nations: Selected Industries and Countries, 1970, 1981, and 1991

	R&D expenditures as a percentage of GDP			Share of U.S. Patenting			Shares of OECD[a] High-Tech Production			Shares of OECD[a] High-Tech Exports		
	1970	1980	1991	1970	1980	1991	1970	1980	1991	1970	1980	1991
United States	2.6	2.3	2.6	73.1	60.4	53.0	50.9	40.4	36.2	28.3	26.9	19.0
Japan	1.8	2.2	3.0	4.1	11.5	21.8	15.6	18.4	28.3	12.1	9.7	22.6
Germany[b]	2.1	2.4	2.8	6.9	9.4	8.0	8.7	11.8	10.2	16.1	16.1	12.3
France	1.9	1.8	2.4	2.7	3.4	3.1	5.5	6.2	5.3	7.0	9.3	7.8
United Kingdom	NA	NA	2.1	4.6	3.9	2.9	7.8	8.1	6.7	9.6	12.6	10.6
Italy	0.8	0.7	1.4	NA	1.3	1.3	NA	3.9	3.4	NA	3.6	3.9
Canada	1.2	1.1	1.4	NA	1.7	2.1						
South Korea				NA	0	0.4						
Taiwan				NA	0.1	0.9						

[a]OECD (Organization for Economic Cooperation and Development) member nations are Australia, Austria, Belgium/Luxembourg, Canada, Denmark, Finland, France, Germany, Greece, Iceland, Ireland, Italy, Japan, The Netherlands, New Zealand, Norway, Portugal, Spain, Sweden, Switzerland, Turkey, the United Kingdom, and the United States.
[b]German data are for the former West Germany only.

SOURCES: National Science Board (1987, 1989, 1991, 1993, 1995).

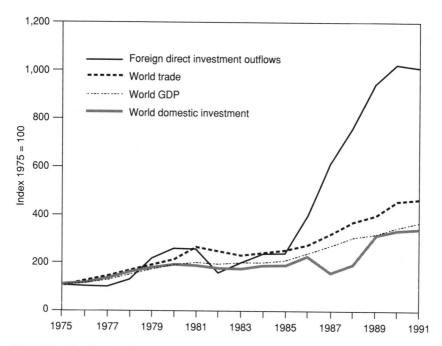

FIGURE 1.1   Growth in world trade, output, domestic investment, and foreign direct investment: 1975–1991.   SOURCE: U.S. Department of Commerce, International Trade Administration, Office of Trade and Economic Analysis, unpublished data, 1993.

U.S. multinational corporations have played a leading role in internationalizing the economies and technology enterprises of the United States and its trading partners. During the 1980s, U.S. direct investment abroad more than doubled. In the process, a rapidly expanding population of U.S.-owned multinational companies greatly expanded their presence in foreign markets and innovation systems. Today, foreign markets account for a large share of the total sales and revenues of U.S.-owned companies in many R&D-intensive industries. For example, more than 60 percent of all revenues of U.S. computer manufacturers derive from foreign markets. As of 1992, U.S.-owned multinational companies[8] were performing $13.6 billion worth of R&D abroad annually, or roughly 10 percent of all U.S.-company financed R&D. American multinationals have been deeply involved in the proliferation of transnational corporate technical alliances during the past decade (Hagedoorn and Schakenraad, 1993; Mowery, 1988a; Peters, 1987).

TABLE 1.2   Three Measures of Foreign Involvement in Manufacturing for Seven Countries, by Percent Share

	Share of Business Enterprise R&D Expenditures 1989	Share of Employment 1989 (1990)	Share of Gross Output 1989 (1990)
United States[a]	10.0	10.0	14.9
France	12.4	(23.8)	(28.4)
United Kingdom	17.0	(16.2)	(25.1)
Sweden	13.6	14.0	15.3
Germany	*	(7.2)	(13.2)
Canada	46.0	37.8[b]	49.0[c]
Japan	1.0	1.1	2.4

*Data not available

[a]The United States defines foreign-controlled firms as nationally incorporated and unincorporated business enterprises in which foreign persons have at least a 10 percent interest. All other nations listed define foreign-controlled firms at a higher level of equity interest.

[b]1980 data

[c]1987 data

SOURCES: Organization for Economic Cooperation and Development (1994) and unpublished data.

The Changing Character of Technology-Based Competition

A second major challenge to the U.S. innovation system stems from rapid changes in corporate and industrial structure and the changing nature of competition in many industries during the past 2 decades. In particular, a virtual revolution has occurred in the human and technical dimensions of industrial production systems, radically redefining the standard of competitive organizational and managerial performance for most companies. At the same time, the technical intensity of many manufacturing and service industries has risen dramatically (Dertouzos et al., 1989; National Academy of Engineering, 1993).

In the context of these trends, product development and product life cycles are shortening in many industries. Time to market has become an increasingly critical measure of competitive success, and R&D costs are rising rapidly. Along with the increasingly important move toward technology fusion—the marriage of disparate technologies—as a source of product innovation, these changes have posed new challenges to the organization and management of public and private R&D in all industrialized countries. Competitive pressure is mounting for companies in many industries to integrate R&D more closely with production and marketing and to look beyond their own institutional and national borders for new sources of innovation (Kodama, 1991; National Academy of Engineering, 1993; Roberts, 1995a, b; Roussel et al., 1991).

The Changing Relationship Between Military and Civilian Technologies

The third major challenge, evident over the last 20 years, is a profound shift in the relationship between military and civilian technology, which has affected dramatically long-standing public R&D priorities and strategies of the U.S. innovation system. For most of the past 40 years, the federal government has directly funded more than half of all R&D performed within the United States (Table 1.3). During this period, defense-related R&D accounted for between 50 and 85 percent of total federal R&D spending. In 1994, the defense share of federally funded R&D stood at roughly 60 percent.

In the 1950s and 1960s, federal defense-related R&D and procurement of advanced technology products created important technology spin-offs in the civilian sector. Indeed, some of those defense spin-offs were seminal to the growth or development of major civilian industries, such as microelectronics, aerospace, computers, and telecommunications.

By the 1980s, however, the rapid growth of global commercial R&D capabilities and civilian markets for advanced technology products had dwarfed federal R&D spending and procurement as contributors to the U.S. innovation system. At the same time, the end of the Cold War weakened considerably the claims of national defense on U.S. technological resources. Today, advances in

TABLE 1.3 Federal Funding of U.S. R&D, in Percent

	1955	1960	1970	1980	1990	1994 (prelim.)
As a share of total U.S. R&D spending	57	65	57	47	41	36
As a share of total U.S. spending in:						
basic research	*	60	70	70	62	58
applied research	*	56	54	45	39	37
development	*	68	55	43	36	30
For defense-related research as a share of total R&D spending	48	52	33	24	25	20
For health-related research as a share of total R&D spending	2	3	4	6	5	6
For space-related research as a share of total R&D spending	1	3	10	5	4	4
For energy-related research as a share of total R&D spending	*	3	2	6	2	2
As share of R&D spending by U.S. industry	47	59	43	32	26	19
As share of R&D spending by the U.S academic sector	54	63	71	68	59	60

*Data not available.

SOURCE: National Science Foundation (1990a, 1992, 1995a,b).

civilian technology set the pace in most fields critical to national defense. As a result, most military weapons systems and subsystems depend on technology developed and applied first in the commercial sphere (Alic et al., 1992).

Recasting U.S. Public- and Private-Sector Technology Strategies

In recent years, these three broad trends in the global economic environment have stimulated a fundamental reassessment of U.S. public- and private-sector strategies for the effective development and exploitation of technology. In particular, these trends have revealed weaknesses in the U.S. technology enterprise that have compromised the nation's ability to develop, organize, and use technology to economic advantage. In some instances, public concern about growing foreign involvement in U.S. R&D has been fueled by these revelations and by the first corrective steps taken by U.S. companies, research universities, and federal and state governments.

U.S. companies have come under increasing pressure to manage more productively their in-house R&D assets and to exploit more aggressively external sources of new knowledge and technology, both at home and abroad. Many companies have taken steps to integrate more effectively in-house R&D activities with design, production, and marketing. In an effort to leverage internal R&D capabilities, a growing number of U.S. companies have entered into technical alliances with competitors, suppliers, and publicly supported research institutions. Indeed, under pressure to cut costs, many U.S. companies in R&D-intensive industries have cut back on long-term basic and applied research, presumably with the expectation that research universities, federal laboratories, and other nonprofit research institutions will fill the gap (Government-University-Industry Research Roundtable, 1989; Roberts, 1995a; Wolff, 1994).

Global economic trends have also forced the United States to reassess the sharp division of roles between government and private-sector participants in the innovation system that emerged following World War II. Under this unwritten compact, the federal government assumed primary responsibility for mobilizing scientific and technical resources for accepted public missions, such as national security, public health, and world leadership in basic research. Responsibility for developing, diffusing, and harnessing technology for national economic development fell almost exclusively to private-sector players and competitive markets. However, in the face of declining U.S. competitiveness, the changing nature of technology-based competition, slow economic growth, and massive economic restructuring promised by the contraction of the defense industry, the federal government has begun to assume a more active role in the nation's civilian innovation system.

Urged on by federal and state lawmakers, other R&D performers in the U.S. innovation system—most notably research universities and federal laboratories—are becoming more directly involved in the nation's quest for improved competitiveness and economic development. Witness, for instance, the proliferation of university-industry cooperative research centers or of cooperative research and development agreements between companies and federal laboratories (Cohen et al., 1994; U.S. General Accounting Office, 1991a, 1995). Similarly, federal legislation and government initiatives of the past decade, such as ATP, TRP, and SEMATECH, have encouraged private firms to enter into collaborative R&D agreements with each other in the interest of enhancing U.S. competitiveness (Committee on Science, Engineering, and Public Policy, 1992).

As efforts to recast the roles of major institutional players in the nation's innovation system proceed,[9] the dividing line between the proprietary R&D activities of companies and the taxpayer-subsidized (and public-mission-oriented) R&D activities of universities and federal laboratories is becoming increasingly blurred. This blurring of roles and mixing of research cultures has raised new concerns about the use of public research monies to advance the economic interests of individual companies, potential conflicts of interest for publicly subsidized researchers, and the accountability of publicly supported research institutions generally (National Institutes of Health, 1994a,b; Rose, 1993a,b; Schmidt, 1993; U.S. General Accounting Office, 1992). Still others question whether closer integration of the nation's diverse public and private research institutions, and other attempts to manage the nation's collective R&D assets more strategically, might in fact undermine the comparative strengths of the U.S. innovation system in a misbegotten effort to compensate for its weaknesses (Brooks, 1993; Dasgupta and David, 1992; Rosenberg and Nelson, 1994). Many of these concerns, in turn, have focused greater attention on the potentially exploitative role of foreign companies in the national innovation system.

Asymmetries of Capability and Access Among National Innovation Systems

Two of the greatest comparative strengths of the U.S. innovation system— the nation's large, highly productive basic research enterprise and its unrivaled capacity for spawning new technology-intensive products, services, and industries—are built on institutions (universities) and markets (financial, labor, corporate security) that are highly accessible to all interested parties—domestic and foreign.

Nevertheless, for various reasons, many U.S. companies have demonstrated a relative inability to exploit some of the system's greatest comparative strengths. Compared to their counterparts in Germany and Japan, for instance, many American companies are weak in the areas of managerial and organizational practice, workforce training, and external technology scanning, and do not invest as much in production processes, plant, and equipment (Competitiveness Policy Council, 1993; Dertouzos et al., 1989; National Academy of Engineering, 1993; Roberts, 1995a,b). Given these findings, it is easy to understand U.S. concerns that foreign-owned companies in certain industries may be better equipped to exploit U.S. basic research capabilities and start-up companies than their U.S.-owned counterparts. These concerns have clearly affected the American outlook on foreign R&D participation.

At the same time, many of the perceived comparative strengths of the Japanese and German innovation systems—in particular, in applied R&D and technology commercialization—are, for various reasons, less accessible to U.S. firms than are the U.S. system's comparative strengths to foreign companies. Not only do these prime foreign-based R&D assets reside in proprietary institutions (rather than publicly accessible universities), but U.S. access to them is often impeded by government policies or corporate practices (Imai, 1990; Keck, 1993; National Research Council, 1989a, b, 1990; U.S. Congress, Office of Technology Assessment, 1994).

Access to foreign markets and technological resources is becoming increasingly important for U.S. firms. Therefore, these long-standing asymmetries in the relative strength and accessibility of national innovation systems have assumed heightened economic and political relevance. Calls for greater international reciprocity and equity in things technical as well as economic resonate much more with the American public, U.S. industrialists, and U.S. policymakers today than they did a decade ago.

The currency of these and related issues suggest the timeliness of an assessment of the causes, nature, and economic consequences of foreign participation in U.S. R&D, in its many guises. Limited understanding of the causes and consequences of foreign involvement in the U.S. R&D enterprise increases the likelihood of ill-conceived public and private policy responses that may actually weaken the enterprise and undermine the economic welfare of U.S. citizens. Lack of understanding may also allow the debate over foreign participation in U.S. R&D to distract our attention from challenges that are arguably much more pressing, such as the need to improve R&D and technology management in U.S. companies or to develop closer links between the R&D capabilities in industry, academe, and the federal government.

Ultimately, public- or private-sector actions to restrict or manage foreign participation in U.S. R&D may be justifiable on a variety of grounds that have little or nothing to do with the costs or benefits of such participation to the U.S. economy. National security, the defense of sovereignty, and the need for reciprocity or fairness may all be legitimate reasons for restricting foreign access to the U.S. R&D enterprise, even if such action would be economically damaging. The aim of this study is to increase public understanding of the nature and economic consequences of foreign involvement in the U.S. R&D enterprise and, by so doing, to improve the quality of the debate and the policy responses that result from that dialogue.

NOTES

1. The U.S. government defines foreign direct investment as the ownership by a foreign person or business of 10 percent or more of the voting equity of a company located in the United States. A 10 percent or more equity interest is considered evidence of a long-term interest in, and a measure of influence over, the management of the company. New foreign direct investment can take two forms—the acquisition of an existing company or the establishment of a new company. (U.S. Department of Commerce, 1991)

2. A national innovation system is defined by Patel and Pavitt (1994) as "the national institutions, their incentive structures and their competencies, that determine the rate and direction of technological learning (or the volume and composition of change-generating activities) in a country."

3. For a discussion of growing foreign involvement in U.S. industrial R&D, see Dalton and Serapio (1993, 1995), Herbert (1989), Kenney and Florida (1993a,b), Peters (1991, 1992, 1993b, 1995), U.S. Congress, Office of Technology Assessment (1994), U.S. Department of Commerce (1993a), Voisey (1992), and Westney (1993). For a discussion of foreign involvement in publicly funded U.S. R&D, see Massachusetts Institute of Technology (1991), National Science Board (1990), Press (1990), Stalson (1989), U.S. Congress, House (1989, 1993), and U.S. General Accounting Office (1988a,b).

4. Although some R&D activities in the United States are supported by a mix of public- and private-sector funding (both direct and indirect), the vast majority are financed predominantly through either public- or private-sector sources.

Privately funded R&D is directed at the generation, assimilation, and application of knowledge and technology to advance the economic interests of stakeholders in the company making the investment. In market economies, it is generally accepted that under most circumstances, private companies should be allowed to dispose of the products of their R&D investments as they see fit. In contrast, publicly funded R&D and its proprietary and nonproprietary outputs are viewed as public property to be used to advance specific U.S. national interests. For the most part, institutions that conduct or use the outputs of publicly funded R&D are subjected to greater public scrutiny than those who conduct or use the outputs of privately funded R&D.

Since only a small fraction of privately funded U.S. R&D is accounted for by private noncommercial/nonprofit organizations, the term "privately funded R&D" is used throughout the report as a synonym for company-funded R&D.

5. For descriptions of each of these programs and supporting references, see Chapter 4, pp. 108, 116-118.

6. For further discussion of these requirements, see Chapter 4, pp.114-116 .

7. There are several legitimate methods for identifying high-technology industries. All rely on some calculation of R&D intensity (typically, R&D expenditures and/or numbers of technical people divided by industry value added or sales). This report draws on data gathered by the U.S. Department of Commerce and the Organization for Economic Cooperation and Development (OECD). The two organizations use different yet comparable definitions of high-technology industries.

The OECD classification of "high-intensity technology products" relies on directly applied R&D expenditures and includes those products with above-average R&D intensities. Direct R&D expenditures are those made by the firms in the product group. The OECD classifies the following industries as high tech: drugs and medicines (ISIC 3522); office machinery, computers (ISIC 3825); electrical machinery (ISIC 383 less 3832); electronic components (ISIC 3832); aerospace (ISIC 3845); and scientific instruments (ISIC 385).

The Department of Commerce definition of high-technology products (DOC-3 high-technology products) includes products that have significantly higher ratios of direct and indirect R&D expenditures to shipments than do other product groups. Direct R&D expenditures are those made by the firms in the product group. Indirect R&D describes the R&D content of input products. The DOC-3 industries include guided missiles and spacecraft (SIC 376); communication equipment and electronic components (SIC 365-367); aircraft and parts (SIC 372); office, computing, and accounting machines (SIC 357); ordnance and accessories (SIC 348); drugs and medicines (SIC 283); industrial inorganic chemicals (SIC 281); professional and scientific instruments (SIC 38 less 3825); engines, turbines, and parts (SIC 351); and plastic materials and synthetic resins, rubber, and fibers (SIC 282).

Comparisons of U.S. production data for high-intensity technology products, as reported to the OECD, with U.S. total shipment data for high-technology products—as reported to the Department of Commerce, according to DOC-3 definition—show that the OECD data represented 96 percent and 100 percent of the DOC-3 data in 1980 and 1986, respectively (National Science Board, 1989).

8. Dalton and Serapio (1995) identify over 100 overseas R&D facilities of U.S.-owned companies. See, also, Peters (1992).

9. With the Congressional elections of November 1994, political support in both the House of Representatives and the Senate for many of these recent technology-policy-for-competitiveness initiatives has waned significantly. Witness, for example, mounting Congressional skepticism regarding the new industrial competitiveness contributions of federal laboratories, and Congress' efforts to "zero out" funding for the Advanced Technology Program, the Technology Reinvestment Project, and the Department of Commerce's Technology Administration. See American Association for the Advancement of Science (1995). Prior to the election, SEMATECH's CEO, William Spencer, announced that the consortium would no longer seek public funding from the Department of Defense (Corcoran, 1994).

2

The Contribution of R&D to U.S. Economic Development

To assess the economic consequences of foreign participation in U.S. R&D, it is essential to understand what activities comprise research and development, how the processes of R&D function, and how readily the outputs of R&D are diffused internationally. At the same time, it is necessary to examine how R&D may affect national economic development and to consider some of the limitations on our understanding of this process. The chapter provides a brief overview of these issues.

RESEARCH AND DEVELOPMENT: A SIMPLIFIED TAXONOMY

The term "research and development" encompasses a range of organized activities directed at the discovery, assimilation, transfer, or application of knowledge. The National Science Foundation (NSF) classifies research and development into three categories: basic research, applied research, and development. Basic research seeks to advance scientific or technical knowledge or understanding of a particular phenomenon or subject without specific applications in mind. In contrast, applied research recognizes a specific need and seeks new knowledge or understanding in order to meet that need. NSF defines development as "the systematic use of the knowledge or understanding gained from research directed toward the production of useful materials, devices, systems, or methods, including design and development of prototypes and processes" (National Science Board, 1993).

In practice, the boundaries between these three broad categories of organized R&D activity are often blurred. In addition, the three are interrelated through complex feedback loops. Sometimes the R&D process moves in a linear fashion, from basic research to applied research to development. Basic research may yield new knowledge that can be usefully applied. In addition, it may enable new applications of existing knowledge as well as suggest new directions for applied research and development. Basic research may also nourish and enhance applied R&D in ways that cannot be traced to a discrete piece of new knowledge. Just as often, however, applied research and development provides the impetus for pursuing new directions in basic research. As noted by Brooks (1994), "Problems arising in industrial development are frequently a rich source of challenging basic science problems which are first picked up with a specific technological problem in mind, but then pursued by a related basic research community well beyond the immediate requirements of the original technological application that motivated them." For example, efforts to understand materials processes and properties critical to the quality and performance of semiconductor devices were largely responsible for the emergence of materials science as a field of academic research.

The role of serendipity in research and development should not be underestimated. Often, major advances in knowledge and new applications of existing knowledge are entirely unexpected by those who fund or perform R&D. Basic and applied research directed at the discovery or application of knowledge in a particular field or industry may yield findings that advance fundamental knowledge in disciplines unrelated to that of the R&D performer or suggest applications of knowledge that are unrelated to the researcher's original objectives.[1]

THE MULTIPLICITY OF R&D OUTPUTS

R&D can have many different outputs, including codified knowledge, know-how or techniques, highly skilled human capital, instrumentation, and technology.[2] However, as the NSF definitions suggest, each type of R&D activity tends to result in particular types of outputs. For example, with the exception of certain fields where direct transfers of knowledge from basic science to technology are frequent (such as in chemistry and molecular biology), basic research yields chiefly new knowledge, new methods, and skilled scientists and engineers—outputs that contribute indirectly to the development and application of technology. By contrast, applied research and development, while creating new knowledge, know-how, and skills, are generally more directly implicated in the generation and application of technology.

Another useful way of classifying R&D outputs is to consider who "owns" them. Some R&D outputs are essentially nonproprietary, or public goods. That is, their use by one party does not diminish their value or utility to others, and they can be exploited freely by anyone possessing the requisite technical capabilities. Much of R&D conducted to advance explicit government missions, such as national defense or the cure of disease, falls into this category. Most of the products of basic research and generic applied research and development, such as new knowledge, know-how and techniques, skilled scientists and engineers, and generic technology (e.g., standards, metrics, manufacturing practices) can also be classified as nonproprietary.

The vast majority of these R&D activities are funded, though not necessarily performed, by the government. The federal government supports roughly 40 percent of applied research and an equal proportion of development work in the United States, most of which is performed by private companies. The government also funds over two-thirds of U.S. basic research. Virtually all publicly funded basic research and over 80 percent of all U.S. publicly and privately funded basic research is performed by not-for-profit institutions, predominantly universities and colleges (National Science Board, 1993).

Other R&D outputs, such as patents, copyrights, and trade secrets, are proprietary in nature. Most proprietary R&D (predominantly applied research and development) tends to be both funded and performed by private companies. U.S. industry supports more than half and performs more than two-thirds of all applied research conducted in the United States. Moreover, industry funds 60 percent and performs nearly 90 percent of all development work in the United States (National Science Board, 1993).

Publicly and privately funded R&D yield both proprietary and nonproprietary outputs. Research universities and federal laboratories, although focused primarily on nonproprietary research, also generate intellectual property that they sell or license to private firms. Collaborative R&D involving publicly funded institutions and private companies also can yield proprietary outputs. Moreover, when federal agencies fund R&D performed by private companies in service of national missions, such as defense, these public investments often enable private companies to develop proprietary technology that confers competitive advantages in commercial and noncommercial markets. At the same time, the private R&D investments of companies yield new knowledge, know-how, skills, and generic technology that are often broadly diffused without direct compensation to the R&D-performing company.[3]

THE POLITICAL-ECONOMIC LOGIC OF PUBLICLY AND PRIVATELY FUNDED R&D

As the preceding discussion suggests, the differences between publicly and privately funded R&D and their respective outputs are clearer in theory than in practice. It is nevertheless useful to distinguish between the two types of R&D, since, within the United States at least, each is shaped by a distinct political-economic logic. Privately funded R&D is directed at the generation, assimilation, and application of knowledge and technology to advance the economic interests of stakeholders in the company making the investment. In market economies, it is generally accepted that, under most circumstances, private companies should be allowed to dispose of the outputs of their R&D investments as they see fit. It is assumed that such firms will pursue their individual economic self-interest with vigilance and, in so doing, collectively advance the interests of the nation as a whole.[4]

In contrast, publicly funded R&D and its proprietary and nonproprietary outputs are viewed as public property to be used to advance specific U.S. national interests. For the most part, institutions that conduct or use the outputs of publicly funded R&D are subjected to greater public scrutiny than those that conduct or use the outputs of privately funded R&D. This is particularly true with regard to how and where the R&D outputs are used, and how the associated public and private benefits are distributed nationally and internationally. Research universities, federal laboratories, and other not-for-profit institutions that perform the majority of publicly funded basic research do not generally commercialize technology or produce products for commercial markets. This has led some observers to question whether these institutions are adequately equipped to assess, let alone capture the true market value of the intellectual property they generate and manage with public money (U.S. Congress, House, 1989, 1993).

R&D, INNOVATION, AND NATIONAL ECONOMIC DEVELOPMENT

R&D activities are a critical, yet relatively small, subset of the many complementary activities and capabilities that contribute to technological innovation, which has been defined as "the processes by which firms master and get into practice product [or process] designs that are new to them, whether or not they are new to the universe, or even to the nation" (Nelson and Rosenberg, 1993). These processes integrate multiple functions, including organized R&D, design, production engineering, manufacturing, marketing, and other value-adding activities in a complex web containing multiple feedback loops (Kline, 1990; Kline and Rosenberg, 1986).[5] Thus, organized R&D activity is not the only source of innovative technology. Much technology, particularly process technology, is generated by other value-adding activities, such as production engineering or manufacturing.

Neither R&D capabilities nor the possession of technology is by itself a reliable indicator of the economic or competitive strength of a company or a nation. Rather, economic and competitive strength are determined by how effectively technology is used and managed in combination with other factors of production, such as labor, capital, and managerial and organizational capabilities. National economic development occurs when these multiple resources are committed and used in a way that causes the value of the economy's output to rise faster than the cost of inputs. This results in profits, however measured, which can be reinvested to the benefit of the nation's citizens.

R&D contributes to a nation's economic development in many ways. The multiple outputs of basic research, applied research, and development yield new products, processes, and industries, as well as improvements in existing products and processes, all of which may contribute to economic growth, rising standards of living, and higher quality of life. These outputs can also provide the infrastructure—knowledge base, human capital, instrumentation—for maintaining and upgrading a nation's capabilities to generate, assimilate, and apply knowledge and skills.

Numerous industry analyses indicate that R&D expenditures have yielded high marginal as well as high median rates of return.[6] Many private-sector investments in R&D yield significant "spillovers"—benefits to society beyond those captured by the individual R&D performer or investor. Therefore, it is generally assumed that the social rate of return (or the return to society as a whole) from private-sector R&D expenditures is substantially higher than the private rate of return to the firms carrying out the R&D. Indeed, estimates of the median social rate of return from private-sector investments in innovations originating from a broad spectrum of industries range from 40 to 99 percent—roughly two to four times the estimated median private rate of return on these investments.[7]

Ultimately, economic returns from R&D investments depend on the complementary assets and competencies of the particular firm or nation. In the case of the individual company, these assets include not only such things as design, production, and marketing, but also the broader technological and economic infrastructure that supports the firm within a given nation. Similarly, the economic or societal returns a nation may gain from a particular R&D investment depends on whether its innovation system can foster the widespread diffusion and effective use of the outputs generated. These factors are, in turn, influenced by the quality (skill level) of a nation's work force; by the size, wealth, and technological sophistication of its domestic market; and, increasingly, by the ability of firms within its borders to access markets and technology abroad.[8]

Different types of R&D make different contributions to economic development. For example, basic research contributes to technological advance and economic growth both directly (through the generation and transfer of commercializable knowledge or technology) and indirectly (by providing generic knowledge and access to skills, methods, and instruments). Only occasionally do the outputs of basic research have intrinsic economic value.[9] Rather, they feed into other investment processes that yield additional research findings and, at times, innovation. Hence, basic and applied research are linked by a complex, recurring cycle of interactions that increase the productivity of both (David et al., 1992; Pavitt, 1991).

For example, as graduate students perform academic research, they develop research skills. Subsequently, many shift from basic to applied work, to which they bring not only knowledge, but also skills, methods, and a web of professional contacts—all developed during their basic research training. This carryover from basic research is important, since instrumentation used in that setting is frequently applied in engineering and more applied disciplines, such as clinical medicine and industrial processes and operations (Brooks, 1994; Nelson and Levin, 1986; Pavitt, 1991; Rosenberg and Nelson, 1994).

Applied research and development generate specific proprietary product or process technologies and innovations. This represents their most obvious and substantial contribution to economic development. At the same time, these activities also yield new knowledge, know-how, skills, and generic technology, some of which are widely, if not freely, diffused throughout a given industrial sector, technological field, or national innovation system. However, most applied R&D takes place in private companies or the nation's defense laboratories, rather than in the more open environment of research universities.

It is possible to describe the contributions of different types of R&D activity to a nation's economy as well as to arrive at very rough estimates of the rate of return to society of aggregate R&D investments or specific innovations in particular sectors. It is virtually impossible to anticipate or trace after the fact the aggregate economic impact of a particular R&D investment. The economic contribution of a particular R&D activity is conditioned by various market, scientific, and technological forces, and certain types of R&D may have much higher value to society than others at a given time. Yet, any attempt to trace the precise roots of a particular economic benefit or stream of benefits—from the customer's needs back through marketing, production, and finally to the germinal R&D—is bound to underestimate the importance of seemingly ancillary research and development and more downstream innovation activities. Add to this the high degree of uncertainty and serendipity involved in R&D and technological innovation generally, and it is virtually impossible to predict which avenues of R&D will yield the greatest returns to society over the long term.

HOW THE BENEFITS OF R&D ARE DISTRIBUTED AT THE NATIONAL AND INTERNATIONAL LEVEL

Every R&D output has multiple beneficiaries. While this observation is generally accepted with regard to the outputs of nonproprietary or public-goods R&D, its validity for the intellectual property generated by private companies is insufficiently appreciated. In fact, the proprietary outputs of R&D, regardless of where it is performed or how it is funded, yield benefits far beyond those that accrue solely to the individual or institution that owns or controls them. For example, the benefits of proprietary product or process innovations that improve the quality and performance of goods and services, or reduce their costs, are widely distributed within national or global economies. Thus, the benefits associated with a firm's proprietary R&D outputs are shared by the company's customers, suppliers, competitors, and the general public (Graham, 1992).

Many factors influence how benefits are distributed among various economic actors within a national economy or among national economies. These include the location of R&D activity, the level of competition, and the relative capacity that a firm, region, or nation has to absorb and make use of R&D outputs. These capacities, in turn, depend on the level, intensity, and sophistication of existing R&D activity and on complementary capabilities and assets.[10]

To understand how each of these factors affects the distribution of benefits, it is useful to consider some of what is currently known about the complex processes of technology and knowledge transfer. In spite of the many advances in communications and information technology, there continue to be significant barriers to the movement of scientific and technological knowledge across national boundaries and among organizations. To be sure, certain types of R&D output, including highly codified knowledge, can be readily transferred long-distance within a firm or between different R&D players. However, most observers agree that the majority of R&D outputs are transferred most efficiently through face-to-face interactions among those who perform R&D and those who apply its results. Indeed, the transfer of knowledge usually involves human interaction in the form of personal contacts, movements among institutions, and participation in national and international networks (David et al., 1992; Gomory, 1989; Pavitt, 1991).

For these reasons, even with the internationalization of industry, R&D activities still tend to occur in proximity to each other, which allows researchers to draw more efficiently on the work of their counterparts in other institutions. Similarly, the economic benefits of R&D activity tend to be much more localized than is commonly assumed. The importance of proximity for capturing R&D outputs has been underscored by recent research on patent licensing and other forms of technology transfer involving research universities and private U.S. companies (Jaffe et al., 1993).

Finally, there is broad consensus among those who study and conduct technology transfer that, in many high-tech sectors, an organization's capacity for absorbing new knowledge and technology depends to a large degree on the level and quality of R&D occurring in that organization. In other words, in order to understand, interpret, and evaluate readily accessible new knowledge generated elsewhere, the recipient organization generally needs to be performing R&D at a level commensurate with that of the organization whose R&D activities it hopes to exploit[11] (Brooks, 1994). Or, as Pavitt (1991) notes, "the most effective way to remain plugged in to the scientific network is to be a participant in the research process."

IMPLICATIONS FOR THE ASSESSMENT OF FOREIGN PARTICIPATION IN U.S. R&D

In earlier decades, the United States occupied a position of global technological and industrial superiority. Many of the issues that today inform debate on foreign access to U.S. R&D and technology were not central. There was little question that Americans would reap most of the economic and technological benefits generated by investment in R&D and other types of technologically innovative activity. Through publications, scholarly exchanges, the activities of U.S.-owned multinational companies, and bilateral agreements the United States exported more new knowledge and technology than any other nation. Nevertheless, the American public generally viewed this predominately one-way transfer of technology and know-how as consistent with both the short- and long-term economic, political, and national security interests of the United States. Moreover, at the time, the research activities of U.S. universities and federal laboratories were not seen as contributing much to the technology strategies and competitive success of American industry. Hence, there was little concern about the relatively limited efforts of foreign entities to gain increased access to these publicly funded R&D activities.

While the United States remains a leader in the generation of new knowledge and technology, its position today is better characterized as first among equals; the gap that once separated the United States from potential competitors has closed. Recent decades have brought increasing convergence in the technological capabilities of industrialized nations as well as growing cross-penetration of national innovation systems through foreign direct investment and transnational industrial alliances. Other shifts have accompanied this convergence. Changes have taken place in the organization and management of R&D, and new links have been forged between different performers of R&D. These changes have included increased emphasis on R&D as a tool for scanning for and exploiting knowledge generated or applied beyond both institutional and national boundaries, as well as closer integration of R&D with activities farther downstream in the value-added process of firms (Kash and Rycroft, 1992; Kodama, 1991; National Academy of Engineering, 1993; Roberts, 1995a).

With these changes have come new questions about the consequences of the continuing net outflow of U.S. technology and know-how and about the growing involvement of foreign nationals in publicly and privately funded U.S.-based R&D. There are both structural and policy reasons that the U.S. innovation system is more accessible than that of most of its foreign counterparts.[12] Therefore, one concern is that foreign nationals may be taking out more knowledge, know-how, and technology and associated economic benefit activity than they return. Growing foreign involvement in U.S. R&D also heightens concerns about national security. For example, military security might be compromised by the unauthorized transfer of certain highly sensitive knowledge or technology. Security may also be threatened if the U.S. government is denied timely access to advanced technology that is controlled by foreign-owned firms.

CONCLUSION

The preceding discussion of R&D activity, technology transfer, and the ways R&D contributes to economic development does not by itself provide clear answers to the many questions that have been raised about the consequences of growing foreign participation in the U.S. research system. It does suggest, however, that the task of appropriating the many valuable outputs of U.S.-based R&D activity is significantly more complex and difficult for foreign nationals than is generally assumed.

Foreign-owned firms that wish to effectively exploit U.S. technology and R&D outputs must establish a significant, technologically sophisticated presence in the United States to do so. Moreover, as the technological sophistication of foreign companies and their home countries increases, so too does the potential for reciprocal transfers of technology and knowledge into the United States. Finally, this discussion suggests that under most circumstances, any country, including the United States, should welcome R&D activity within its borders, regardless of the nationality of the R&D performer. If a large share of the returns to R&D investments is captured by those proximate to the R&D activity, and these returns are beneficial, clearly it is better to have R&D performed within one's borders than beyond them.

The two chapters that follow examine in some detail the causes, scope, and character of foreign involvement in U.S.-based R&D in an attempt to address questions about the costs and benefits to the United States of such participation. Proceeding from a belief that foreign involvement in publicly funded U.S. R&D is governed by a different political-economic logic than is foreign participation in privately funded U.S. R&D, the committee evaluates these two intertwined halves of the nation's R&D enterprise in separate chapters. The distinction between these two types of R&D is in many instances artificial—at least some of the R&D activities of both private companies and not-for-profit institutions are sustained by both public and private monies. Still, the committee believes that separating the two helps clarify and delineate the public-policy issues that are involved.

NOTES

1. Summarizing Rosenberg (1990), Brooks (1994) notes that, "[l]aboratory techniques or analytical methods used in basic research, particularly in physics, often find their way either directly, or indirectly via other disciplines, into industrial processes and process controls largely unrelated either to their original use or to the concepts and results of the research for which they were originally devised."

2. Expanding on Nelson's (1992) working definition, Brooks (1994) defines technology "both as 'specific designs and practices' and as 'generic understanding that provides knowledge of how and why things work' . . . and what are the most promising approaches to further advances."

3. For further discussion of the complex relationships between publicly and privately funded R&D and their proprietary and nonproprietary outputs, see Committee on Science, Engineering, and Public Policy (1992); Kash (1989); Mansfield (1986); and Nelson (1989).

4. Indeed, the very concept of intellectual property rights is premised on the assumptions that technological innovation yields significant benefits to society and that without the promise of temporary monopoly rights, individuals and institutions would have insufficient incentive to invest or engage in R&D activity and technological innovation more broadly.

5. Characterizing a representative allocation of effort in the introduction of a new product, a seminal study of the management of technological innovation sponsored by the U.S. Department of Commerce in 1967 (known as the Charpie report) estimated that product conception and the associated generation of primary knowledge (research, advanced development, basic invention) accounted for roughly 5 to 10 percent of the total effort. The remaining effort was devoted to "downstream" activities, including product design and engineering (10 to 20 percent); production layout, tooling, and process design (40 to 60 percent); manufacturing start-up and debugging (5 to 15 percent); and marketing start-up (10 to 20 percent). (See U.S. Department of Commerce, 1967, chart 7, p. 9.)

Commenting on the Commerce study, Brooks (1994) notes that since many of the projects launched never get beyond the R&D/product-conception phase, and even a smaller share of total project launches make it all the way to marketing start-up, the 5 to 10 percent estimate probably understates the amount of activity devoted to R&D. Indeed, most companies engaged in R&D also conduct background research unrelated to any particular product.

6. The marginal rate of return is the rate of return from an additional dollar spent on R&D. Evaluating the rate of return on a number of industrial innovations and then calculating the median provides the median rate of return.

7. Mansfield (1986) compares the results of several independent studies, including his own research, of the median and marginal rates of return on private investment in particular innovations. He notes that the marginal social rate of return for private-sector investments in R&D is estimated to be in excess of 30 percent.

8. For further discussion of the concept of a national innovation system and the many factors that influence its performance, see Lundvall (1992) and Nelson (1993).

9. The extent to which knowledge is transferred directly from basic to applied science varies according to the economic sector and scientific field. In the development of chemicals and drugs, knowledge gained through basic research frequently results directly in industrially useful technology, including intellectual property. In transport and mechanical technologies, however, the link between basic science and technology is relatively weak (Pavitt, 1991).

10. Many factors play a role in the allocation of benefits among nations, including the quality of interaction and exchange between the various public- and private-sector R&D-performing institutions, the quality of the education system, the size and wealth of the domestic market, and other structural and regulatory factors.

11. Clearly, a company does not need to be doing advanced R&D (or any R&D for that matter) to exploit technology developed by somebody else very effectively and profitably. However, effective assimilation and use of a technology that is already developed, or "stabilized" (in effect, "codified"), requires a much lower level of technical sophistication on the part of the acquirer than does the assimilation and use of advanced R&D outputs (i.e., new knowledge, know-how, or technology in the making). In the recent past, the Japanese have proved themselves world leaders in reverse engineering products and commercializing technology developed abroad. The new dimension of the Japanese challenge is their growing ability to access and use the fruits of U.S. basic and long-term applied research to both develop and commercialize new technology more competitively than U.S.-based companies.

12. For further discussion of the relative openness of the U.S. innovation system, see Chapter 3, pp. 70-74, and Chapter 4, pp. 90-91, 124-126.

3

Foreign Participation in
Privately Funded U.S. R&D

Foreign participation in privately funded U.S. R&D[1] has grown rapidly since the early 1980s. This growth is primarily the result of a surge in direct investment by foreign entities in existing or newly established manufacturing facilities based in the United States. During the 1980s, foreign investors nearly tripled their ownership share—from 7.2 to 19.2 percent—of U.S. manufacturing assets (Graham and Krugman, 1995). Also during this period, U.S.-based affiliates of foreign-owned firms increased their share of total private U.S. R&D spending from 6.4 percent (in 1980) to 14.5 percent (in 1992).[2]

A second major source of growing foreign involvement in privately funded U.S. R&D has been the proliferation of international alliances. Between 1980 and 1989, U.S. companies entered into over 1,500 technical alliances with European and Japanese firms in R&D-intensive industries, such as microelectronics, telecommunications, aerospace, and pharmaceuticals (Hagedoorn and Schakenraad, 1993).

The rapid growth of foreign participation in privately funded U.S. R&D has generated four major concerns related to the economic welfare and military security of U.S. citizens.

First, foreign-owned companies and their stakeholders abroad may be extracting more intellectual property and associated economic value from the United States than they contribute to it.

Second, U.S.-owned companies may not enjoy reciprocal access to privately funded R&D activities and assets abroad. These asymmetries of access may put U.S.-owned companies at a competitive disadvantage, thereby penalizing their U.S. stakeholders.

39

Third, the rapid increase in foreign direct investment in U.S.-based high-technology companies may leave the nation hostage to a small number of foreign-controlled suppliers for technically advanced components and subsystems critical to U.S. military security. Furthermore, growing foreign direct investment and international corporate alliances may make it increasingly difficult for the United States to prevent the transfer of militarily sensitive technology to potential enemies.

Fourth, it is possible that increased foreign direct investment and transnational alliances in high-technology industries will foster monopolies. Such monopolies might injure U.S. consumers and compromise U.S.-based companies' access to key components and subsystems they require to make their products competitive with those produced abroad.

In an effort to assess the validity and significance of these and related issues, the following discussion explores the causes, scope, and nature of growing foreign participation in privately funded U.S. R&D.

THE CAUSES OF GROWING FOREIGN PARTICIPATION

Three related trends have fostered the recent surge of foreign participation in privately funded U.S. R&D:[3]

• The increase in foreign industrial, financial, and technological strength compared to that of the United States;
• The internationalization and changing nature of competition and innovation in most manufacturing and service industries; and
• Recent U.S. trade and technology policies that have raised barriers to foreign imports of R&D-intensive products and restricted foreign access to U.S. research in certain critical-technology areas.

Collectively, these developments have provided powerful economic, technological, and political incentives for foreign-owned firms to access U.S. markets and technological capabilities.

The rapid expansion in the number of foreign firms with the requisite technical and financial resources to exploit as well as contribute to U.S.-based R&D activities has been a key aspect of the trend. The growing presence of foreign multinationals in the U.S. economy reflects a general narrowing of the gap in scientific and technological capabilities between the United States and other industrialized countries. Since the mid-1970s, many foreign companies have successfully entered the U.S. market by utilizing both their unique organizational and technological strengths as well as their newfound financial clout. (See Chapter 1, Table 1.1.)

Reflecting the growing commercial importance of technology, industrial demand for scientists and engineers has outstripped the supply of these professionals in some countries, most notably Japan. This, in turn, has provided another impetus for foreign-owned multinational companies to locate advanced technological activities in the United States, where there is an abundance of scientific and engineering talent (Hakanson and Zander, 1988; Serapio, 1994).

Intense global competition, shortening product life cycles, the growing complexity of technologies, and spiralling R&D costs have also fostered the internationalization of industrial R&D. Today, firms in most R&D-intensive industries must compete in all major international markets as well as exploit worldwide economies of scale and sources of innovation. In this evolving global competition, firms need the ability to respond quickly to and anticipate customer needs and wants across highly diverse national markets. To achieve this objective, more and more R&D-intensive companies are locating production facilities and a range of advanced technological capabilities, including R&D and design, in the foreign markets they wish to serve.[4]

The increasingly rapid, interdisciplinary, and costly nature of technological advance in many industries demands that firms seek out and acquire technology developed elsewhere. Yet, the very pace and complexity of technological advance in many industries has made it difficult for firms based in one country to effectively assess and acquire technology developed in another without establishing an R&D capability within the nation of interest. The United States has become a prime target of foreign multinational activity because of the sheer size, wealth, and sophistication of its domestic market, the strength of its basic research enterprise, and its unrivaled capacity for incubating new industries and products (National Academy of Engineering, 1993).

In addition to these economic and technological factors, U.S. trade and technology policies have also provided incentives for foreign firms to expand their manufacturing and R&D presence in the United States. Many analysts believe that existing or threatened nontariff barriers to trade, such as voluntary export restraints, buy-American procurement laws, and domestic-content requirements, have fostered the growth of foreign direct investment in production facilities and subsequently in R&D in some U.S. industries, including steel, automobiles, electronics, and telecommunications equipment. Efforts by the federal government to prevent or regulate foreign access to certain areas of commercially promising U.S. R&D, particularly government-funded R&D, also appear to have encouraged foreign firms to establish or acquire U.S.-based R&D facilities and enter into marketing and technical alliances with U.S.-owned companies (Chesnais, 1988; Mowery, 1991; Serapio and Dalton, 1994).[5]

Responding to many of the same factors that have pushed their foreign counterparts into U.S. markets, U.S.-owned companies are looking increasingly to foreign firms and markets both as potential customers and as sources of complementary capital, manufacturing capability, and technology.[6]

FOREIGN DIRECT INVESTMENT

Foreign direct investment has been the principal way foreign firms and individuals have become involved in privately funded U.S. R&D.[7] Between 1982 and 1992, the cumulative stock of foreign direct investment in the United States grew from $124.7 billion to $430.2 billion. As a share of the total net worth of U.S. nonfinancial corporations, this type of investment increased more than threefold during the decade, from 3.5 percent to 11.6 percent (Graham and Krugman, 1995). Roughly 80 percent of foreign direct investment in the United States during this period was used to acquire existing U.S.-based businesses; the remaining 20 percent went to establish new businesses.[8]

In U.S. manufacturing industries, which account for nearly 90 percent of total U.S. industrial R&D expenditures, the growing importance of foreign direct investment has been even more pronounced. In 1982, U.S. affiliates of foreign-owned companies accounted for 9.8 percent of U.S. manufacturing assets, 6.6 percent of manufacturing employment, and 7.3 percent of manufacturing value-added. By 1991, affiliates claimed 19.2 percent of manufacturing assets, and by 1992, they accounted for 11.6 percent of employment and 15 percent of value-added in U.S. manufacturing industries (Graham and Krugman, 1995; U.S. Department of Commerce, 1994b).

As foreign direct investment in U.S. industries has increased, so too has the share of industrial R&D funded by U.S. affiliates of foreign-owned firms. From 1982 to 1992, affiliates' share of spending on private-sector U.S. R&D increased from 9.3 percent to 14.5 percent (Figure 3.1). Over this period, R&D spending by affiliates grew nearly twice as fast as did the domestic R&D expenditures of all U.S.-based companies.[9] In 1992, U.S. affiliates of foreign-owned firms performed $13.7 billion worth of R&D, employed 104,500 people in U.S.-based R&D activity, and accounted for 12 percent of U.S. jobs in high-technology manufacturing industries (Florida, 1994; U.S. Department of Commerce, 1993a, 1995a).[10] As of 1993, foreign nationals owned 1,482, or 6.5 percent, of the nearly 23,000 U.S.-based companies active in high-technology fields (Table 3.1).

Affiliate R&D Expenditures

In 1992, U.S. affiliates of European-owned manufacturers accounted for roughly two-thirds of all affiliate expenditures on U.S. R&D. British-owned affiliates accounted for 15.9 percent of such spending, followed by the Swiss at 15.8 percent, the Germans at 14.4 percent, and the French at 9.3 percent. U.S. affiliates of Canadian companies accounted for 15.7 percent of R&D expenditures, and spending by Japanese-owned affiliates represented 12.1 percent of the total. Spending by Japanese-owned affiliates on U.S. R&D has increased much more rapidly than that of other major investing countries since the early 1980s (Table 3.2).

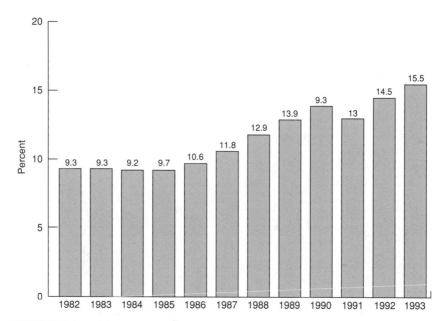

FIGURE 3.1 R&D spending by U.S. affiliates of foreign-owned firms as a percentage of all privately funded U.S. R&D, 1982–1993. SOURCE: National Science Board (1993); National Science Foundation (1996); U.S. Department of Commerce (1995a).

Nearly 42 percent of all affiliate spending on U.S. R&D in 1992 was concentrated in two industries: drugs and medicines (24.8 percent) and industrial chemicals (17.0 percent) (Figure 3.2). Roughly another fifth of total expenditures was for R&D in the audio, video, and communications equipment (8.4 percent), computers and office equipment (5.5 percent), and instruments and related products (4.4 percent) industries. Spending in each of two other categories, all other manufacturing industries and all nonmanufacturing industries (the latter comprising wholesale and retail trade, services, public utilities, mining, and agriculture), accounted for roughly 17 percent of the total.

Data on R&D spending and product sales for U.S. affiliates in high-technology industries underline distinct patterns of specialization among firms of different national origins (Table 3.3). For example, Swiss- and British-owned affiliates together accounted for more than 71 percent of all affiliate R&D spending and over 75 percent of affiliate sales in the U.S. pharmaceutical industry. Likewise, affiliates of European companies, led by the British, accounted for roughly 90 percent of affiliate R&D spending and sales in the instruments and related products sector. Affiliates of German and Canadian companies performed more than 72 percent of affiliate R&D and claimed more than half of all affiliate sales in the industrial chemicals sector. In the computer and electronic component

TABLE 3.1 Ownership of Companies Active in High-Technology Fields Operating in the United States in 1993, Percent of Total, by Country

Country	All fields	Automation	Biotechnology	Computer hardware	Advanced materials	Photonics & optics	Software	Electronic components	Telecom- munications	Other fields[a]
United States	93.5	90.3	92.7	91.8	87.8	91.5	97.9	92.1	92.7	92.9
Foreign	6.5	9.7	7.3	8.2	12.2	8.5	2.1	7.9	7.3	7.1
United Kingdom	1.6	2.0	1.4	1.2	2.9	2.4	0.7	2.2	1.3	2.1
Japan	1.2	1.6	1.1	2.6	2.3	2.1	0.1	2.0	2.1	0.8
Germany	1.0	2.5	0.7	0.6	3.2	2.1	0.1	1.1	0.6	1.1
France	0.5	0.7	0.0	0.5	1.3	0.5	0.3	0.6	0.5	0.7
Switzerland	0.5	1.1	0.5	0.2	0.5	0.4	0.1	0.7	0.2	0.9
Canada	0.4	0.3	0.2	0.4	0.3	0.4	0.3	0.2	1.2	0.4
Sweden	0.3	0.5	1.1	0.3	0.3	0.1	0.1	0.2	0.2	0.3
Taiwan	0.1	*	*	0.7	*	0.2	*	0.0	0.5	0.0
South Korea	*	*	0.2	0.1	*	*	*	0.1	0.1	0.0
					Number of companies					
Total	22,728	1,534	558	2,176	869	823	5,644	2,611	1,267	7,246

* = less than 0.05 percent.

NOTE: Data reflect information collected on high-technology companies formed through June 1993.

[a]Other fields are chemicals, defense-related, energy, environmental, manufacturing equipment, medical, pharmaceuticals, subassemblies and components, test and measurement, and transportation.

SOURCE: National Science Board (1993).

TABLE 3.2 R&D Spending by U.S. Affiliates of Foreign-Owned Companies, Volume and Percent of Total by Country, 1980, 1985, and 1992

	1980		1985		1992	
	$ Millions[a]	Percent of Total	$ Millions[a]	Percent of Total	$ Millions[a]	Percent of Total
United Kingdom	312	16.0	748	14.3	2,178	15.9
Germany[b]	380	19.5	671	12.8	1,968	14.4
Switzerland	338	17.4	625	11.9	2,159	15.8
France	146	5.4	166	3.2	1,272	9.3
All Europe	1,544	79.3	2,918	55.7	8,956	65.4
Canada	135	6.9	1,550[c]	29.6	2,151[c]	15.7
Japan	88	4.5	267	5.1	1,656	12.1

[a]Current dollars.

[b]German data are for the former West Germany only.

[c]Data include roughly $1 billion of R&D spending by Du Pont, a U.S. majority-owned company in which the Canadian company Seagrams held roughly 20 percent equity. Seagrams sold its holdings in Du Pont in 1995.

SOURCE: National Science Board (1993); U.S. Department of Commerce (1995a).

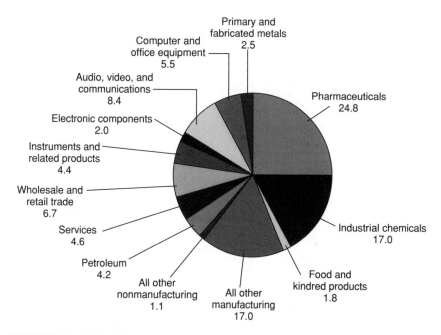

FIGURE 3.2 U.S. affiliates of foreign-owned firms, percent of total, by industry, 1992. SOURCE: U.S. Department of Commerce (1995a).

TABLE 3.3 R&D Spending and Sales by U.S. Affiliates of Foreign-Owned High-Technology Firms, by Country and Industry, 1992

Industry	All Countries (in millions of dollars)		Canada		Japan		Europe		France		Germany		Switzerland		United Kingdom	
	R&D	Sales	R&D	Sales	R&D	Sales	R&D	Sales	R&D	Sales	R&D	Sales	R&D	Sales	R&D	Sales
							(Percent share of All Countries)									
Manufacturing:																
Industrial chemicals and synthetics	2,333	67,657	>40[a]	>32[a]	2.7	5.7	50.7	59.7	(D)	9.7	32.4	26.2	(D)	0.5	4.5	14.4
Pharmaceuticals	3,391	27,939	>10[a]	>5[a]	2.3	3.8	81.6	87.3	(D)	(D)	(D)	2.7	42.7	43.1	28.5	32.2
Computers and office equipment	759	8,558	0.4	>1[a]	61.0	51.1	28.7	33.5	25[b]	>16[b]	(D)	(D)	0.9	(D)	1.6	4.9
Audio, video and communications equipment	1,146	21,318	(D)	>18[a]	1.9	19.8	47.9	55.8	(D)	19.8	(D)	(D)	1.0	(D)	6.3	4.3
Electronic components	269	7,960	1.5	3.4	44.2	48.1	46.1	46.0	(D)	4.5	13.4	16.6	0.4	0.8	11.9	13.6
Other transportation equipment	139	6,266	(D)	14.6	1.5	<8[a]	66.9	76.9	(D)	(D)	11.5	6.0	-0-	0.3	46.8[b]	46.0
Instruments and related products	608	15,238	1.3	0.3	6.1	6.1	90.0	92.7	8.6	6.2	20.6	12.6	16.8	9.4	32.4	56.7
Services:																
Computer and data processing	389	4,726	4.1	7.1	3.3	6.4	76.1	77.1	(D)	11.4	(D)	(D)	(D)	(D)	17.5	23.7
Engineering and architectural	25	5,572	(D)	4.5	8.0	8.5	84.0	86.5	56.0	22.2	4.0	14.2	<0.4	5.4	12.0	(D)
All manufacturing	11,413	431,223	18.2	13.4	10.4	16.3	66.6	63.8	10.6	9.6	15.7	12.0	16.4	8.4	16.0	19.8
All industries	13,695	1,231,972	15.7	9.1	12.1	27.3	65.4	53.2	9.3	7.5	14.4	9.8	15.8	6.0	15.9	16.3

(D) = Data suppressed by the Bureau of Economic Analysis (BEA) to avoid disclosure of information on an individual company.

[a]Data suppressed by BEA. Estimate obtained by subtracting available R&D or sales data for individual countries from the amount in the All Countries column.

[b]Estimate based on preliminary 1992 R&D data.

SOURCE: U.S. Department of Commerce (1995a).

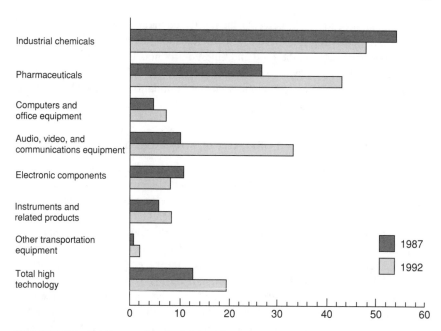

FIGURE 3.3 R&D spending by U.S. affiliates of foreign-owned firms in U.S. high-technology industries as a percentage of all privately funded U.S. R&D, 1987, and 1992. SOURCE: National Science Board (1993), National Science Foundation (1996); U.S. Department of Commerce (1995a).

industries, Japanese-owned affiliates claimed the largest shares of R&D spending and sales. For the most part, data on foreign direct investment and on R&D spending by U.S. affiliates indicate that foreign parent companies have invested in areas in which they have a demonstrated competitive advantage (U.S. Department of Commerce, 1993a).[11]

Sector-by-sector comparisons of R&D spending by affiliates as a share of all privately funded U.S. R&D show considerable variations among industries (Figure 3.3). Overall in 1992, affiliate spending accounted for 19.3 percent of the total invested by U.S. high-technology companies in R&D. U.S. affiliates of foreign companies accounted for the largest share of total U.S. R&D expenditures in industrial chemicals (47.5 percent) and pharmaceuticals (42.7 percent). Affiliate spending on audio, video, and communications equipment R&D (33 percent of the total) also represented a significant share of U.S. R&D expenditures in that industry. Affiliates' shares of private-sector R&D spending in electronic components, instrumentation, and in computers and office equipment were 8.1, 8.2 and 7.2 percent, respectively.

U.S. affiliates of foreign-owned companies also accounted for a significant proportion of U.S. privately-funded R&D in several other sectors, including the primary metal industry (37.2 percent), the fabricated metal products industry (20.2 percent), the petroleum industry (25.4 percent), the nonelectrical machinery industry (10.1 percent), and the food and kindred products industry (17.8 percent). In the automotive industry, affiliates accounted for less than 4 percent of total privately funded U.S. R&D (National Science Foundation, 1995b; U.S. Department of Commerce, 1995a).[12]

Organization and Character of Affiliate R&D Activity

The R&D activities of U.S. affiliates of foreign-owned companies generally are of three types. First, there is R&D performed by freestanding facilities. Their activities range from basic research and product development to general technical support. These facilities are engaged primarily in R&D, operate under their own budgets, are overseen by their own group of officers, and are located separately from other U.S. facilities of the parent company (Dalton and Serapio, 1993, 1995). Second, there is R&D—predominantly development engineering—performed within the business units of U.S.-based manufacturing affiliates. Generally, this R&D is managed by the manufacturing facility or business unit to provide general technical and organizational support to production. Third, there is R&D performed by third-party contractors to foreign-owned companies. Such contractors may include universities and public- and private-sector laboratories.

Few data have been collected on the scope and nature of R&D that supports the U.S. manufacturing affiliates of foreign-owned firms or on the amount of R&D that affiliates contract out to unaffiliated U.S.-based companies.[13] Contracting between affiliates and U.S. universities and federal laboratories is examined in detail in Chapter 4. The following discussion focuses on the first type of affiliate R&D, that which is performed in freestanding laboratories. These facilities account for the majority of all affiliate expenditures on R&D and have been more extensively inventoried and evaluated (Dalton and Serapio, 1993, 1995; Directory of American Research and Technology, 1994; Florida and Kenney, 1993).[14]

Freestanding Industrial R&D Facilities

Research by Dalton and Serapio (1995) documents that as of 1994, nearly 301 foreign companies had established 645 freestanding R&D facilities in the United States.[15] Of these, 375 were owned by European companies, 225 by Japanese companies, 27 by Korean companies, and 8 by Canadian companies (Figure 3.4). Two industries—pharmaceuticals and biotechnology, with 115 facilities, and chemical, rubber and materials, with 110 facilities—accounted for more than one-third of all freestanding R&D operations. Another third of all such facilities (238 in total) was in industries in the electronics and information technology fields. The remaining third was dominated by three industry groups—automo-

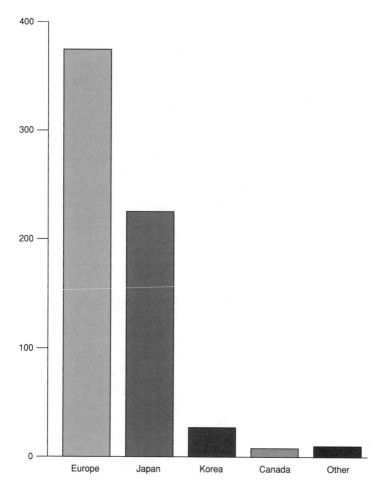

FIGURE 3.4 Number of freestanding R&D facilities in the United States owned by foreign parent companies, 1992. SOURCE: Dalton and Serapio (1995).

tive (53 facilities), instrumentation (43 facilities), and foods, consumer goods, and miscellaneous (55 facilities) (Figure 3.5). Japanese firms owned 50 percent or more of all freestanding R&D facilities in 6 of the 13 major industrial groupings defined by Dalton and Serapio. European firms owned the vast majority of facilities in six industry areas (Table 3.4).

In terms of the size of their professional staff, the largest foreign R&D facilities are in pharmaceuticals and biotechnology (Table 3.5). On average, Japanese R&D facilities in the United States are much smaller than those of their European counterparts. Limited 1993 data on freestanding R&D centers (excluding those in the automotive industry) show an average staff size of 160 at European facili-

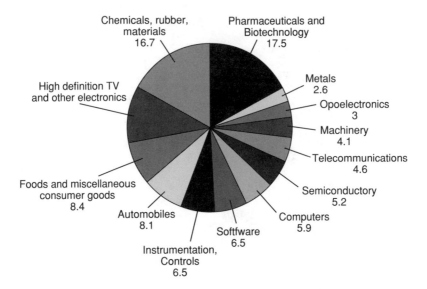

FIGURE 3.5 Foreign ownership of freestanding U.S. R&D facilities, percent by industry, 1992. SOURCE: Dalton and Serapio (1995).

ties and 45 at Japanese facilities (Dalton and Serapio, 1993). Eleven of 23 Japanese-owned automotive R&D facilities and 4 of 12 Japanese-owned electronics R&D facilities surveyed in 1992 had 20 or fewer employees (Dalton and Serapio, 1993).[16] Data collected by Dibner et al. (1992) indicate that the average number of professional staff (207) working in European-owned pharmaceutical/biotechnology R&D facilities is roughly 15 times that working in Japanese-owned centers.

Most foreign-owned R&D facilities are clustered near major U.S. geographic centers of R&D activity—Silicon Valley/Stanford University (computers, semiconductors, and computer software), greater Los Angeles (auto design and styling), Detroit (automobiles), Boston/MIT (biotechnology and computers), Princeton, New Jersey/Princeton University (software and high-definition television), and Research Triangle Park, North Carolina (biotechnology) (Figure 3.6).

The Nature of Affiliate R&D Activity

Surveys of affiliate R&D laboratories and their parent companies, case studies of individual companies, and patent data offer some insight into the nature of R&D conducted by U.S. affiliates of foreign firms in different industries. Although there are important differences among industrial sectors, most affiliate R&D activity in the United States appears to have two major objectives: to help the local manufacturing affiliate and the parent company meet the demands of

TABLE 3.4 Number of Freestanding R&D Facilities in the United States Owned by Foreign Parent Companies, by Industry, 1994

Industry	Japan	United Kingdom	Germany	France	Switzerland	Netherlands	Korea	Sweden	Others	Industry Total
Drugs, biotechnology	25	23	18	11	17	5	1	6	9	115
Chemicals, rubber, materials	24	19	28	17	10	4			8	110
High-definition TV, other electronics	33	10	9	4	5	4	4		3	72
Software	27	6	4	3		1	1		1	43
Computers	22		4			3	7		3	39
Semiconductors	19		3			2	10			34
Telecommunications	15	2	4	2	1		1	2	3	30
Optoelectronics	11	2	3					1	3	20
Instrumentation, controls	1	23	3	6	6	3		1		43
Automotive	34	1	11	2			3	2		53
Metals	5	3	1	4	1			1	2	17
Machinery	7	4	2	3				6	5	27
Foods, consumer goods, miscellaneous	7	19	6	2	6	7		1	7	55

SOURCE: Adapted from Dalton and Serapio (1995). Columns include double counting of facilities that perform R&D in more than one industry.

TABLE 3.5   Largest Foreign-Owned Freestanding R&D Facilities in the United States

Company (Home Country)	Location	Staff[a]
1. Pharmacia (SWE)	Upjohn Laboratories: Kalamazoo, MI	1,318
2. Northern Telecom (CAN)	Farmington, Ann Arbor, MI; Los Angeles, CA	1,260
3. SmithKline Beecham (UK)	King of Prussia, PA	1,198
4. Siemens (GER)	Iselin, NJ	1,100
5. Glaxo (UK)	Research Triangle Park, NC	1,000
6. Burroughs Wellcome (UK)	Research Triangle Park, NC	891
7. Honda (JA)	Marysville, OH (2); Torrance, CA; Denver, CO	800
8. Hoechst (GER)	Somerville, NJ	716
9. Hoffman-LaRoche (SW)	Genentech: San Francisco, CA	672
10. Sony (JA)	San Jose, CA	600
11. Bayer (GER)	Miles: West Haven, CT	500
12. Glaxo (UK)	Sterling Drug: Rensselaer, NY	450
13. Hoechst (GER)	Marion Merrill Dow, Kansas City, MO	411
14. Nestle (SW)	Westreco: New Milford, CT	410
15. Nestle (SW)	Alcon Labs: Fort Worth, TX	404
16. Rhone-Poulenc (FR)	Fort Washington, PA	400
17. Bayer (GER)	Miles: Pittsburgh, PA	389
18. Hoffman-LaRoche (SW)	Nutley, NJ	350
19. Toyota (JA)	California (4); Ann Arbor, MI	350
20. Rhone-Poulenc (FR)	Research Triangle Park, NC	350
21. Unilever (NE)	Edgewater, NJ	329
22. Nissan (JA)	Farmington, Ann Arbor, MI; Los Angeles, CA	320
23. Northern Telecom (CAN)	San Ramon, CA	319
24. Northern Telecom (CAN)	Rochester, NY	280
25. PA Consulting (UK)	Hightstown, NJ	250
26. Zeneca (UK)	Wilmington, DE	245
27. Moore (CAN)	Grand Island, NY	235
28. Thomson (FR)	Indianapolis, IN	230
29. Mazda (JA)	Flat Rock, Ann Arbor, MI; Irvine, CA	213
30. Racal (UK)	Sunrise, FL	209
31. Goldstar (KO)	United Micro Tech: NJ	200
32. Siemens (GER)	Gammasonics: Hoffman Estates, IL	200
33. Siemens (GER)	Rolm: Boca Raton, FL	200
34. OSRAM (GER)	Sylvania: Danver, MA	200
35. Dainippon Ink & Chemicals (JA)	Reichold Chemicals: Research Triangle Park, NC	186

NOTE: CAN = Canada, FR = France, GER = Germany, JA = Japan, KO = Korea, NE = Netherlands, SW = Switzerland, SWE = Sweden, UK = United Kingdom.

[a]Professional.

SOURCE: Adapted from Dalton and Serapio (1995).

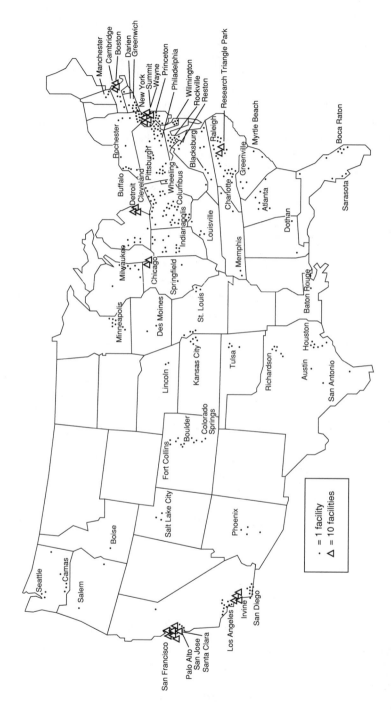

FIGURE 3.6 The location of foreign-owned industrial R&D facilities in the United States, 1994. SOURCE: Dalton and Serapio (1995).

U.S. customers more effectively (e.g., by working both to adapt existing products and processes to U.S. markets, and to design and develop new products); and to facilitate foreign firms' access to the scientific and technical talent in established U.S. centers of technology and innovation (Dalton and Serapio, 1993, 1995; Florida, 1994; Organization for Economic Cooperation and Development, 1994).

In their 1988 survey of the overseas R&D activities of 560 large companies, Pearce and Singh (1992) found that the most prevalent type of R&D activity among U.S. affiliates of foreign firms was applied research to derive new manufacturing technologies in the industry of the parent company.[17] Less prevalent (in descending order of importance) was applied research intended to: adapt existing products to the local market; derive additional products in new areas of specialization; derive new products in a current area of specialization; and adapt existing manufacturing technology to the local market.

Not surprisingly, the relative importance of different types of applied R&D varied among industrial sectors. For instance, applied research to derive new products was seen as very important by affiliate laboratories in the food, drink, tobacco, and metals industries, and less important in pharmaceuticals, consumer chemicals, motor vehicles, industrial and farm machinery, and electronics and electrical machinery. In contrast, applied research to adapt existing products to local markets was considered particularly important in industrial and agricultural chemicals, motor vehicles, and electronics and electrical appliances, and less significant in pharmaceuticals and consumer chemicals, and photographic and scientific equipment. Research to adapt production processes to local requirements was particularly relevant in food, drink and tobacco, metal manufacturing, and industrial and agricultural chemicals. Such research was least important in pharmaceuticals and consumer chemicals, and industrial and farm machinery (Pearce and Singh, 1992).

Overall, basic research was the least prevalent R&D activity. It was significantly more common in the pharmaceuticals and consumer chemicals industries, however, than it was in any other manufacturing sector. Survey data also indicate that a significant number of foreign-owned laboratories in the United States, which were established originally to perform applied research, had since added basic research to their portfolios (Pearce and Singh, 1992).

More recent surveys and case studies of affiliate R&D activity document an increase since the late 1980s in the number of research facilities devoted exclusively to basic and long-term applied research (Dibner et al., 1992; Florida and Kenney, 1993; Peters, 1991; Voisey, 1992; Westney, 1993). For example, since 1989, NEC, Canon, Philips, Matsushita/Panasonic, and Mitsubishi Electric have all established basic research centers in the United States.[18] Westney (1993) notes that Japanese basic research laboratories appear to cultivate close interactions with other U.S.-based basic research institutions. The goal seems to be to support the R&D strategy of the parent company rather than to assist the firm's U.S.-based manufacturing affiliates. Most of these laboratories have relatively small research staffs and so are believed to be primarily monitoring research and technology developments, not conducting much basic research themselves. (Their small staffs also significantly limit the extent to which these laboratories can reach out and draw upon the work of other U.S.-based researchers.[19]) A notable exception is the Princeton-based NEC Research Institute, a facility established in 1988 by the Japanese computer company. As of fiscal 1994, the institute had a permanent staff of approximately 80 scientists and engineers engaged in basic research in the computer and physical sciences.[20]

There are similarities as well as differences in the objectives and the focus of R&D conducted by U.S. affiliates of foreign-owned firms. For example, Japanese affiliates in the automotive, biotechnology, and electronics industries identified acquiring technology and keeping abreast of technological developments and competitors as major objectives for their U.S.-based R&D facilities (Table 3.6). However, the Japanese biotechnology and electronics industries considered the opportunity to employ U.S. scientists and engineers and to cooperate with other U.S. R&D facilities more important than did the Japanese automotive industry. The automotive and electronics industries assigned far greater importance to assisting the parent company to meet customer needs than did the biotechnology industry. Only the biotechnology industry attached significance to the opportunities to take advantage of a favorable research environment and engage in basic

TABLE 3.6 Reasons Cited by Technical Executives of Japanese-Owned Firms for R&D Investments in the United States (1=extremely important, 2=important, 3=neutral, 4=unimportant)

	Automotive	Electronics	Biotechnology
Acquire technology	2	1	1
Keep abreast of technological developments	2	2	1
Assist parent company in meeting U.S. customer needs	1	1	3
Employ U.S. scientists and engineers	3	2	2
Follow the competition	3	3	4
Take advantage of favorable research environment	4	4	1
Cooperate with other U.S. R&D laboratories	3	2	2
Assist parent company in meeting U.S. environmental regulations	1	4	4
Assist parent company's U.S. manufacturing plants in procurement	2	4	4
Engage in basic research	4	3	2

SOURCE: Adapted from Dalton and Serapio (1995).

research. At the same time, the automotive industry placed much more emphasis on assisting its manufacturing affiliates with local procurement, and assisting the parent company in meeting U.S. environmental regulations than did the other two industries.[21]

The U.S.-based R&D facilities of European automotive and electronics companies have not received as much scholarly attention as those of the Japanese, therefore it is difficult to draw cross-national comparisons in these sectors. Data gathered by Dalton and Serapio (1995) indicate that European-owned automotive R&D facilities are engaged in a narrower range of activities (mostly automotive design and styling) than their Japanese-owned counterparts. In the electronics industry, U.S. affiliates of European-owned companies tend to concentrate their R&D activities in fewer but larger R&D laboratories than is true for the Japanese. This is also the case in the biotechnology, pharmaceuticals, and chemicals sectors, industries in which European-owned firms are world technological leaders (Dalton and Serapio, 1995; Dibner et al., 1992; Peters, 1991, 1992).

In the electronics, pharmaceuticals, and biotechnology industries, European-owned freestanding R&D facilities appear to be less specialized (focusing on more than one product or technology area) and enjoy greater autonomy than those owned by the Japanese.[22] Compared to their Japanese counterparts, European-owned U.S. research laboratories in both sectors appear to be more heavily oriented toward supporting the technical needs of their U.S.-based manufacturing affiliates and less focused on drawing on U.S. research and technical talent to support the technology strategies of their parent companies (Dalton and Serapio, 1995; Kümmerle, 1993a,b; Peters, 1991; Pisano et al., 1988; Westney, 1993).[23] These observations are consistent with the reliance of Japanese-owned firms in most industries on licensing technology developed overseas.[24] Finally, although a lack of data makes it difficult to draw comparisons between European and Japanese affiliates in this regard, several of the newly established Japanese electronics R&D facilities in the United States appear to be focused on technology or research that is deemed critical to the long-term technology strategy of the parent company but is in an area in which the parent company does not yet possess significant capabilities (Kümmerle, 1993a,b; Voisey, 1992).[25]

INTERNATIONAL CORPORATE ALLIANCES

A second major vehicle for foreign participation in U.S. industrial R&D has been corporate technical alliances. Corporate alliances involve sustained collaboration between independent firms in R&D, product development, production, or marketing. They demand ongoing contributions of technology, capital, or other assets by the participants.

International corporate alliances have a long history in many U.S. industries—from oil and chemicals to power generation and automobiles. Indeed, since 1945, such alliances have accounted for a large share of foreign investment by

U.S. manufacturing companies (Hladik, 1985). Since the mid-1970s, the number of domestic and international corporate alliances involving U.S. companies has grown rapidly, particularly in R&D-intensive industries. This trend is a result of companies' efforts to respond to increasing international competition, the rising costs and risks of applied research and product development, and the increasingly interdisciplinary nature of innovation in many industrial sectors.[26] Since the early 1980s, alliances between U.S.- and foreign-owned companies in the United States has also been encouraged by changes in U.S. antitrust law.[27]

During the 1950s and 1960s, corporate alliances were based nearly exclusively on joint marketing ventures. Today, the emphasis is on more technology-intensive activities, such as joint R&D, development, and production. Corporate technical alliances can assume many forms, including technology cross-licensing agreements, joint technology development, technology-acquisition (equity) investments, second-sourcing agreements, servicing contracts, and outright joint ventures.

Between 1976 and 1987, the number of international R&D joint ventures entered into by U.S. companies grew on average by more than 17 percent per year (Hladik and Linden, 1989). As of 1987, nearly half of such joint ventures tracked by Hladik and Linden were in four R&D-intensive industries: electronics, computers, semiconductors, and instrumentation. More recent surveys (Peters, 1992) indicate that licensing is the predominant form of technical alliance in the pharmaceuticals industry, joint ventures are preferred in telecommunications, and the chemical industry relies on both approaches equally.

In another analysis, Hagedoorn and Schakenraad (1993) documented a surge during the 1980s in the number of newly established international technical alliances (both equity and nonequity arrangements) involving U.S. firms. Most of these alliances were concentrated in three areas: information technology, biotechnology, and new materials (Figure 3.7).[28] However, other U.S. industries, such as aerospace, automobiles, chemicals, and steel, also experienced a proliferation of transnational technical alliances in the 1980s (Mowery, 1988a; Peters, 1991; Vonortas, 1989).

Technical alliances between U.S. and European companies have been concentrated in the areas of information technology, instrumentation, and medical technology. Most U.S.-Japanese corporate technical alliances have been in the areas of automotive technology, instrumentation, and medical technology.[29] Technical alliances between U.S. and European firms have generally focused more on R&D and less on enhancing market access than those between U.S. and Japanese firms (Hagedoorn and Schakenraad, 1993). A 1990 Department of Commerce survey (Dalton and Genther, 1991) of U.S.-Japanese corporate linkages in six industrial sectors[30] found that most of the alliances were concerned with the production or development of new products rather than with research.

As the preceding discussion indicates, corporate technical alliances (whether national or international in scope) may yield significant benefits to the companies

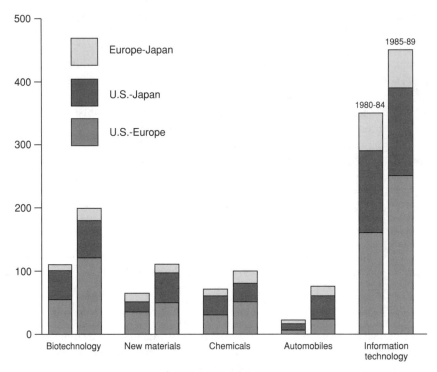

FIGURE 3.7   Number of new transnational corporate technology alliances in the United States, by industry and partnership nations or region, 1980–1984 and 1985–1989. SOURCE: National Science Board (1993).

involved and society in general by fostering innovation, technology transfer, productivity gains, new products and processes, and economic growth more broadly. At the same time, increased alliance activity in high-technology industries that are already highly concentrated at the national and international level also carries with it a greater potential for collusive behavior by the firms involved.   There has been little effort to assess or document the anticompetitive effects of the most recent wave of corporate alliances.   However, the history of cartelization in many industries during the first half of the twentieth century illustrates the potential costs to society of domestic or international alliances that result in monopoly abuse (Hexner, 1945; Stocking and Watkins, 1946).

OPPORTUNITIES AND RISKS

The committee finds little value in debating whether foreign participation in U.S.-based privately funded R&D, either through foreign direct investment or corporate alliances, is generally good or bad for U.S. economic and national security interests. Clearly, growing foreign involvement in the United States' industrial R&D base has costs and risks as well as benefits and opportunities. While the positive and negative consequences of this foreign involvement can be readily described, it is virtually impossible to quantify the associated benefits and costs. The committee nonetheless believes it worthwhile to explore whether specific costs and risks can be isolated. If so, these may then be assessed and either reduced, eliminated, or at least better managed through policy actions in the public or private sector.

Debate over the costs and risks of growing foreign participation in U.S. industrial R&D activity has focused on four major issues:

- the failure of foreign participants to provide an adequate economic or technological quid pro quo for the benefits they receive;
- the lack of reciprocal U.S. access to foreign-based privately funded R&D assets and activities;
- the dangers of such participation to U.S. military security; and
- the dangers of such participation to U.S. economic security (i.e., its effect on the ability of U.S.-owned companies to access technologies critical to their competitiveness in world markets).

The following discussion assesses each of these four concerns, and it identifies the benefits and opportunities of foreign investment in privately funded U.S. R&D that policymakers may need to consider as they shape responses to the concerns.

Do Foreign Participants Offer an Adequate Quid Pro Quo?

The growth and nature of foreign-controlled industrial R&D have led a number of observers to challenge its net contribution to the U.S. economy and technology base. Since more than 80 percent of foreign direct investment in the United States during the 1980s went to acquire existing U.S.-based businesses, it is estimated that a majority of the recent increase in affiliate R&D spending in the United States has come from the acquisition of existing U.S. R&D operations rather than the establishment of new R&D operations by foreign-owned companies.[31] This has led some to question whether foreign participation in U.S. industrial R&D has been truly additive or has merely displaced would-be U.S. owners of R&D assets, technology, knowledge, and their associated revenue streams.

Limited evidence suggests that several recently established U.S. R&D facilities owned by Japanese firms in the electronics and pharmaceutical/biotechnology industries are drawing on areas of U.S. research strength that are relatively new to the Japanese parent company yet are viewed as critical to the parent's long-term technology strategy (Kümmerle, 1993a,b; Voisey, 1992; Westney, 1993). For the most part, however, data on foreign direct investment suggest that foreign parent companies have invested in U.S.-based high-technology assets in areas in which the parent company has a strong export position or demonstrated competitive advantage. In other words, foreign companies appear to be trying to exploit their company-specific competitive advantages in the U.S. market rather than trying to buy their way in to areas of U.S. competitive advantage (U.S. Department of Commerce, 1993a).

Nevertheless, two issues remain troubling. First, are the U.S. affiliates of foreign-owned firms performing enough high-yield R&D in the United States given the volume of their sales in the U.S. market? Second, are they removing more intellectual property and associated economic value than they are contributing?

R&D Intensity of Affiliates

Some argue that foreign-owned firms with U.S.-based manufacturing facilities are not performing their fair share of R&D in the United States. Indeed, the average R&D-to-sales ratio (one measure of R&D intensity) of affiliates was lower than that for all U.S.-based firms in five of seven major high-technology manufacturing industries and in manufacturing industries as a whole in 1992 (National Science Foundation, 1994; U.S. Department of Commerce, 1993a, 1995a). This has led several analysts to suggest that the foreign parent companies of U.S.-based affiliates are deliberately and unfairly retaining in the home country certain R&D projects and other high-value-adding activities (and their associated jobs) that might otherwise be conducted in the United States. This argument has also been used to support policies that would place performance requirements or other restrictions on foreign firms seeking to invest in U.S. high-technology industries (Gaster, 1992; U.S. Congress, Office of Technology Assessment, 1994).

In 1992, foreign-owned manufacturing affiliates spent less on R&D relative to their total sales than did U.S.-based manufacturing companies overall (Figure 3.8). Nevertheless, the average intensity of all affiliate R&D doubled during the past decade, from 0.5 percent in 1980 to 1.1 percent in 1992.[32] There is significant variation among industries, however. For example, in the pharmaceuticals , industrial chemicals, and primary metals sectors, the R&D intensity of U.S. affiliates was slightly higher than or equal to the average for all U.S.-based firms in these industries. Affiliate R&D intensities were only marginally lower than those of all U.S.-based companies in the audio, visual, and communications equipment, electronic components, and instruments and related products sectors. However, the R&D intensities of affiliates that manufacture computers and office equipment, motor vehicles and equipment, and other (nonautomotive) transportation equipment were far below the U.S. industry average in these sectors.

There are also significant international differences in the R&D intensity of U.S. affiliates of foreign-owned firms (Table 3.7). To a large extent, these differences reflect international variations in the composition of foreign direct investment and affiliate sales in the United States. For example, Swiss and German

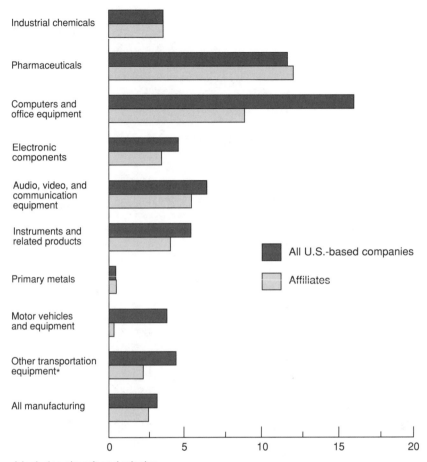

* Includes aircraft and missles.

FIGURE 3.8 Ratios of R&D to sales in percent for all U.S.-based companies and U.S. affiliates of foreign firms, by industry, 1992. SOURCE: National Science Foundation (1996); U.S. Department of Commerce (1995a,b).

direct investment in U.S. industry is concentrated in pharmaceuticals and industrial chemicals—industries that account for nearly half of all U.S. affiliate R&D spending. These same two industries were responsible for 34.4 percent and 35.7 percent, respectively, of Swiss- and German-owned affiliates' total U.S. manufacturing sales in 1992. By contrast, much direct investment in the United States by British and Japanese manufacturing firms as well as sales by their U.S. affiliates are in significantly less R&D intensive industries (U.S. Department of Commerce, 1995a).

Even within industries that are heavily dependent on research and develop-

TABLE 3.7 Ratio of R&D to Sales in Percent for U.S. Affiliates of Foreign-Owned Firms, by Industry and Home Country of Parent Company, 1992

	All Countries	Japan	Europe	France	Germany	Switzerland	United Kingdom
Total Manufacturing	2.6	1.7	2.8	2.9	3.5	5.2	2.1
Industrial chemicals	3.4	1.7	2.9	(D)	4.3	(D)	1.1
Pharmaceuticals	12.1	7.2	11.3	(D)	(D)	11.9	10.7
Computer and office equipment	8.9	10.6	7.6	12.1	(D)	(D)	2.9
Electronic components	3.4	3.1	3.4	(D)	2.7	1.5	2.9
Audio, video, communications equipment	5.4	0.5	4.6	(D)	(D)	(D)	7.5[a]
Instrumentation and related products	4.0	4.0	3.9	5.5	6.5	8.7	2.3
Motor vehicles and equipment[b]	0.3	0.2	0.9	(D)	1.3	(D)	(D)
Other transportation equipment	2.2	6.1[a]	1.9	(D)	4.3	(D)	2.3[a]

(D) = Data suppressed by Bureau of Economic Analysis to avoid disclosure of information on an individual company.

[a]Preliminary 1992 data.
[b]Sales and R&D data for affiliates classified by the Bureau of Economic Analysis as belonging to the manufacturing and wholesale trade industry groups.

SOURCE: U.S. Department of Commerce (1994a, 1995a).

ment, there are major differences in R&D intensity among U.S.-based affiliates of different national origin. For instance, the R&D-to-sales ratios of Japanese-owned affiliates in industries that manufacture computers and office equipment, and instruments and related products in the United States are slightly higher than the average for all foreign-owned affiliates. The Japanese ratios are higher than the average for all affiliates that manufacture computers and office equipment, and other (non-automotive) transportation equipment and are significantly lower than the affiliate average for the industrial chemicals, pharmaceuticals, and audio, video, and communications equipment industries (Table 3.7).

The fact that the average R&D intensity of affiliates is currently lower than that of all U.S.-based companies and that international variations exist in affiliate R&D intensities does not, in the committee's view, shed much light on either the motives of foreign companies, "equity" issues in general, or, most important, the economic consequences of foreign direct investment (including investments in R&D) for U.S. citizens.

The committee does not place much stock in the argument that lower affiliate R&D intensity is the result of "conspiracy" by foreign firms (or by foreign industry-government collaborations) to retain high-value-added activity within their home markets. To begin with, the vast majority of industrial R&D in all major industrialized countries is conducted within the home markets of the R&D-performing firms (Patel, 1995; Roberts, 1995a). As noted above, an individual company's decisions about undertaking R&D in a given market, the level of that investment, and how this activity should be managed are shaped by many different factors. These include, among other things, the relative size, projected growth, and special regulatory or other requirements of the target market, as well as the availability of trained scientists, engineers, and technicians, and other elements of a strong technological infrastructure in that market. The potential for economies of scale and scope may also figure in, as may the firm's sense of how important it is to conduct R&D proximate to foreign customers, suppliers, or competitors.

Numerous case studies make clear the significant variation in both R&D intensity and spatial organization of R&D activity among firms—even firms of the same national origin—within virtually every industry. This is not to say that corporate nationality is irrelevant to the scope, organization, and character of affiliate R&D activity. As noted, leading Japanese electronics companies as a group appear to retain more of their R&D activity within their home market and exercise greater centralized control over R&D activities abroad than do their U.S. and European counterparts (Kümmerle, 1993a,b; Westney, 1993). Nevertheless, the motives behind any single firm's decision to conduct R&D in the United States are multivariate and highly specific to the needs of that firm. Indeed, the realities of corporate R&D practice are much at odds with the rather simplistic notion that a single "appropriate" or "fair" R&D-investment-to-sales ratio exists for companies within a given industry in a given geographic area.[33]

Fairness or equity arguments regarding affiliate R&D intensities are not entirely compelling either. After all, the R&D intensities of U.S.-owned overseas affiliates are significantly lower for all manufacturing industries as a whole as well as for most high-technology industries individually than are those of foreign-owned affiliates in the United States (U.S. Congress, Office of Technology Assessment, 1994).

Finally, although affiliate R&D activity can yield multiple direct and indirect economic benefits to the United States (see Chapter 2), the R&D intensity of an individual affiliate in and of itself says little about the overall contribution of that affiliate to the U.S. economy or technology base. Indeed, the correlation between R&D spending levels and commercial performance is at best weak at the level of the firm within any given industry (Roberts, 1995a,b).

For these reasons, as well as because of the complexity and variability of the highly firm-specific calculus involved in decisions regarding R&D investments, the committee believes strongly that the U.S. government should avoid imposing R&D performance standards or taking other policy actions aimed at compelling private companies to increase the R&D intensity of their activities in the United States.

The Value of Affiliate R&D

Limited data suggest that most of the R&D performed in the United States by foreign-owned firms, whether in freestanding laboratories or in production facilities, appears to be oriented toward meeting the immediate technical needs of the firm's U.S.-based production efforts—design work, incremental, process-oriented, applied R&D, and applied R&D related to U.S. technical standards or regulation.

No industrywide or sector-specific data exist on the level of basic or long-term applied research performed by U.S. affiliates of foreign-owned companies. Surveys and case studies suggest such research is rather limited in scope in all but the pharmaceuticals and biotechnology industries. These studies also indicate that a growing number of foreign firms are developing a resident capacity for basic research. Such capacity appears designed primarily to draw more effectively on the research competence and creativity of U.S.-trained scientists and engineers as well as on the basic research activities of U.S. companies, universities, and federal laboratories (Brooks, 1994; Pearce and Singh, 1992; Voisey, 1992; Westney, 1993).

U.S. affiliates of foreign-owned firm have increased their patenting activity in recent years. Nevertheless, the proportion of foreign-owned patents awarded to laboratories of U.S. affiliates remains relatively small overall (Table 3.8). Affiliates of European-owned firms account for a significantly larger share of their parent companies' patenting activity than do affiliates of Japanese companies (Patel, 1995; Patel and Pavitt, 1991).[34] This is consistent with the findings of Roberts (1995a), which show that major Japanese companies spend less than their leading U.S. and European competitors on overseas R&D as a percentage of their total R&D investment.

There is little reason to believe that the privately funded R&D conducted by U.S. affiliates of foreign-owned firms differs significantly from that of U.S.-owned affiliates abroad. Indeed, what limited comparative evidence there is suggests that the importance of different types of R&D varies significantly among industries and among firms within the same industry—both for U.S.- and foreign-owned multinational companies. Several studies have noted differences in R&D focus between European- and Japanese-owned affiliates in the U.S. biotechnology and electronics industries. However, for the most part, there is relatively little variation in R&D type among companies of different nationality within the same industry (National Science Foundation, 1991; Pearce and Singh, 1992; Serapio, 1994).

There are few data to support the notion that U.S.-owned firms in a given industry do significantly more basic and long-term applied research overseas than do their foreign-owned competitors in the United States. In fact, patenting data suggest that as a group, U.S.-owned firms do a notably smaller share of their total patent-yielding R&D work in foreign markets than do European-owned firms in the United States (Patel, 1995) (Table 3.8). Nevertheless, there is one aspect of international R&D activity in which Japanese companies on average appear to

TABLE 3.8   Geographic Location of Large R&D Firms' Patenting Activities, By Home Country

Firm's Home Country (number of firms)	Location of Patenting Activity		Region or Nation in Which "Abroad" Patenting Activity Took Place			
	Home	Abroad	United States	Europe	Japan	Other
Japan (139)	99.0	1.0	0.8	0.2	-	0.0
United States (243)	92.2	7.8	-	6.0	0.5	1.3
Italy (7)	88.2	11.8	5.3	6.2	0.0	0.3
France (25)	85.7	14.3	4.8	8.7	0.3	0.6
Germany (42)	85.1	14.9	10.4	3.9	0.2	0.4
Finland (7)	82.0	18.0	1.6	11.5	0.0	4.9
Norway (3)	67.9	32.1	12.7	19.4	0.0	0.0
Canada (16)	67.0	33.0	24.9	7.3	0.3	0.5
Sweden (13)	60.8	39.2	12.6	25.6	0.2	0.8
United Kingdom (54)	57.9	42.1	31.9	7.1	0.2	3.0
Switzerland (8)	53.3	46.7	19.6	26.0	0.6	0.5
Netherlands (8)	42.2	57.8	26.1	30.6	0.5	0.6
Belgium (4)	37.2	62.8	22.2	39.9	0.0	0.6
All Firms (569)	89.1	10.9	4.1	5.6	0.3	0.8

SOURCE: Patel (1995).

invest greater resources, if not always perform more effectively, than do their U.S. or European counterparts: monitoring and drawing upon R&D activity and technology beyond their corporate and national boundaries (Mansfield, 1988a,b; Roberts, 1995a).[35]

The Balance of Technology Flows

The United States exports significantly more technology than it imports from abroad, and U.S.-owned multinationals are the principal gateways through which technology enters and leaves the country. Nearly 80 percent of the flow of U.S. technology exports, as measured by the receipt of royalties and licensing fees, is between U.S.-owned parent companies and their foreign-based affiliates.[36]

Unaffiliated foreign-owned companies paid U.S. organizations and individuals $3 billion for the use of proprietary technology and know-how in 1991, roughly $2 billion more than unaffiliated foreign firms received from U.S. citizens for the use of foreign technology. In unaffiliated technology trade, the United States runs a net deficit with Europe and a large surplus with Japan (Figure 3.9).

In contrast, royalty and licensing fee data show that the U.S. affiliates of foreign-owned firms import significantly more technology from their foreign parent companies than they export to them or to other unaffiliated firms abroad. Net payments by U.S. affiliates to their foreign parents increased from $378 million in 1980 to $2.1 billion in 1991 (U.S. Department of Commerce, 1993a). That year, payments of royalties and licensing fees to parent firms were largest for affiliates of British-owned companies (Figure 3.10). Japanese, Swiss, and German parent firms received fewer payments from their affiliates.

In addition to imports of patented or copyrighted technology, which can be readily quantified by data on royalties and licensing fees, U.S. affiliates of foreign companies, particularly Japanese companies, have also imported into the United States advanced production technologies and methodologies. These have included technologies embodied in advanced manufacturing equipment, unpatented production technology and know-how, and organizational innovations, such as concurrent engineering and just-in-time and total quality management techniques. Collectively, these less quantifiable flows of technology and know-how are believed to have contributed significantly to increased productivity in many U.S.-based industries (Florida, 1994; Jaikumar, 1989; Kenney and Florida, 1993a; National Academy of Engineering, 1993; Westney, 1993).

Contributions to the technological strength of the United States by U.S. affiliates of foreign-owned firms appear to vary from industry to industry. For example, a U.S. General Accounting Office study (1990b) concluded that foreign direct investment in the U.S. chemical industry, which represented more than 30 percent of the industry's assets in 1990, would bring a flow of new technology to the United States. Similarly, sectoral studies of U.S.-Japan technological linkages conducted during the late 1980s and early 1990s suggest that the transfer to

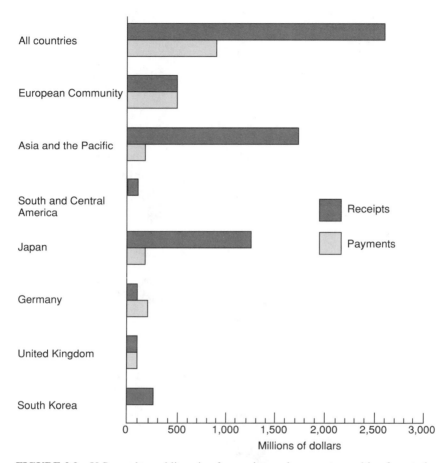

FIGURE 3.9   U.S. royalty and licensing fee receipts and payments resulting from technology trade between unaffiliated U.S. and foreign companies, 1991. SOURCE: National Science Board (1993). NOTE: U.S. payments to both South and Central America and to South Korea were less than $500,000.

U.S. businesses of organizational and managerial innovations by the U.S. affiliates of Japanese companies has been significant in the automotive and steel industries but relatively inconsequential in the consumer electronics industry (Cusumano and Takeishi, 1991; Florida and Kenney, 1992; Kenney and Florida, 1993a; National Research Council, 1992a).

Similarly, case studies of international corporate alliances indicate that the United States is a net technology importer in some industries and a net exporter in others. Most technology transfer within international corporate alliances in the aircraft and biotechnology industries, for example, has consisted of exports of U.S. technology to other countries (Mowery, 1988b; National Research Council,

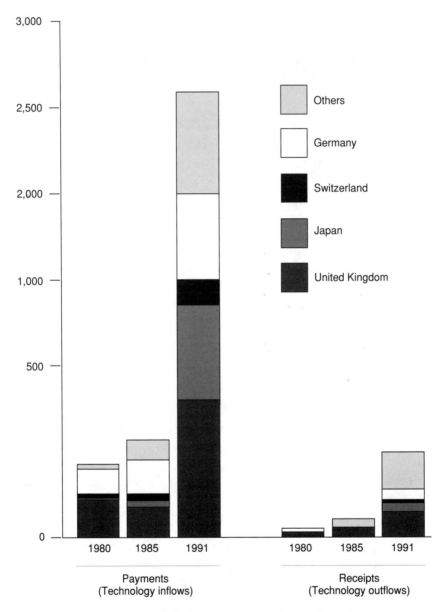

FIGURE 3.10 Affiliate royalty and licensing fee payments and receipts, by country of Ultimate Beneficial Owner, 1980, 1985, and 1991. SOURCE: U.S. Department of Commerce (1993a).

1992c, 1994b; Pisano et al., 1988). However, case studies of alliances in the automotive, steel, integrated circuits, and robotics industries reveal that U.S. firms which collaborate with foreign companies gain access to not only financial resources, but also technology—particularly production technology—and other assets not available from other U.S. firms (Lynn, 1988; National Research Council, 1992b; Steinmuller, 1988; Womack, 1988; Womack et al., 1990). Christelow (1989) has observed that most U.S.-Japanese joint ventures have occurred in industries in which Japanese companies appear to have a demonstrated competitive advantage.

An exclusive focus on technology imports and exports ignores the technology and know-how that foreign-owned companies underwrite, develop, apply, and diffuse throughout the U.S. economy. In U.S. industries that are net exporters of technology as well as in those that are net importers, foreign-owned firms have complemented existing U.S. assets with valuable assets of their own. These include capital, intellectual property, managerial and organizational know-how, advanced manufacturing equipment, and knowledge of and access to foreign markets. In many industries, these assets have enhanced the productivity of existing U.S.-based assets, including indigenous R&D capabilities. This has occurred both directly, as those assets are used in foreign-owned facilities, and indirectly, as affiliates of foreign-owned firms increase the competitive pressure on indigenous U.S. producers in many industries (McKinsey Global Institute, 1993; Organization for Economic Cooperation and Development, 1994). Without the complementary R&D assets provided by affiliates of foreign-parent companies, there likely would have been significant delays in the commercialization and diffusion of many important product and process innovations developed within the United States.

The recent experience of the U.S. biotechnology industry is illustrative. Analysts generally agree that foreign direct investment in and technical alliances with foreign firms have resulted in a net export of technology by U.S. companies. Industry analysts also find that foreign direct investment in the biotechnology sector has had a net beneficial effect on the industry itself (Dibner et al., 1992; National Research Council, 1992c; Pisano et al., 1988). As a recent Commerce Department study concluded, foreign direct investment "allowed [U.S.-based] companies to survive, retained jobs, [and] increased investment in plant and equipment and R&D to develop new products that might have been dropped due to lack of funding" (U.S. Department of Commerce, 1991).

"Lost Opportunities" and Technology Stripping

There has been considerable discussion in recent years about the so-called lost opportunities resulting from foreign direct investment in the United States, particularly from foreign acquisitions of U.S. high-technology start-up companies (Koprowski, 1991; Schrage, 1990). In the opinion of the committee, however, this is a highly speculative concern based largely on faulty assumptions. For example, many of those who decry such supposed lost opportunities seem to assume that an American purchaser of the now-foreign-owned high-tech company would have managed that firm more effectively than the foreign purchaser.

At the same time, while virtually impossible to verify empirically, foreign acquisitions of U.S. high-technology companies probably have in some cases resulted in the transfer of profits and economic activity abroad that might otherwise have remained in the United States. However, the committee believes it is equally if not more likely that in the absence of a foreign investor, the U.S. R&D assets or intellectual property in question might have remained idle, moved abroad, or been less effectively managed, thus yielding smaller economic returns to U.S. citizens. Indeed, many of the most celebrated instances of foreign acquisitions of U.S.-owned companies attest to the fact that there were no U.S. buyers waiting in the wings.[37]

Some observers also assert that foreign firms deliberately "strip" U.S. technologies by buying small U.S. high-technology companies. However, there are few data to either confirm or refute this claim. Clearly, nothing prevents foreign firms from transferring codified or otherwise readily transferrable technology from the U.S. companies they have acquired to production or R&D sites overseas. Neither is there anything stopping U.S.-owned companies from licensing, selling, or otherwise transferring proprietary technology to affiliated and unaffiliated firms abroad. Yet, the principal R&D assets of these small high-technology firms are the individual and collective capabilities of the highly motivated entrepreneurial scientists and engineers who work in them, not the companies' patent portfolios. And, as any manager of U.S. industrial R&D will attest, these highly specialized human assets are very difficult to move from one region of the United States to another, let alone across national borders (Mowery and Teece, 1993).

Ultimately, the committee believes it would be ill-advised for the federal government to attempt to second-guess or otherwise shelter U.S. corporate security markets in the hope of preempting lost opportunities or technology stripping caused by foreign acquisitions of U.S. companies. This opinion is based on the high degree of risk and uncertainty associated with the development and commercialization of any new technology, and on the highly complex process firms undertake when deciding to invest in a particular technology or set of R&D assets.

Asymmetries of Access

The debate over the costs and benefits of foreign participation in privately funded U.S. R&D has focused primarily on the lack of reciprocal access, its costs to U.S. citizens, and the need to level the playing field internationally. Whether the result of discriminatory public policies, collusive private practices, or long-standing differences among national systems of corporate finance and governance, barriers that deny U.S.-owned companies access to privately owned R&D capabilities in other nations are seen to impose costs both on those firms and on their U.S.-based stakeholders. These costs take the form of foregone exports, market share, profits, and economies of scale and scope. There are also costs associated with more limited or less timely access to leading-edge technological capabilities of foreign suppliers, competitors, scientists, engineers, and customers.

The United States has long been the leading proponent of liberal treatment of foreign direct investment worldwide. In international forums, as well as in its bilateral economic relations with other countries, the United States has consistently advocated liberalization of international trade and investment, and has supported the national, or nondiscriminatory, treatment of the affiliates of multinational companies by their host governments. Furthermore, the United States' market-driven, shareholder-based system of corporate finance and governance has greatly facilitated foreign investment.

Until relatively recently, most of America's trading partners in Europe, Asia, and Latin America have to varying degrees regulated and restricted foreign direct investment as well as discriminated against foreign-owned firms operating within their borders. During the past decade, however, public policies governing foreign direct investment in most industrialized and industrializing countries have been significantly liberalized. Explicit restrictions on foreign investment have been eased or lifted in most industrial sectors. Moreover, in many countries, these changes have been accompanied by privatization of state-owned industries and a general opening up and development of domestic financial markets, including those for corporate securities (Organization for Economic Cooperation and Development, 1992a, 1993). At the international level, there has also been significant progress toward liberalizing the treatment of foreign direct investment. Most notable in this regard are the recent efforts of the Organization for Economic Cooperation and Development (OECD) aimed at liberalization of international capital movements, and the market-opening investment provisions of the U.S.-Canada Free Trade Agreement, the North American Free Trade Agreement (NAFTA), and the Uruguay round of multilateral trade negotiations under the General Agreement on Tariffs and Trade (GATT).[38]

Despite these trends, however, significant impediments to foreign direct investment remain in a number of major economies. For example, in Germany and Japan, complex cross-shareholding and bank-holding arrangements continue to impede foreign acquisitions of indigenous companies (Organization for Economic Cooperation and Development, 1992a; U.S. Congress, Office of Technology Assessment, 1994).[39]

The impact of these impediments on the flow of foreign direct investment appears very pronounced in the case of Japan but is difficult to discern in the case of Germany. Comparisons of foreign direct investment in the major industrialized countries with direct investments they make in other nations' economic systems reveal relatively moderate investment asymmetries for Germany, Great Britain, and the United States (Figure 3.11). Japan, in contrast, invests more than 20 times as much in other countries as it permits in foreign direct investment within its own borders.

The causes of Japan's anomalous position are the subject of intense debate.[40] At the same time, the success of some U.S. firms in gaining access to the Japanese market suggests that the "access problem" may be at least in part the result of U.S. corporate practices in some industries. Inwardly focused technology development strategies, the "not-invented-here" syndrome, and a general lack of

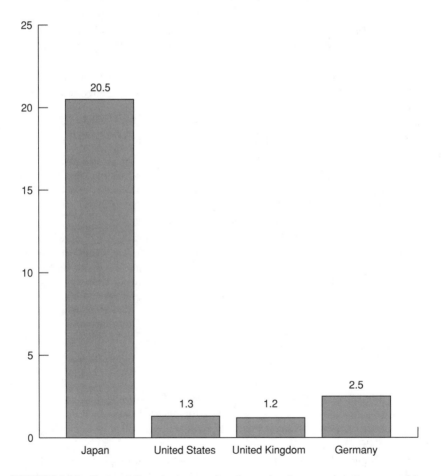

FIGURE 3.11 Ratio of direct investment in other nations' economies to amount of foreign direct investment in home nation, selected countries, 1990. SOURCE: U.S. Congress, Office of Technology Assessment (1993).

tools with which to learn from joint ventures and alliances have been self-imposed barriers for many U.S. firms.

Regardless of its origins, for many Americans Japan's impenetrability to foreign direct investment raises serious questions about the merits of continuing to provide foreign investors free entry into the United States. Moreover, in some quarters, the access problem contributes to growing skepticism regarding the effectiveness of international economic negotiations in this area.

The costs associated with asymmetries of access are relatively easy to describe, but they are difficult to quantify and allocate among the various U.S. and foreign stakeholders (i.e., customers, company shareholders, and workers). At a time when foreign direct investment is an increasingly important engine of growth in world trade,[41] sheltered foreign markets impose costs on most U.S. stakeholders as well as on many foreign consumers. In large foreign markets that are particularly rich in technological resources, such as Japan, one would expect there to be substantial costs to the United States imposed by barriers to foreign investment. Indeed, in some cases, asymmetries in access to markets have weakened the bargaining position of U.S.-owned companies in the negotiation of alliances with foreign-owned firms.[42] Moreover, barriers to foreign direct investment may undercut the competitiveness of U.S.-owned firms, both in the protected market and in global markets generally, by denying them access to important material, financial, and technological resources.

The continuing existence of barriers to foreign direct investment has caused some observers to challenge the effectiveness of U.S. government efforts to negotiate reductions in these barriers within various bilateral and multilateral forums, such as the GATT, the OECD, the Asian-Pacific Economic Cooperation (APEC) Forum, the NAFTA, the U.S.-Japan Structural Impediments Initiative (SII), and bilateral investment treaties. In order to force the pace of progress in this area, particularly with the Japanese, the federal government has resorted to more aggressive unilateral actions, such as sanctions imposed under Section 301 of the 1988 Trade Act, quasi-extraterritorial application of U.S. antitrust law, and the use of legal standards based on principles of reciprocity[43] and conditional national treatment (Bayard and Elliott, 1994; Beltz, 1995; Coalition for Open Trade, 1994: Graham and Krugman, 1995; Tyson, 1992). Some advocate even more forceful changes in U.S. policy, such as imposing more extensive disclosure requirements on foreign-owned affiliates, increasing the screening of foreign acquisitions in the name of broadly defined national economic interests, or imposing extensive economic performance requirements on foreign-owned firms (Gaster, 1992; Gaster and Prestowitz, 1994; Tolchin, 1993; U.S. Congress, Office of Technology Assessment, 1994).

While some of these unilateral actions may appeal to a collective sense of fairness, it is not at all clear to the committee that they will advance the short- or long-term economic interests of U.S. citizens. Such measures run a serious risk of discouraging more "good" foreign direct investment (with its associated benefits to the U.S. economy) than "bad." In many respects, these unilateral measures undercut the efforts of the United States to champion open markets and the free flow of goods, services, investments, and technology in bilateral and multi-lateral negotiations. There is also a risk that such measures will invite retaliation by America's major trading partners at significant cost to U.S.-owned multinational companies and their U.S.-based stakeholders. Given the magnitude of U.S. direct investment abroad, the dominant role of U.S.-owned multinational companies in U.S. exports, and the growing importance of overseas markets and sources of technology to virtually all U.S. industries, the potential costs to U.S. citizens of retaliatory actions are not trivial.

Ultimately, the committee believes that the benefits to U.S. citizens of foreign direct investment and of U.S. direct investment overseas are substantial and, on balance, outweigh the associated costs. Moreover, the committee believes that more restrictive unilateral actions designed to force U.S. access to closed markets abroad—actions beyond those already provided for in existing U.S. trade law—are more likely to delay rather than advance progress toward more liberal treatment of foreign direct investment and trade worldwide.

Implications for U.S. Military Security

The U.S. military is perceived to be heavily dependent on the industrial and technological capabilities of resident and nonresident foreign-owned companies.[44] The scope and nature of this relationship are poorly documented, however. Procurement regulations that place particularly stringent security requirements on foreign prime contractors generally discourage these firms from working directly with the Department of Defense (DOD). Nevertheless, with DOD's tacit blessing, U.S.-owned prime contractors routinely subcontract with foreign-owned suppliers for critical components and subsystems. The U.S. military's reliance on foreign-owned companies is certain to increase with time, given the growing importance to the military of technologies that have both civilian and military applications and the current and growing strength of foreign-owned firms in many of these dual-use technologies (Alic et al., 1992; National Research Council, 1995).

The growth of foreign participation in privately funded U.S. R&D may have a positive effect on U.S. national security. Given the global leadership position occupied by many foreign-owned firms in many areas of dual-use technology, foreign direct investment and international corporate alliances can improve DOD access to innovative technological capabilities important to national defense. For example, Sony Corporation's 1989 acquisition of the U.S. semiconductor equipment manufacturer Materials Research Corporation (MRC) prevented the U.S.-owned company from going bankrupt, thereby maintaining a "domestic location and relatively assured [U.S.] access to 60 percent of the world's production capability for sputtering materials" (Defense Science Board, 1990). According to the

Defense Science Board, had MRC gone bankrupt, the United States might have had assured access to only 2 percent of world production capability. Similarly, both the Defense Science Board (1990) and the National Research Council (1992c) have concluded that joint ventures and other types of technical alliances between U.S. and Japanese companies in the semiconductor industry have helped strengthen resident U.S. capabilities in important areas of dual-use technology.[45]

On the other hand, America's national security may be jeopardized in several ways by increasing foreign involvement in the U.S. dual-use technology base. First, when foreign firms acquire or establish U.S.-based companies in high-technology industries that serve both civilian and military markets or enter into technical alliances with U.S.-owned companies in these sectors, militarily sensitive technology may be more easily transferred (intentionally or not) to current or potential future enemies of the United States.

Second, despite the possible benefits to the United States, foreign acquisitions of privately held U.S. technological capabilities may reduce the timeliness or increase the expense associated with gaining access to leading-edge or emerging technologies controlled by these companies. Foreign-owned companies may withhold or delay access to dual-use technologies either because they are compelled to do so by their government or are seeking a competitive advantage.

Third, foreign participation in the nation's dual-use industrial base may pose a more long-term national security risk. As a result of their expanding presence in U.S. commercial markets, foreign-owned firms may be better positioned to take away domestic market share from U.S.-owned competitors in critical dual-use industrial sectors. This, in turn, would enable them to shift sourcing for advanced technological components away from U.S.-based suppliers to suppliers located overseas or beyond the reach of U.S. national security laws and regulations.

The federal government has several options for reducing the risks associated with foreign involvement in the nation's defense technology base. The risk of intentional or unintentional transfer of militarily sensitive U.S. technology by foreign-owned companies appears to be fairly well contained by current laws and procedures.[46] All companies operating within the United States are subject to U.S. export control laws (Export Administration Act of 1979, P.L. 96-72). The Committee on Foreign Investment in the United States (CFIUS), established by executive order in 1975 and formalized by Congress in the 1988 Omnibus Trade and Competitiveness Act, is charged with reviewing foreign acquisitions that might constitute a threat to national security. Under the same 1988 law, the president was given the authority to investigate and block foreign investments that threaten national security. (See box.)

Current rules governing DOD contracting impose stringent security requirements on foreign firms and their U.S. subsidiaries. Under the DOD's program on foreign investment, control, and influence (FOCI), the Defense Investigative Service can require foreign owners of U.S.-based affiliates that want to work on

The Committee on Foreign Investment in the United States

In May 1975, in response to concerns over a surge in foreign petrodollar investment in the United States by members of the Organization of Petroleum Exporting Countries (OPEC), President Ford established the interagency Committee on Foreign Investment in the United States (CFIUS). CFIUS was intended to serve as a central point for gathering and analyzing information on national security-related foreign investments in U.S. firms. CFIUS is run out of the Treasury Department and relies on data collected by other agencies, including the Commerce and Defense Departments, the Securities and Exchange Commission, and the Census Bureau, as well as on the voluntary filings by companies involved in a planned foreign acquisition of potentially militarily sensitive U.S. industrial assets.

In 1988, Congress formalized the CFIUS as part the Exon-Florio amendment to the Omnibus Trade and Competitiveness Act, which expanded the authority of the president to investigate and stop investments that threaten U.S. national security. Exon-Florio established two key requirements for blocking proposed foreign investment: 1) there must be a finding that the foreign entity might take action that could impair U.S. security; and 2) there must be a finding that provisions of law other than the International Emergency Economic Powers Act do not provide adequate authority to protect national security.

CFIUS does not have the authority or resources to assess broad concerns about foreign involvement in the U.S. defense industrial base or technologically strategic industries. In practice, this means that CFIUS first considers whether a proposed foreign investment is linked to national security. (However, Exon-Florio does not define the term "national security." The legislation also does not provide a precise definition of what firms and technologies are considered critical to U.S. national security.)

If CFIUS concludes that a foreign investment would hurt the national interest, the situation may be reviewed by more senior government officials. Over the years, CFIUS has attempted, apparently with some degree of success although without legislative authority, to modify objectionable aspects of particular foreign investments, such as the unauthorized access to classified information or technology, rather than preventing the investment altogether.

CFIUS also must assess whether other U.S. laws are inadequate to protect national security. It can use provisions in other laws, such as the Export Administration Act, the Defense Production Act, and antitrust laws, to block foreign investment, when necessary.

The CFIUS process has been criticized as reactive and case specific. Exon-Florio does not require foreign investors to notify CFIUS of proposed investments, although fear of forced divestiture at a later date may motivate foreign investors to notify CFIUS in advance of any transaction. The Exon-Florio amendment has also been criticized because it does not require foreign investments in nonpublicly traded companies to undergo CFIUS review (Graham and Krugman, 1995; U.S. General Accounting Office, 1990a, 1994b).

classified contracts to either relinquish managerial control of their defense businesses to U.S. citizens or to meet other demanding performance or control criteria. The FOCI program appears generally effective in protecting classified information (Defense Science Board, 1990). However, the program is a disincentive to foreign acquisitions of U.S. companies involved in defense work and discourages affiliates of foreign firms from contracting directly with the Department of Defense (Defense Science Board, 1990; Graham and Krugman, 1991).

Recent trends raise doubts about the ability of U.S. policies to assure access to militarily critical technologies over both the short and long term. Under the federal government's emergency powers authority (Defense Production Act), the DOD may requisition materiel or services from any domestic firm in times of national crisis. However, as in other situations, the United States seems to have little recourse should foreign-owned firms withhold their most advanced technology from their U.S.-based affiliates and customers.

Although there are a number of economic and political disincentives for doing so, at least one or two times in recent decades foreign-owned firms have either been compelled by their home governments or opted on their own to withhold or delay the transfer to the United States of technologies deemed important to U.S. defense. In 1983, the Japanese government reportedly pressured the leading Japanese producer of ceramic materials, Kyocera, to stop supplying through its U.S. subsidiary ceramic nose cones to the U.S. Tomahawk Missile program (Graham and Krugman, 1991). More recently, Japanese semiconductor equipment and materials manufacturers may have withheld their most advanced technologies (many of them considered dual use) from some of their U.S. customers, including the semiconductor, semiconductor manufacturing equipment, and computer industries (U.S. General Accounting Office, 1991b).

Similarly, questions have been raised about the ability of U.S. antitrust law as currently enforced to anticipate and prevent the emergence of monopolies in niche defense markets—highly specialized markets served by a small number of suppliers. Accordingly, mergers and acquisitions, whether by U.S.-owned or foreign-owned firms, pose a risk of monopoly if they further diminish the number of competitors within a given segment of the defense supplier base.

Because of the limited data available, it is difficult to draw general conclusions about the risks to national security posed by denied, delayed, or monopoly-priced access to private technological capabilities, all of which can result from foreign direct investment or mergers and acquisitions. Several observers believe that in the niche defense markets, current monitoring efforts and enforcement of U.S. antitrust law may be inadequate to address the monopoly risks posed by mergers and acquisitions, whether instigated by foreign- or U.S.-owned companies (Graham and Krugman, 1991, 1995). The task of identifying vulnerable niche sectors is hampered by the federal government's lack of clearly defined, agreed-upon criteria or procedures for determining whether the technological capabilities of a particular company are, in fact, militarily critical.[47]

Even more difficult to assess is the impact of foreign direct investment on the long-term health of domestic suppliers of dual-use technologies. Although U.S.-owned firms have been displaced in world markets by foreign-owned companies in a number of high-technology product areas, one can only speculate whether the influx of direct foreign investments has accelerated or helped slow this trend. In some instances, foreign parent companies have probably diminished U.S. technological capabilities in certain dual-use areas, either by shifting the R&D activities of acquired U.S.-based companies abroad or by shifting sourcing of advanced technological components from U.S.- to overseas-based suppliers. There is no reason to assume, however, that U.S.-owned firms or resident capabilities more generally would not have experienced a similar contraction when exposed to export competition from abroad.

In other instances, such as the Sony takeover of Materials Research Corporation or the U.S-Japanese joint ventures in semiconductor manufacturing mentioned above, foreign direct investment and the associated pressure of new competition have probably helped strengthen important domestic capabilities in the area of dual-use technologies.

Despite the difficulty of assessing the long-term consequences of foreign direct investment for particular industry niches, the committee believes that U.S. regulations that discourage foreign-owned firms from contracting directly with the DOD or investing in existing U.S.-based defense contractors may pose greater costs and risks to U.S. national security than they prevent.

The committee also believes that the federal government must develop more sophisticated capabilities for assessing and addressing the risks and capitalizing on the opportunities presented by the growth of foreign involvement in the nation's dual-use technology base. Greater scrutiny of mergers, acquisitions, and corporate alliances in dual-use industries, particularly in niche technology areas, might reduce the risk of anticompetitive behavior by both foreign- and U.S.-owned firms (Graham and Krugman, 1991, 1995). More important, to serve U.S. national security interests more effectively, DOD needs to define clearly the criteria and procedures for identifying militarily critical technological assets and broaden its portfolio of strategies for managing inevitable U.S. dependence on foreign technological capabilities.

Implications for U.S. Economic Security

Closely related to the above concerns is the broader question of whether foreign direct investment may help foreign-owned firms acquire monopoly control of established and emerging commercial technological capabilities critical to U.S. long-term economic growth and development. Again, however, there are few data that validate this concern.

As noted, some evidence suggests that Japanese firms have withheld their most advanced technologies from some U.S.-owned companies in the semiconductor, semiconductor manufacturing equipment, and computer industries (U.S. General Accounting Office, 1991b). Without timely access to these technologies, most U.S. companies in these industry sectors could not serve as effectively as they might the needs of their worldwide customers. The effect on the Japanese firms involved is less clear. Their growing involvement in U.S.-based R&D activity in these industries, through direct investment or joint ventures, may have either enhanced or weakened their ability to manipulate the market to gain commercial advantage (National Research Council, 1992c).

Furthermore, broader concerns have been raised about the long-term effects of foreign acquisitions of U.S. niche technology companies or high-technology start-ups on the ability of U.S.-owned companies to access emerging critical civilian technologies. Much more than any other industrialized country, the United States has relied since World War II on technology niche companies for a disproportionate share of major product and process innovation (Mowery and Rosenberg, 1993). Since the mid-1980s, foreign acquisitions of these firms appear to have increased significantly. Data gathered by Spencer (1991) and the U.S. Department of Commerce (1993a) underline the particularly large appetite of Japanese investors for U.S. high-technology start-up companies during the late 1980s and early 1990s (Table 3.9). These data also suggest that foreign investors have targeted U.S. companies in a select number of technology areas deemed critical or emerging by the U.S. government (Council on Competitiveness, 1991; National Critical Technologies Panel, 1993; U.S. Department of Commerce, 1990).

Still, inventories of foreign acquisitions of U.S. high-technology firms offer little if any insight into the relative importance of the technological capabilities acquired, let alone the cumulative effect of these purchases on the nation's capabilities in a given area of technology. For example, such data do not provide information on sales, assets, or employment for either the firms acquired or their niche industrial sector. Nor do these data shed any light on the performance of the acquired firms subsequent to their takeover. Without such information, it is impossible to assess the extent and significance of foreign control in any high-technology niche sector.

Many high-technology industries are already highly concentrated at the national and global levels. Hence, it is likely that at least some of the many recent mergers and acquisitions have significantly reduced competition in particular civilian industry sectors. For this reason, the committee believes that the federal government should intensify its scrutiny and regulation of all U.S.-based mergers and acquisitions. However, there is no evidence to suggest that foreign-owned firms are any more likely than their U.S.-owned counterparts to engage in anticompetitive activity in the United States. Indeed, in terms of the sheer number of acquisitions and mergers concluded in U.S. technology-intensive industries each year, foreign acquisitions are dwarfed by those involving U.S.-owned firms.

TABLE 3.9 Foreign Acquisitions of U.S. High-Technology Companies, by Industry and by Purchasing Country, October 1988 to March 1993

	Materials	Aerospace	Chemicals	Computers	Electronics	Semiconductor Equipment	Semiconductors	Telecommunications	Biotech	Other	Total
Japan	42	18	25	108	36	34	53	32	27	62	437
United Kingdom	12	6	7	14	14	1	2	13	7	6	82
France	3	5	11	10	3	2	1	5	2	6	49
Germany	0	1	6	1	3	1	3	6	6	2	29
Canada	1	3	3	7	2	0	1	2	0	0	19
Switzerland	1	0	1	3	0	1	0	2	5	1	14
Taiwan	1	0	0	8	0	0	2	1	0	0	12
Australia	2	0	0	1	1	1	0	2	1	0	8
S. Korea	0	0	0	4	1	0	2	0	0	0	7
Netherlands	1	0	2	2	1	0	0	0	0	1	7
Total	70	34	61	171	71	43	65	69	55	83	722

SOURCE: Adapted from Gaster and Prestowitz (1994).

SUMMARY

During the past decade, foreign participation in privately funded U.S. R&D has grown significantly, both through direct investment and intercorporate technical alliances. In 1990, U.S. affiliates of foreign-owned firms accounted for a sizeable fraction (20 percent or more) of U.S.-based R&D activity in several large manufacturing industries. These included industrial chemicals, pharmaceuticals, audio, video, and communications equipment, and primary and fabricated metals. Roughly two-thirds of total affiliate R&D spending in the United States is accounted for by companies based in Canada, the United Kingdom, Germany, Switzerland, and Japan. Since 1980, Japanese-owned affiliates have increased their share of total affiliate R&D activity faster than has any other major investing country. For the most part, foreign parent companies have invested in areas in which they have a strong export position or demonstrated competitive advantage.

Comparative surveys of U.S.- and foreign-owned multinational companies across a range of industries suggest that the motives for engaging in R&D in a foreign market, as well as the type of R&D activity, vary in importance primarily according to the industry sector, not the company's nationality. Overall, the two most frequently cited motives are to help the local manufacturing affiliate and the parent company meet the demands of U.S. customers, and to improve access to U.S. scientific and technical talent.

Most major foreign-owned R&D facilities are clustered near major U.S. centers of R&D activity, and most affiliate R&D performed in the United States appears oriented toward meeting the more immediate technical needs of the affiliates' U.S.-based production facilities. Thus, affiliates concentrate largely on design work, incremental process-oriented applied R&D, and applied R&D related to U.S. technical standards or domestic regulation.

Growing foreign involvement in the nation's industrial R&D base brings with it costs and risks as well as benefits and opportunities. One key question, however, cannot be answered definitively: Do foreign nationals take away more technology and associated economic value than they return to the United States through their participation in U.S. industrial R&D? The evidence suggests that in general, the technological contributions of foreign-owned firms through affiliates or technical alliances vary from industry to industry. Thus, in some industries, foreign firms are net exporters of technology; in others, they are net importers. The few quantitative measures that exist confirm that overall, U.S.-based affiliates of foreign-owned firms import significantly more codified technology from their parent companies than they export to them or to unaffiliated firms abroad. Case studies show that foreign-owned companies, and Japanese companies in particular, have imported significant amounts of advanced production technology and methodologies into the United States in several industries.

Foreign involvement in U.S.-based industrial R&D has in some cases resulted in lost opportunities for U.S.-owned firms, as well as in foregone wealth for their U.S.-based stakeholders. In other cases, however, foreign firms have created opportunities and wealth for U.S.-owned firms and Americans generally as they transfer technology, know-how, capital, and other complementary assets to the United States.

On balance, the committee considers the growth of foreign direct investment in the United States and the proliferation of transnational corporate alliances to be generally positive trends that enhance the productivity and wealth of the United States and its trading and investing partners overseas. Furthermore, the committee believes that for the purpose of assessing its consequences for the U.S. economy, foreign participation in privately funded U.S. R&D cannot be separated meaningfully from the larger trends that carry it.

Asymmetries of access to the economies and innovation systems of the United States and other industrialized nations have affected profoundly public perceptions and federal policies on foreign involvement in U.S.-based R&D. During the past decade, America's trading partners have liberalized their policies on foreign direct investment—the most important avenue of access to privately funded R&D activities abroad—making them more similar to those of the United States. Nevertheless, significant impediments to open access—the product of structural barriers, public policies, or collusive or discriminatory corporate practices—remain in some major economies. These impediments have led some to call for aggressive unilateral action by the U.S. government. The committee, however, considers many such proposals ill advised and, in their stead, urges the government to use existing policies to hold itself and its trading partners accountable to international agreements. The government should also redouble its efforts to negotiate solutions to these asymmetries of access in bilateral and multilateral forums.

The public debate about national security has focused almost exclusively on the difficult-to-assess risks that accompany growing foreign involvement in particular R&D-intensive industries. Current national security regulations and procedures appear to minimize the risk that militarily sensitive U.S. technology will be transferred to foreign-owned companies. However, the utility of these rules and procedures is of questionable value for addressing the medium- to long-term risks of delayed or denied access to militarily critical technological capabilities posed by foreign direct investment or mergers and acquisitions.

Two sets of issues inform the debate on whether existing measures intended to protect national security are sufficient. On the one hand, current monitoring efforts and methodologies associated with the enforcement of U.S. antitrust laws may be neither extensive nor strong enough to address the monopoly risks that mergers, acquisitions, and corporate alliances pose in niche defense markets, whether instigated by foreign- or U.S.-owned companies. Moreover, the task of identifying vulnerable niche sectors is made difficult by the federal government's lack of clearly defined, agreed-upon criteria or procedures to determine whether a particular company's technological capabilities are critical to the military.

On the other hand, little consideration has been given to the costs and risks to national security posed by existing procurement regulations, which discourage foreign-owned firms from contracting directly with DOD or investing in existing U.S.-based defense contractors. The committee believes such concerns merit greater attention in the national security debate. This is especially true given the current relatively high level of U.S. dependence on foreign sources of component technology, the growing importance of technologies that have both civilian and military applications to the nation's military needs, and the growing strength of foreign-owned firms in many of these dual-use technologies.

There is little evidence that increasing foreign involvement in U.S. industrial R&D through direct investment and alliances has damaged U.S. economic security. The ability of U.S.-based companies to access the technologies, components, and subsystems required to make their major products competitive with foreign producers does not appear to be impaired. Many high-technology industries are already very concentrated at the national and global levels. Hence, it is likely that at least some of the many recent mergers, acquisitions, and alliances have fostered monopolies in particular civilian high-technology industries. However, the actions of foreign-owned firms within the U.S. economy do not suggest that they are any more likely to engage in anticompetitive activity than their U.S.-owned counterparts.

The committee anticipates that the fundamental trends that have fueled the experience of foreign involvement in privately funded U.S. R&D will continue to spur its growth into the next century. Carried by expanding international trade and foreign direct investment, global technical and economic capabilities will be distributed more evenly among an expanding population of industrialized countries, and competition and innovation in most manufacturing and service industries will become increasingly internationalized.

NOTES

1. Privately owned U.S. companies financed 59 percent of all R&D performed in the United States in 1994 and an estimated 90 to 95 percent of all privately funded R&D (National Science Foundation, 1995b).

2. Data on R&D spending by U.S. affiliates of foreign-owned firms come from the Annual Survey of Foreign Direct Investment in the United States, conducted by the Department of Commerce's Bureau of Economic Analysis. The Survey of Industrial Research and Development, conducted by the Bureau of the Census for the National Science Foundation, provides data on the total amount of privately funded U.S. R&D.

Changes introduced recently in the methodology and scope of the Survey of Industrial Research and Development have resulted in significant upward revisions in estimates of R&D funded by U.S. companies. Beginning in 1992, survey statistics are based on annual sampling. Previously, samples were selected every 5 to 7 years. In addition, "For 1992, the sample size was increased from approximately 14,000 to approximately 23,000 firms to better account for births of new R&D-performing establishments in the survey universe, to survey more fully and accurately R&D activity in the service sector, and to gather more current information about potential R&D performers" (National Science Foundation, 1993b). With the upward revision in the volume of U.S. company-funded R&D,

there has been a corresponding downward revision of the share of R&D conducted by U.S. affiliates of foreign-owned firms. For instance, the proportion of R&D conducted by affiliates in 1992 fell from 17.1 percent in the old data series to 14.5 percent in the new data series (National Science Foundation, 1995b, 1996; U.S. Department of Commerce, 1995a).

3. For a more extensive overview of the many factors that have contributed to the internationalization of industrial R&D, or more specifically to the decisions of many multinational firms to establish R&D subsidiaries abroad, and an extensive bibliography on the subject, see the review article by Cheng and Bolon (1993).

4. Illustrating the expectations that some foreign firms have of their U.S.-based R&D facilities, Serapio and Dalton (1994) quote the following observation of an executive of a large Japanese automotive company: "Prior to establishing an R&D center in [the United States], our engineers in [the U.S. plant] had to work with the R&D and technical centers in Japan. We were sending faxes to each other all the time and our engineers took many trips between Japan and the United States. The process of developing and producing a car for the U.S. market or correcting an engineering problem was very time consuming. We have eliminated this lengthy process by establishing a U.S. technical center [in close proximity] to our U.S. plant, sales office and suppliers in the United States. We expect to shorten the time needed for concurrent design and development, concurrent development and engineering, and working on design and engineering issues for our vehicles in or near production." (p. 29)

5. Recent surveys of Japanese multinationals in a number of industries suggest that the fear of diminished access to U.S. technology has played an important role in the decision of many Japanese companies to establish an R&D presence in the United States (Ministry of International Trade and Industry, 1992; Serapio, 1994). As discussed in greater detail in Chapter 4, the U.S. Congress has placed restrictions on foreign corporate involvement in publicly funded R&D in American universities, federal laboratories, and other U.S.-based institutions performing government-funded research. For example, foreign participation in the Department of Commerce Advanced Technology Program, Advanced Research Projects Agency-coordinated Technology Reinvestment Project, and cooperative research and development agreements with federal laboratories is conditioned on reciprocal access to comparable government-funded R&D initiatives abroad. Several U.S. industry-led consortia, including the Semiconductor Manufacturing Technology Research Corporation (SEMATECH), the National Center for Manufacturing Sciences, the U.S. Display Consortium—all partially funded with public monies—exclude foreign participants.

In 1987, a U.S. government-sponsored symposium on high-temperature superconductivity (HTS) excluded foreign participants. Subsequent Reagan administration proposals for additional research funding for HTS included provisions designed to prohibit or restrict foreign access to the results of publicly funded research in this area (Mowery, 1991).

6. For documentation of the growing interest and involvement of U.S.-owned multinational companies in the advanced technological capabilities of foreign firms and foreign countries see, for example, Dalton and Serapio (1995), Mansfield et al. (1979), Mowery (1991), National Science Foundation (1990c, 1991), and Peters (1992, 1993b).

7. The U.S. Department of Commerce defines a foreign investment as direct when a foreign investor acquires a stake of 10 percent or more in a U.S. firm. The 10-percent criterion, although arbitrary, is meant to reflect the idea that a large stockholder will generally have a strong say in the operations of a company, even if that stockholder does not have a majority stake. Data from 1988 show that on average, the foreign parent controlled 78.8 percent of its U.S. affiliate's equity. Calculations by analysts at Commerce's Bureau of Economic Analysis indicate that raising the definitional cutoff for direct investment to 20 percent or even 50 percent would increase only slightly estimates of the amount of foreign direct investment in the United States (Graham and Krugman, 1991, pp. 9-11). Hence, most experts consider the potential for understating or overstating the level of foreign control with the 10 percent criterion to be small. There is one notable case of relevance to this study in which a foreign firm with a moderate equity share in a U.S. company, according to the Department of Commerce criterion, "controls" a very large R&D portfolio. Until spring of 1995, the Canadian

Bronfman (Seagram) family owned a 23 percent stake in DuPont, which invests over $1 billion annually in R&D worldwide. On April 7, 1995, the Bronfman family sold its stake in DuPont, thereby removing DuPont and its R&D spending from the ledger of foreign-owned affiliates.

8. See U.S. Department of Commerce, Survey of Current Business, May issue, various years, for data regarding the share of foreign direct investment accounted for by foreign acquisitions of existing U.S.-based firms and that accounted for by the establishment of new U.S.-based companies by foreigners.

9. "Special tabulations were prepared by [the Commerce Department's Bureau of Economic Analysis] to reveal R&D expenditures in the United States of those firms in which there is majority foreign ownership—i.e., 50 percent or more. For 1990, the 10-percent foreign ownership threshold results in an estimated $11.3 billion foreign R&D investment total. R&D expenditures of majority owned U.S. affiliates of foreign companies were $8.4 billion.

"Funding trends of these two groupings are quite similar. From 1980 to 1990, inflation-adjusted R&D spending of majority-owned foreign firms was up 350 percent, whereas that of firms with 10 percent or more foreign ownership (including majority-owned firms) rose slightly more, 370 percent" (National Science Board, 1993, p. 125, footnote 77).

The particularly rapid growth of affiliate R&D spending between 1987 and 1990 included several multimillion dollar acquisitions by foreign firms of U.S. pharmaceutical companies with large R&D budgets, such as Glaxo, SmithKline Beecham, and Genentech (Dalton and Serapio, 1993).

10. Majority-owned affiliates of foreign companies performed approximately $10.7 billion of R&D in 1992, roughly $750 million more than was spent by U.S. companies and their foreign subsidiaries on overseas R&D that year (National Science Foundation, 1994, Table SD-5; U.S. Department of Commerce, 1994a, Table N-1).

11. Florida and Kenney (1993) go so far as to conclude that "foreign R&D investment in the U.S. is largely the province of corporations which are global technology leaders and that it is primarily used to consolidate that position of technological advantage." (p. 30)

12. The volume of affiliate R&D spending in the U.S. motor vehicle and equipment industry is arrived at by adding affiliate R&D expenditures that are classified in the Bureau of Economic Analysis' survey of affiliate R&D as "manufacturing R&D" with those that are classified as "wholesale trade R&D." Department of Commerce analysts acknowledge that much of the R&D spending classified as "wholesale trade R&D" by affiliates in the motor vehicles and equipment industry is, in fact, R&D performed by U.S. manufacturing establishments of foreign-owned firms.

13. In 1992, U.S. affiliates of foreign-owned firms performed $170 million of R&D for the U.S. federal government and $689 million of R&D for other unaffiliated U.S.-based organizations. Ninety-four percent of the R&D performed by affiliates in 1992 was for the affiliates themselves (U.S. Department of Commerce, 1995a).

For one of the most extensive, though by no means comprehensive, inventory of U.S.-based organizations that perform industrial research, development, and design, see the *Directory of American Research: Organizations Active in Product Development for Business,* published annually by R. R. Bowker, New Providence, New Jersey.

14. Freestanding R&D facilities appear to play the greatest role in two industries: pharmaceuticals and chemicals, which together account for nearly half of all affiliate R&D expenditures. Whether freestanding facilities account for a majority of affiliate R&D expenditures in discrete manufacturing industries (i.e., automobiles or consumer electronics) is more of an open question (Peters, 1992).

15. Dalton and Serapio (1995) define a foreign R&D facility in the United States "as a freestanding R&D company (i.e., a company engaged mainly in R&D) of which 50 percent or more is owned by a foreign parent company." (pp. 16-17)

A 1993 Department of Commerce report (1993a) noted that data collected earlier by Dalton and Serapio (1993) "include numbers of design studios, which are not considered research facilities by the National Science Foundation, and thus, possibly represent a significant overstatement of research facilities in the United States—as much as 80 percent above actual R&D facilities, according to one NSF analyst." Research by Peters (1991, 1992) also suggests that data gathered by Dalton and Serapio considerably overstate the number of "true" R&D facilities owned by foreign companies in the United States.

16. The relatively small size of many Japanese-owned freestanding R&D facilities in the United States has led some observers to suggest that these facilities may serve mainly as "listening posts" rather than research units (Fusfeld, 1994; Peters, 1991). Serapio (1994), however, notes that the smaller size of Japanese R&D facilities in the United States could be explained by their more specialized orientation and relative newness. This may be true in the case of many recently established Japanese-owned R&D facilities in the U.S. biotechnology and electronics industries, which conduct mainly basic research. For further discussion, see pp. 54-55.

17. The overall response rate to the Pearce and Singh survey was 28.9 percent. Parent companies supplied 163 of 296 usable responses; subsidiaries supplied the remaining 133 responses. The response rate from 181 U.S.-based affiliates that were sent the survey was roughly 30 percent. The authors note that response rates were poor for French-owned companies and that there were too few Japanese companies in their sample to say much about them.

18. NEC Research Institute was established in Princeton, New Jersey, in 1989. It focuses on software development, artificial intelligence, and machine learning (Noguchi, 1989). Matsushita established its Information Technology Laboratory in Princeton the following year to conduct basic research in computer graphics, document processing, and systems software. In 1991, Hitachi set up a high-definition television research laboratory in Princeton. That same year, Mitsubishi Electric set up a basic research laboratory in Cambridge, Massachusetts, that focused on next-generation parallel processing and supercomputers. Canon established the Canon Research Center in Palo Alto, California, in 1990 to do research on data compression, optical recognition, and network architecture. Florida and Kenney (1993) note that these facilities tend to focus on areas of research "where Japanese industry lags the United States, such as parallel computing, software development, and artificial intelligence." This may explain their proximity to leading U.S. centers of R&D in these fields. Florida and Kenney also note that these laboratories "are designed to generate and harness new sources of knowledge, which leverages existing corporate technological capabilities and enhances long-range corporate development efforts."

19. Dibner et al. (1992) note that because of their large staffs, European-owned biotechnology R&D facilities have many more interactions with U.S. university- and industry-based researchers than Japanese-owned facilities with smaller R&D staffs.

R&D managers generally agree that there is a minimum efficient size for R&D laboratories that varies from industry to industry. Below this minimum, laboratories are unlikely to be successful either at performing in-house research or drawing upon extramural research.

20. From comments by NEC Research Institute Director William Gear before the NAE study committee at a November 9, 1993, workshop. See, also, Chapter 4, p. 110.

21. Of the 12 Japanese-owned electronics R&D facilities surveyed by Dalton and Serapio (1993), six focused on applied research (new applications for existing technology, design customization), two performed basic research exclusively, and four conducted both basic and applied research, although basic research was limited. Ten R&D facilities performed prototype testing, evaluation, and production, designed new products or modified existing product designs; seven did parts evaluation; five designed parts; seven conducted joint R&D with other research organizations; and seven employed university research professors as consultants.

In contrast, six Japanese automotive affiliates performed vehicle testing and evaluation, emissions certification, scanning of regulatory trends, technology scanning, and advanced concept design; four of the six firms surveyed did parts and materials evaluation and design; two performed joint research with a U.S. partner and produced prototypes of near-production vehicles; and three companies were involved in the development of local parts suppliers.

22. See, for example, Dibner et al. (1992) and National Research Council (1992c) for a discussion of affiliate-conducted R&D in the pharmaceuticals and biotechnology industries. For affiliate R&D

in electronics, see Florida and Kenney (1993), Kümmerle (1993a,b), Peters (1991, 1992), Voisey (1992), and Westney (1993).

23. According to Serapio (1994), Japanese companies are under additional pressure to internationalize their R&D activities as a result of a growing shortage of highly skilled scientific and engineering manpower in Japan.

24. See, for example, National Research Council (1992b), U.S. Congress, Office of Technology Assessment (1993, 1994), Organization for Economic Cooperation and Development (1994). See, also, Figure 3.9.

25. Summarizing the results of a 1992 Mitsubishi Research Institute survey of Japanese companies with overseas R&D facilities, Kümmerle (1993b) notes the following:

> Out of 28 labs which the 7 leading Japanese electronics companies have established abroad during the last 5 years, 15 were built with the intention to create new knowledge in targeted areas, 7 facilitate local adaptation of products, 3 support complex local production facilities, and 3 were built because of local political pressure. These figures mean that more than half of the new labs serve as facilitators for learning and creating new knowledge abroad. In the pharmaceutical sector, numbers are even more striking: 7 out of 9 labs abroad were established for purposes of local learning and local creation of new knowledge. Moreover, the majority of electronics and pharmaceutical companies expressed an intent to establish at least one more laboratory abroad during the next 5 years. . . . The research focus of the new 'learning-creating laboratories' is generally on areas with strategic importance for the firm but which are still mastered insufficiently by the company. Out of 5 laboratories that Canon has founded in Europe and the United States since 1988, none is concerned with research in optics: the focus is on either computer languages, image processing software, or telecommunications. This is in line with Canon's intent to shift from an 'Optical Technology Company' to a 'Total Image and Information Processing Company.'

26. Hagedoorn and Schakenraad (1993) attribute the recent growth of corporate interest in technical alliances to three primary motives. First, firms view alliances as a way to strengthen their research capabilities in the face of rapid technological change and the need to monitor and exploit external sources of science and technology. Second, by leveraging the know-how of alliance partners, companies can expand their ability to develop and apply new technologies. Third, alliances enhance firms' access to foreign markets and help them to seek out new business opportunities abroad.

27. Under the National Cooperative Production Amendments of 1993 [P.L. 103-42], which amended the National Cooperative Research Act of 1984 [P.L. 98-462], R&D and production joint ventures located within the United States and registered with the U.S. Department of Justice are exempted from the treble damages liability of U.S. antitrust laws. If any of the firms involved in a joint venture are foreign-owned, the home country of that firm must accord national treatment to U.S. firms with respect to antitrust treatment of similar joint ventures in the country.

28. The Department of Commerce (1991) found that the number of alliances involving biotechnology firms in the United States increased from 30 in 1981 to 400 in 1988. In 1981, 30 percent of such alliances included a foreign partner and in 1988, 45 percent had one. Peters (1992) notes that during the 1980s, the number of international strategic alliances grew eightfold in the telecommunications industry, around sevenfold in the pharmaceuticals industry, and sixfold in the biotechnology industry.

29. Peters (1993a) cites the example of NEC to show the complementary relationship between the growth of Japanese R&D facilities in the United States and the growth of technical alliances in the computer industry. In 1991, 2 years after establishing its basic research facility in Princeton, New Jersey, "NEC signed a contract with AT&T for a comprehensive package in semiconductor development for the next 5 years. NEC also entered a joint development agreement with Hewlett Packard to develop tools for microprocessors and microcomputers. Other companies having joint technology agreements with NEC include Grumman (supercomputer), American Microsystems (microprocessors), 3M (optical memory system), Summit Micro Circuit (a venture company to develop high-speed static random access memory chips), Hughes (weather satellite), Adobe Systems (desktop publishing software), General Electric (international PC network), Tektronix (gate array design software)." (pp. 6-7)

30. The six industrial sectors were aerospace, computers and peripherals, computer software, semiconductors, semiconductor manufacturing equipment, and biotechnology.

31. See note 8. Graham (1992) "guesstimates" that roughly two-thirds of the increase in Japanese-controlled R&D activity in the United States during the late 1980s resulted from Japanese acquisitions of existing U.S. operations.

32. Between 1980 and 1992 the average R&D/sales ratio for manufacturing affiliates increased from 1.6 percent to 2.6 percent (U.S. Department of Commerce, 1993a, 1995a).

33. For further discussion, see Graham and Krugman (1995), Organization for Economic Cooperation and Development (1994), Ozawa (1991), and U.S. Congress, Office of Technology Assessment (1994).

34. A number of factors may explain this variation between European and Japanese firms. Differences in the industrial composition of European and Japanese foreign direct investment may be one determining factor. The fact that direct investment by the Japanese is more recent in most U.S. industries than is that by European firms may also play a role. (Many U.S. affiliates of European-owned companies have added R&D capabilities after having had a U.S. manufacturing presence for decades.) Westney (1993) also points out that Japanese organization and management of affiliate R&D in the electronics industry may have a negative effect on Japanese patenting activity in the United States. Specifically, Japanese electronics firms have chosen to establish large numbers of small highly specialized facilities in the United States, each with a narrow technology mandate yet networked to the parent companies to provide input into technologies developed at the parent firms' facilities in Japan.

35. It should be noted that there is nothing unfair or unethical about foreign companies establishing technology scanning capabilities in the United States, or U.S. companies doing the same abroad. Indeed, the rapid pace of technological innovation in many sectors and the high costs of R&D have made it imperative that companies become much more effective at scanning for and acquiring technology developed beyond their institutional borders.

36. Royalties and license fees are payments for the sale and use of intangible property rights, such as patents, copyrights, franchises, trademarks, industrial processes, know-how, and other intellectual property rights. Some observers argue that multinational corporations, U.S. and foreign, frequently use these fees as a form of "transfer pricing," that is, shifting costs from subsidiaries in low-tax countries to a high-tax country in order to minimize tax obligations. (U.S. Department of Commerce, 1993a, p. 73).

37. See, for example, the Council on Competitiveness (1993) case study of the Committee on Foreign Investment in the United States (CFIUS) review of the sale of Semi-Gas System Inc. to the Japanese company, Nippon Sanso KK (pp. 137-155). Dalton and Genther's (1991) survey of foreign acquisition of U.S. electronics companies notes that most acquired companies were small, in need of a capital infusion, and were having difficulty obtaining credit or raising equity. See also the reflections of Materials Research Corporation's CEO Sheldon Weinig (1990) on his company's purchase by Sony. Graham and Krugman (1995) also review several CFIUS cases.

38. The Organization for Economic Cooperation and Development (OECD) has adopted two codes directed at international investment, the Code of Liberalization of Capital Movements and the Code of Liberalization of Current Invisible Operations, which are, in principle, binding on all OECD member states. In addition to these codes, all member states currently adhere to a "National Treatment Instrument," which obligates them to grant national treatment, with some exceptions, to companies controlled by investors from other OECD countries. The OECD is presently considering a "Wider Investment Instrument" that would, among other things, bolster national treatment provisions.

Both the U.S.-Canada Free Trade Agreement (FTA) and the North American Free Trade Agreement (NAFTA) commit (with some exceptions) their respective signatory states to national treatment of enterprises owned by nationals of other signatory states, limit the screening of acquisitions by nationals from other signatory states, call for free repatriation of capital and earnings, restrict recourse to performance requirements on investments that affect trade between signatories, and provide for dispute settlement mechanisms (the option of binding arbitration). Finally, the Uruguay Round agreement signed in mid-1994 obliges signatories, in principle, to refrain from imposing local-content requirements and export performance requirements on foreign-owned firms operating within their borders. For a detailed assessment of these and related initiatives, see Graham and Krugman (1995).

39 For a more comprehensive review of foreign barriers to international trade and investment, see Office of the U.S. Trade Representative (1995).

40. To get a feel for this debate, see Japan Economic Institute (1991), Krugman (1991), Lawrence (1991a,b), and Saxonhouse (1991).

41. It is estimated that intrafirm trade (IFT)—trade between the affiliates and parent multinational companies—now accounts for more than 40 percent of total world trade. Between 1983 and 1992, U.S.-Europe IFT accounted for 43 percent of all U.S.-European merchandise trade, with U.S.-owned multinationals claiming 43 percent of total U.S.-Europe IFT and European-owned multinationals 57 percent. During the same period U.S.-Japan IFT accounted for 71 percent of total U.S.-Japan merchandise trade. However, reflecting a large asymmetry in the volume of U.S. foreign direct investment in Japan compared to Japanese foreign direct investment in the United States, Japanese multinationals accounted for 92 percent of total U.S.-Japan IFT (U.S. Congress, Office of Technology Assessment, 1994).

42. Many U.S. companies enter into alliances with foreign firms in order to achieve greater access to their foreign partner's home market. In some cases, policy-related or structural barriers to access provide the foreign company with additional leverage in its negotiations with its U.S. partner. On the whole, however, transnational corporate alliances appear to have eased the entry of U.S.-owned and U.S.-based companies into foreign markets and national innovation systems.

43. The recent focus within segments of the U.S. trade community on "specific" or "tit-for-tat" reciprocity (with its emphasis on reciprocity in absolute levels of protection) marks a significant departure from the pursuit of "general" reciprocity (i.e., reciprocal changes in the level of protection with a commitment to unconditional Most-Favored-Nation treatment) that has characterized the negotiation of multilateral trade agreements during the post-World War II era. The former focuses on outcomes, such as comparable market access, while the latter focuses on the process of liberalization, such as market opening. For further discussion, see Bayard and Elliott (1994), and Cline (1982).

44. See Defense Science Board (1990), Institute for Defense Analysis (1990), Moran (1993), National Defense University (1987), The Analytic Sciences Corporation (1990), and U.S. General Accounting Office (1991b, 1994b).

45. In May 1993, the only remaining U.S.-owned supplier of mainstream semiconductor lithography equipment, SVG Lithography Systems, Inc. (SVGL), announced its intention to enter into a 10-year contract with the Japanese firm Canon. The contract would have given Canon access to all of SVGL's current and future Micrascan scan-and-step technology in return for an infusion of capital and Canon's assistance with manufacturing lithographic steppers. Negotiations between the two firms became protracted, and ultimately the deal fell through when the SEMATECH consortium members put together an alternative financing package that SVGL accepted . . . Nevertheless, many observers agree that the SEMATECH alternative would not have materialized had Canon not given SVGL its seal of approval by entering into negotiations with the small U.S. company in the first place. Ultimately, it was Canon's reputation and the prospect of Canon backing up the struggling U.S. company with its deep pockets, manufacturing technology, distribution networks, etc., that turned the tide in customer perceptions of the company's viability. See Randazzese (1994) for a well-documented assessment of the SVGL-Canon deal.

46. Aside from the oft-cited sale of sensitive U.S. submarine technology to the Soviets by Toshiba Corporation in the early 1980s, there is only limited anecdotal evidence to suggest that foreign-owned firms have leaked sensitive U.S. technologies to potential adversaries (Graham and Krugman, 1991).

47. See, for example, the criteria and procedures put forward in Graham and Krugman (1991, 1995), Moran (1990), and U.S. General Accounting Office (1994b).

4

Foreign Participation in Publicly Funded U.S. R&D

The past 10 to 15 years have also witnessed the growth of foreign involvement in publicly supported U.S. R&D activities at U.S. universities and federal laboratories.[1] This trend is less well documented than is the growth of foreign participation in privately funded U.S. R&D, and it has stimulated intense controversy. This is because these institutions, the two main pillars of the nation's publicly funded basic research enterprise and a unique source of national competitive advantage, are viewed as particularly vulnerable to foreign exploitation.

At a time when many elements of the nation's innovation system are perceived to be faltering in the face of increasing global competition, publicly funded U.S. basic research capabilities remain internationally preeminent. This is particularly true of those resident in the nation's academic institutions. In an effort to capitalize on this strength, the federal government is trying to enlist the research assets of universities and federal laboratories to bolster the competitiveness of U.S.-based companies in world markets. However, the internationalization of U.S. industry and the general openness of the nation's basic research enterprise have heightened concerns about losing government-funded intellectual property and its associated economic value to foreign entities.

The strength of the U.S. basic research enterprise is due primarily to its scale, its highly decentralized and pluralistic structure (i.e., multiple institutional players with different research agendas), and its openness to the free flow of ideas and talent from throughout the world. Underlying these sources of strength is the fact that most basic research is conducted in publicly funded, noncommercial institutions with reward systems that provide powerful incentives for researchers to share rapidly and widely the results of their research. Ironically, these very sources of strength make the U.S. basic research enterprise relatively easy for foreign nationals to access and exploit (National Academy of Engineering, 1993).

To date, three concerns have driven debate and policy on foreign involvement in publicly supported U.S. R&D, whether conducted by foreign firms, governments, academic institutions, or individual researchers. First, the United States may not receive an adequate quid pro quo for allowing various foreign entities to participate in publicly funded U.S. R&D. Second, some foreign governments appear to deny U.S. researchers reciprocal access to comparable publicly funded research within their borders. Third, some foreign countries do not appear to carry their fair share of the global basic research burden. Faced with these concerns, the American public and the Congress have become increasingly willing to restrict foreign access to U.S. government-supported research.

This chapter examines the scope and nature of foreign participation in three areas of publicly funded R&D activity: research universities, federal laboratories, and federally funded industrial R&D programs and industry-led consortia. It concludes with an assessment of the costs and benefits of this participation.

UNIVERSITY-BASED RESEARCH

The primary locus of foreign participation in U.S. publicly funded research and development has been the nation's academic research enterprise—home to roughly half of the nation's basic research activity. In 1994, American universities and colleges are estimated to have performed $21 billion worth of research and development, or roughly 12 percent of total U.S. R&D performed that year. Also in 1994, academic institutions performed more than 48 percent of all basic research, 13 percent of all applied research, but less than 2 percent of all development work conducted in the United States. Sixty percent of all academic R&D conducted in 1994 was paid for by the federal government (National Science Foundation, 1995b).

Foreign entities establish ties with U.S. universities for many reasons. Foreign students, visiting scholars, and company researchers are drawn to U.S. research universities to learn about some of the most advanced and creative research methods in the world. Foreign governments, companies, and nonprofit institutions establish ties with research universities to gain timely access to new knowledge and technology in particular fields or to engage university-based researchers in the solution of particular technical problems. Foreign firms license technology generated and owned by U.S. universities, and their U.S. affiliates look to U.S. research universities for highly trained science and engineering talent.[2] Often, foreign firms look upon their investments in U.S. research universities as a way to build goodwill and enhance their reputations in the U.S. research community.[3]

At the same time, several related factors have encouraged U.S. research universities to solicit more foreign participation in recent years. The nation's indigenous supply of advanced degree students, postdoctoral researchers, and faculty in science and engineering has fallen behind demand, forcing universities to turn increasingly to foreign talent to make up the shortfall. Similarly, the failure of federal R&D budgets to keep pace with the rising fiscal demands of research universities has encouraged these institutions to seek other patrons and clients, including foreigners. Finally, rapid growth in the scope, quality, and accessibility of foreign-based science and engineering capabilities has encouraged U.S.-based academic researchers to seek out foreign collaborators in many fields.

Foreign participation in U.S. academic R&D has manifested itself in multiple ways in recent years. These include:

• The involvement of foreign students, postgraduates, and visiting scholars and researchers from foreign firms in university research activities;

• Collaborations between foreign academic institutions/researchers and their U.S.-based counterparts;

• Sponsored and open-ended underwriting of university research by foreign governments, foreign corporations and their U.S. subsidiaries, and foreign nonprofit institutions;

• The cooperative activities of foreign corporate laboratories operating near U.S. research universities;

• Foreign support for the construction of buildings, purchase of equipment, and other in-kind contributions; and

• The hiring of U.S. faculty as consultants or advisors to foreign corporations and governments.

Foreign Students, Researchers, and Faculty

One measure of expanding foreign participation in U.S. university research and development has been the growing dependence of these institutions on foreign-born graduate students, postdoctoral researchers, and faculty. In 1980, non-U.S. citizens accounted for 12.8 percent of graduate enrollments in U.S. science and engineering fields, 21 percent of all science and engineering doctorate recipients, and a third of all postdoctoral researchers in science and engineering fields at U.S. universities. By 1991, non-U.S. citizens accounted for 23 percent of enrollments, 37 percent of doctorates, and more than half of postdocs working in science and engineering fields (Figure 4.1) (National Science Foundation, 1993a).

U.S. engineering schools are particularly dependent on foreign talent (Figure 4.2). As of 1991, 47 percent of all graduate students, 59 percent of all doctorate recipients, and 69 percent of all university-based postdoctoral researchers in engineering were non-U.S. citizens. The extent of foreign participation at the graduate level varies among engineering fields, with significantly more participation in petroleum, mining, and agricultural engineering, and significantly less in aerospace and biomedical engineering, and in engineering science (Figure 4.3).

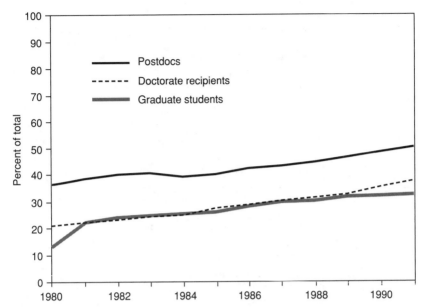

FIGURE 4.1 Foreign postdocs, doctorate recipients, and graduate students in science and engineering fields, 1980 through 1991. SOURCE: National Science Foundation (1993a).

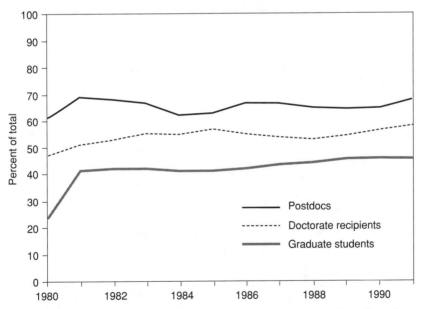

FIGURE 4.2 Foreign postdocs, doctorate recipients, and graduate students in engineering, 1980 through 1991. SOURCE: National Science Foundation (1993a).

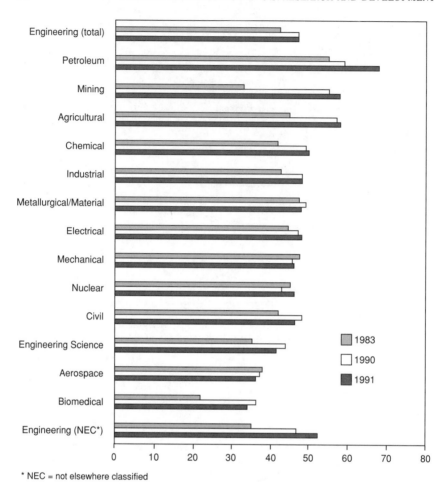

* NEC = not elsewhere classified

FIGURE 4.3 Non-U.S. citizens enrolled full-time in graduate engineering programs, percent of total enrollees by field of study, 1983, 1990, and 1991. SOURCE: National Science Foundation (1993a).

During the past 15 years, U.S. engineering faculties have experienced similar growth in the level of foreign involvement. In 1975, only 10 percent of engineering faculty under 36 years of age were from other countries. In 1985, the latest year for which data are available, the foreign-born share stood at 50 percent (National Research Council, 1988).[4]

The sudden rise in foreign graduate enrollment, postdoctoral research, and faculty employment is a function of three inter-related developments: the rapid growth of university research activities during the past decade and the resulting increase in demand for research personnel; a rapid increase in American industry's demand for science and engineering graduates, mostly those with B.S. degrees; and an absolute decline in the number of U.S.-born science and engineering students who pursue advanced engineering degrees or academic careers (National Research Council, 1988).

In contrast to the well-documented situation with foreign students, post-doctoral researchers, and resident faculty, little is known about the number, research focus, or duration of stay of foreign researchers visiting U.S. universities. Because most U.S. universities are highly decentralized, they do not keep tabs on foreign visitors, unless these individuals have an appointment at the host university or require contact with the federal government. In 1991, for example, the Massachusetts Institute of Technology (MIT) reported hosting 1,250 foreign scholars, "including professors, visiting scientists and engineers, post-docs, research affiliates and others" on campus, of whom 91 were paid fully or partially by foreign industrial firms (Massachusetts Institute of Technology, 1991).[5]

Collaboration between Foreign and U.S. Academic Researchers

Another dimension of deepening foreign involvement in U.S. academic research is the increase in research collaboration between U.S. academic researchers and their counterparts abroad in many science and engineering fields. One measure of this growth is the number of journal citations that include the names of both U.S. and foreign researchers (Figure 4.4). Between 1980 and 1991, the share of scientific and technical articles with international coauthorship more than doubled, from 5.2 percent to 11.0 percent. Papers in the earth and space sciences, mathematics, and physics were more likely than those in other fields to exhibit coauthorship.

Although no national data are collected on the extent of research collaboration between U.S. universities or university-based research centers and their counterparts overseas, anecdotal evidence suggests an increase in such linkages (Godfrey, 1991). For example, in testimony at a December 1993 National Academy of Engineering workshop on the flat panel display industry, Jay William Doane, director of the Liquid Crystal Institute at Kent State University, underlined the importance of his institution's research collaboration—with the University of Stuttgart, Tokyo University of Agriculture and Technology, and the Slovenian J. Stefan Institute—to active matrix display research and development.[6]

Foreign Funding of U.S. University Research

Between 1975 and 1994, the share of university research funded by the federal government fell from 67 to 60 percent and that supported by state and local governments decreased from 10 to 8 percent. Over the same period, industry more than doubled its contributions to academic research, from 3 to 7 percent of the total; the share of academic research supported by nonprofit institutions re-

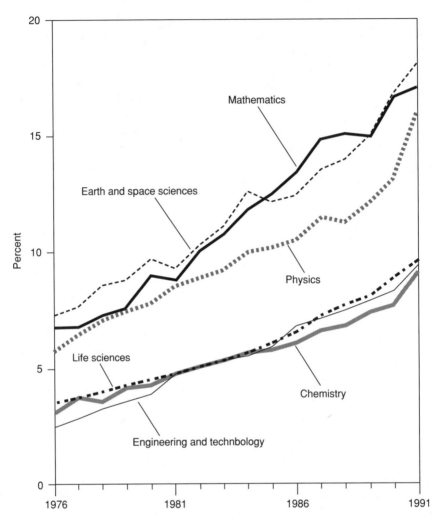

FIGURE 4.4   Internationally coauthored articles as a percent of all articles, by science and engineering field, 1976 through 1991. SOURCE: National Science Board (1993).

mained virtually unchanged, between 7 and 8 percent, while the contributions by universities themselves increased from 12 to 18 percent (Table 4.1). Within the context of these shifts, foreign governments, nonprofit institutions, and companies have begun to play a small role in underwriting U.S. academic R&D.

Data on foreign funding of U.S. university-based research are scant and dated. Although some public institutions are required by state law to report the receipt of foreign funds, most do not differentiate support obtained from domestic versus foreign sources. Factors that contribute to the haphazard tracking of foreign fi-

TABLE 4-1 Support for U.S. Academic R&D, Percent by Contributing Sector, 1975, 1980, 1985, 1990, and 1994

	1975	1980	1985	1990	1994
Federal government	67.1	67.5	62.6	59.2	60.1
State and local governments	9.7	8.2	7.8	8.1	7.6
Industry	3.3	3.9	5.8	6.9	6.9
Academic institutions	12.2	13.8	16.7	18.5	17.9
All other sources	7.6	6.6	7.2	7.3	7.4

NOTE: Columns do not necessarily total to 100 due to rounding.

SOURCE: National Science Board (1993) and data from the National Science Foundation Science Resource Series, National Patterns of R&D Resources series, accessed via the World Wide Web.

nancial support include the lack of uniform university accounting procedures, the multiplicity of funding sources and channels, and the decentralized nature of exchanges between donors and a broad spectrum of university offices, departments, and individual researchers.

According to the most recently published survey, foreign-sponsored research stood at $74.3 million in fiscal 1986, or roughly 1 percent of total university R&D expenditures (U.S. General Accounting Office, 1988a).[7] An informal inquiry by the National Science Foundation (NSF) found that foreign support of university R&D had not changed as of fiscal 1988 (National Science Foundation, 1990c).[8] More recent data collected from leading research universities by the study committee suggest that the foreign share of academic research funding has not grown appreciably since the GAO survey was conducted (Table 4.2).

Also in fiscal 1986, more than half of foreign funds for U.S. academic R&D were concentrated in five institutions: Texas A&M University, Harvard University, MIT, Oregon State University, and the University of Wisconsin. Foreign support ranged from 1 to 9 percent of total R&D expenditures at these institutions and averaged 4 percent. In fiscal 1988, three top-20 research universities, Texas A&M, the University of Michigan, and Harvard, reported receiving more than 2 percent of their research funding from foreign sources (National Science Foundation, 1990c). Another nine top-20 institutions received between 1 and 2 percent of their research funding from foreign sources. Six years later, in fiscal 1994, the foreign share of total sponsored research at most of the nation's top research universities had not changed significantly.[9]

In fiscal year 1986, Japanese entities sponsored more university-based R&D in the United States ($9.5 million) than did those of any other foreign country, although the United Kingdom and Germany were also major contributors to U.S. academic research (U.S. General Accounting Office, 1988a). That year, foreign funding of U.S. academic R&D was concentrated in a relatively small number of universities (Table 4.3).

TABLE 4.2 R&D Expenditures and Foreign Support for R&D at the Top 20 U.S. Research Universities,[a] Fiscal Years 1986, 1988, and 1993/1994

	FY 1986		FY 1988		FY 1993/1994	
	Total R&D Exp. ($1,000s)	Foreign R&D Support (% of Total)	Total R&D Exp. ($1,000s)	Foreign R&D Support (% of Total)	Total Sponsored R&D[b] ($1,000s)	Foreign R&D Support (% of Total)
1. Univ. of Michigan	182,400	<1	250,169	>2	333,340	2
2. Univ. of Minnesota	126,000	<1	252,027	<1	222,145	<1
3. Univ. of Wisconsin-Madison	231,000	1-2	271,418	<1	326,471	<1
4. Massachusetts Institute of Technology	256,096	>2	270,584	1-2	359,700	2-3
5. Stanford Univ.	218,219	<1	277,504	<1	293,000	<1
6. Cornell Univ.	216,286	<1	271,659	1-2	251,116	<1
7. Texas A&M Univ.	165,400	>2	231,161	1-2	355,800	N/A
8. Univ. of Washington	159,815	1-2	190,735	1-2	458,000	1-2
9. Johns Hopkins Univ.	164,914	1-2	557,016	<1		
10. Univ. of California-San Francisco	N/A		193,289	1-2	347,494	4-5
11. Pennsylvania State Univ.	151,196	<1	188,444	1-2	292,575	<1
12. Univ. of California-San Diego	138,900	<1	200,472	1-2	312,860	<1
13. Univ. of California-Berkeley	114,787	<1	186,372	<1	213,164	1-2
14. Univ. of California-Los Angeles	160,402	<1	209,338	1-2	342,098	<1
15. Univ. of Illinois-Urbana	119,619	<1	197,393	1-2	185,673	<1
16. Univ. of Texas-Austin	119,611	<1	172,608	<1	203,278	N/A
17. Harvard Univ.	185,688	>2	190,429	>2	328,787	4-5
18. Univ. of Arizona	124,790	<1	155,464	<1	202,082	2-3
19. Univ. of Maryland-College Park		-0-	135,531	<1	138,153	<1
20. Univ. of California-Davis	100,723	1-2	154,655	1-2	160,328	N/A

[a]Universities ranked according to volume of R&D expenditures in 1991.

[b]Total sponsored research includes all contracts and grants awarded in a given fiscal year and does not necessarily equal total R&D expenditures for that year.

SOURCE: U.S. General Accounting Office (1988a); National Science Foundation (1990b); and National Academy of Engineering, unpublished data.

Three fields—geology ($16.4 million), agriculture ($11.5 million), and medicine ($8.4 million)—accounted for nearly half of all foreign support for U.S. academic R&D in fiscal 1986 (Table 4.4). There were very few similarities in either the research fields funded or the source of foreign support among the top five recipient institutions. An international ocean-drilling research program funded in part by NSF at Texas A&M University received 93 percent of all foreign support directed to U.S. university-based geology research. Four universities accounted for nearly 80 percent of all foreign-funded research in agriculture, most of which focused on the agricultural research needs of developing countries (U.S. General Accounting Office, 1988a).

In fiscal 1986, a little more than a third of all foreign funds for university research came from businesses; the remaining two-thirds came from foreign governments and nonprofit organizations. Of the top five U.S. recipients of foreign R&D funding, Texas A&M, Harvard, and Oregon State received the majority of such support from governments and nonprofit institutions (99 percent, 95 percent, and 78 percent, respectively). In contrast, nearly all foreign support of research at MIT and the University of Wisconsin came from private companies (98 and 89 percent, respectively). Indeed, foreign firms accounted for more than half of all foreign R&D funding at 13 of the top 20 U.S. research universities in fiscal 1986 (Table 4.5).

Foreign Corporate Participation in U.S. Academic R&D

The most controversial aspect of foreign involvement in U.S. university R&D centers on the participation of foreign corporations and their U.S. subsidiaries. This is because foreign firms—unlike foreign governments, nonprofit institutions, and academic researchers—are well equipped to acquire and apply commercially valuable outputs of publicly funded U.S. academic research, thereby appropriating a significant share of their associated economic returns.[10]

There are five major ways foreign corporations can participate in U.S. university-based R&D: through company-sponsored research, either in the form of contracts or grants; by working with university patent and technology licensing offices; via university industrial liaison or affiliates' programs; by involvement in university-industry research centers; and through activities in formal or de facto industrial technology parks located near prominent U.S. research universities.

Data on the current magnitude, disciplinary focus, and national shares of foreign sponsored research at individual U.S. universities and federal laboratories are fragmentary. Limited survey data (National Research Council, 1994a; Roberts, 1995a) and anecdotal evidence indicate that Japanese companies are more diligent than their U.S. or European counterparts with regard to accessing, monitoring, and drawing upon the research capabilities of these publicly funded institutions.

TABLE 4.3 Foreign Support of U.S. Academic R&D, by Country and Top Four Recipient Universities, FY 1986

Contributing Country/Region[a]	Support for University R&D (Millions of $)	Number of Universities Receiving Funds	Number of Universities Receiving $100,000 or More	Top Four Recipient Universities	University Share of Foreign Country's R&D Contribution
Canada	5.7	45	13	Texas A&M Univ.[b]	43
				Massachusetts Institute of Technology	7
				North Carolina State Univ.	7
				Oregon Health Science Univ.	5
Japan	9.5	53	15	Texas A&M Univ.[b]	26
				Massachusetts Institute of Technology	23
				Univ. of Washington	14
				Univ. of Arizona	4
Other Far East	8.8	22	8	Harvard Univ.	79
				Univ. of Wisconsin	4
				Univ. of Washington	3
				Massachusetts Institute of Technology	3
Middle East (excludes Israel)	7.2	24	6	Harvard Univ.	39
				Univ. of California-Davis	19
				Georgia Tech	18
				Oregon State Univ.	14

United Kingdom	7.0	40	13	Texas A&M Univ.[b]	37
				Univ. of Alabama	13
				Massachusetts Institute of Technology	11
				Johns Hopkins Univ.	10
West Germany	5.6	40	9	Texas A&M Univ.[b]	46
				Univ. of Arkansas	7
				Massachusetts Institute of Technology	6
				Univ. of Texas-Austin	5
Other Western Europe	16.3	80	34	Texas A&M Univ.[b]	16
				Univ. of Arkansas	9
				Massachusetts Institute of Technology	7
				Univ. of Wisconsin	7
All Other Countries	12.5				

[a] Excludes multinational sources because of their small size.

[b] Texas A&M University received about $2.5 million in 1986 from each of these countries for an ocean-drilling program which is sponsored by the National Science Foundation.

SOURCE: U.S. General Accounting Office (1988a).

TABLE 4.4   Foreign Support for U.S. Academic
R&D, by University Department, Fiscal 1986

Field	$ in Millions
Geology	16.4
Agriculture	11.5
Medicine	8.4
Civil engineering	2.7
Biology	2.6
Chemistry	1.5
Chemical engineering	1.5
Materials engineering	1.3
Computer engineering	1.1
Other engineering	1.1
Mechanical engineering	.8
Electrical engineering	.7
Physics	.5
Nuclear engineering	.4
Aeronautical engineering	.3
Psychology	.1
Other	21.3

SOURCE: U.S. General Accounting Office (1988a).

Research Contracts and Grants

As noted, foreign-owned companies accounted for approximately one-third of all foreign-sponsored research at U.S. universities, or one-third of one percent of total academic research funding in 1986, the latest year for which aggregate data are available. Company-sponsored research at U.S. universities comprises research contracts and research grants. The distinction between the two instruments is subtle and varies among institutions. In general, research contracts obligate university-based researchers to provide their corporate sponsor with more-frequent and more-formal reports on their progress than are required with grants. Contracts also usually specify particular deliverables, whereas grants are generally more open ended. National statistics on the sponsorship of academic research do not distinguish between contracts and grants because of the definitional vagaries and reporting inconsistencies among institutions.

Research grants may demand more of a quid pro quo from university-based researchers than the term "grant" implies. For example, companies providing research grants to university-based researchers may receive favorable consideration in licensing negotiations, even though they do not receive royaltyfree or exclusive rights. For example, at the University of California at Berkeley and MIT, some engineering departments have agreed to accept visiting fellows from major industrial donors. During the 1991–92 academic year, Berkeley's College

TABLE 4.5 Total Foreign Support for R&D and Corporate Share of that Support at the Top 20 U.S. Research Universities, Fiscal 1986[a]

	Total Foreign R&D Support ($1,000s)	Corporate Share (% of Total)
1. Massachusetts Institute of Technology	5,304	98.2
2. Univ. of Wisconsin-Madison	2,380	89.5
3. Stanford Univ.	562	93.2
4. Cornell Univ.	245	29.4
5. Harvard Univ.	10,781	4.8
6. Univ. of Michigan	450	83.9
7. Texas A&M Univ.	15,200	1.3
8. Johns Hopkins Univ.	2,118	n/a
9. Univ. of California-Los Angeles	782	50.4
10. Univ. of Washington	2,068	38.3
11. Pennsylvania State Univ.	673	69.4
12. Univ. of Pennsylvania	228	100.0
13. Univ. of California-San Diego	728	96.5
14. Univ. of Minnesota	268	61.9
15. Univ. of Arizona	586	100.0
16. Yale Univ.	194	87.6
17. Univ. of Illinois-Urbana	206	0
18. Univ. of Texas-Austin	752	96.9
19. Univ. of Southern California	30	n/a
20. Univ. of California-Berkeley	187	52.5

[a]Universities ranked according to volume of R&D expenditures in 1986.

SOURCE: U.S. General Accounting Office (1988a).

of Engineering hosted 17 fellows from Japanese companies as part of a research program funded with between $2 and $3 million in grants. The salaries and expenses of these fellows were paid by their sponsor companies.[11]

There are no recent national aggregate data on the disciplinary focus of foreign corporate sponsorship of university research. However, in fiscal 1986, nearly 50 percent of foreign support of university research, including funding by foreign governments, companies, and nonprofit organizations, was concentrated in geology, agriculture, and medicine (see Table 4.3). Stalson's (1989) survey of eight leading engineering schools found that foreign corporate sponsors demonstrated an interest in research from all of the traditional engineering disciplines, as well as the science-oriented fields of biotechnology and computer science. Although Japanese firms awarded the majority of foreign-sponsored contracts in these disciplines, German and French companies were significantly represented, with a smaller presence of Canadian, British, Dutch, Italian, and other European firms. According to Stalson, there was no discernible pattern of national specialization in any field of engineering research except civil engineering and construction, which appeared to be the exclusive province of the Japanese.[12]

As of 1993, over 60 percent of all foreign company-sponsored research at the University of California at Berkeley was concentrated in three locations: the department of chemistry, the electronics research laboratory, and the space sciences laboratory. The largest single research contract by a foreign firm, $1.8 million to the space sciences laboratory, came from French-owned Fairchild Space Company, itself a contractor to NASA. British companies accounted for almost all the foreign corporate research support in chemistry. The German company, Siemens, provided 85 percent of all foreign funds that went to the electronics research laboratory; the remaining 15 percent came from Japanese firms. All foreign corporate support of the university's Engineering Systems Research Center and department of optometry came from Japanese companies, as did a majority of foreign research support for the department of mechanical engineering and mechanical design.[13]

For the most part, foreign firms appear to be sensitive to the charge that they are taking more from U.S. research institutions than they are contributing. They have sought ways to avoid even the appearance of impropriety by concentrating on "precompetitive" research and seeking U.S. corporate partners when engaging universities in contract research (Stalson, 1989; U.S. Congress, House, 1993). Nevertheless, in recent years, a small number of controversial agreements between U.S. universities and foreign firms have had a negative effect on the public's perception of foreign involvement in U.S. government-funded R&D.

A case in point was the 1988 agreement between Hitachi Chemical Research (HCR), a subsidiary of the Japanese firm Hitachi Chemical Company, Ltd., and the University of California, Irvine (UCI). Under the terms of this agreement, the Japanese company agreed to build a facility on university-owned property to house rentfree the basic research laboratories of the university's department of biological chemistry and a basic research laboratory for the company's proprietary programs. Normally, intellectual property developed using University of California resources, including facilities and equipment, is owned by the university. In this case, however, Hitachi owns all intellectual property developed within its proprietary research laboratory, and in the case of "joint investigations of at least one UCI investor and at least one HCR inventor," UCI and HCR will each own an equal interest in the invention (National Research Council, 1992c).

From the outset, public criticism of the UCI-HCR agreement was intense. Many questioned whether the two institutions could keep their research activities separate or whether the U.S. taxpayer was being called upon to subsidize the proprietary research of a Japanese company. Others doubted whether UCI faculty collaborating with HCR could avoid potentially harmful conflicts of interest. Although little has transpired to substantiate these fears since the shared research facility opened its doors in 1990, public skepticism about the arrangement lingers.

It is not unusual for U.S. or foreign-owned firms to establish R&D facilities proximate to leading research universities in order to draw upon their resident technical expertise and research activities. (See discussion of industrial technology parks, below.) It is also fairly common for companies to supply instrumentation, equipment, and other in-kind support to academic research projects in exchange for facilitated or preferential access to intellectual property resulting from the research. In the committee's view, what has made the UCI-HRC agreement so controversial is that it is such an obvious attempt by a privately owned Japanese firm to draw upon the intellectual resources of a university that are underwritten by the U.S. government.

Also controversial have been cases in which universities or university-affiliated research institutions have effectively sold to foreign-owned firms the right of first refusal to all intellectual property resulting from a broad stream of research that has been partially, and in some cases largely, subsidized by U.S. public monies. Some of the more highly publicized agreements of this type include the 1989 deal between Harvard Medical School, its teaching hospital Massachusetts General Hospital, and the Japanese cosmetics firm Shiseido Co. Ltd., in the area of skin research;[14] the 1990 agreement between the University of California at San Diego and the Swiss pharmaceutical company, Ciba-Geigy;[15] the 1992 agreement between Scripps Research Institute and the Swiss pharmaceutical company Sandoz Pharma;[16] and the 1993 agreement between the University of California at San Francisco and the Japanese firm Daiichi Pharmaceuticals, involving research on atherosclerosis.[17]

The Scripps-Sandoz Pharma agreement has been the most controversial of the four. This is so in part because it was the largest research agreement ever concluded between a U.S. research institution and an industrial partner, and also because its terms were so expansive. Under the original agreement, which was to begin in 1997 and continue for 10 years, Scripps would receive $300 million and in exchange would grant Sandoz the right of first refusal to license any intellectual property resulting from institute's research. The agreement included the option to extend the agreement for an additional 6 years. Controversy arose because Scripps receives 60 percent of its funding from the National Institutes of Health (NIH). The agreement was subsequently modified at NIH's insistence (National Institutes of Health, 1994a,b).

In the opinion of the committee, it is in the best interests of the United States for publicly supported research universities and other publicly funded institutions to offer to private-sector investors the right of first refusal for intellectual property resulting from specific research supported by these investors. Such provisions offer an important incentive to private companies to invest in high-risk research activities that leverage public R&D monies. They also can yield substantial benefits to society at large, in the form of better trained science and engineering graduates, advances in knowledge, and improvements in instrumentation. If the intellectual property includes technology that may be commercialized, another effect may be higher performance and lower-cost products and services.

At the same time, the public interest is poorly served when universities grant to a private firm rights of first refusal to all intellectual property that might follow from an extremely broad stream of publicly subsidized research—in effect providing the firm with a windfall and potentially preventing or delaying useful application of the resulting intellectual property by other companies.[18] Each of the cases that received extensive public scrutiny has involved different circumstances and different trade-offs, whose implications for the public interest are difficult to assess. Nevertheless, universities and other performers of publicly funded R&D need to recognize and address the public perception that they are giving away the store.

Patent and Technology Licensing Programs

In 1980, Congress passed amendments to the Patent and Trademark Act, known as the Bayh-Dole Act (P.L. 96-480). This legislation made it possible for universities, other nonprofit organizations, and small businesses to retain rights to most of their federally funded inventions. Universities are granted considerable autonomy in commercializing these technologies under the act. In return for this autonomy, the amendments require that universities meet two provisions. First, they must give preference to U.S.-based businesses, particularly small companies, in licensing federally funded technologies. Second, they may grant exclusive rights or sell these technologies only to companies willing and able to manufacture substantially in the United States products embodying the invention or produced through application of the invention (U.S. General Accounting Office, 1992).[19]

In response to this change in law, U.S. research universities have greatly expanded their patenting and technology licensing programs during the past 14 years. What few data exist suggest that foreign companies played an appreciable role in this increased activity. A 1991 GAO survey of patent licensing by 35 leading U.S. research universities found that roughly 15 percent (29 of 197) of all exclusive licenses issued by universities for technologies developed with NSF or NIH funds were sold to foreign companies (18) or to their U.S. subsidiaries (11) (U.S. General Accounting Office, 1992).[20] As of May 1994, foreign companies held 21 (or 8 percent) of MIT's 225 active exclusive licenses. European firms held 13 of these and Japanese and Canadian firms claimed 4 each. Foreign companies also claimed 23 (roughly 16 percent) of MIT's 145 currently active nonexclusive licenses. By way of comparison, foreign-owned companies held just 3 of 27 active exclusive licenses from the University of California at San Diego, 5 of 65 exclusive licenses from the University of Michigan, and only 1 of 34 active exclusive licenses issued by the Georgia Institute of Technology.[21] Neither the

GAO data nor those provided by individual research universities provide information on the nature or relative importance of exclusive licenses granted to foreign and domestic firms.

When universities turn to foreign firms to license their technologies, they seem to do so for reasons specific to each transaction. In his testimony at a November 9, 1993, NAE workshop on access by foreign companies to U.S. technology, John Wiley, then dean of graduate studies and vice president for research at the University of Wisconsin at Madison, illustrated this point with two examples. In the first case, the university licensed a technology for making a silicon-backbone polymer to a Japanese firm after having spent several years attempting unsuccessfully to interest U.S. chemical, fiber, and other companies in the process. In the second case, the university licensed to a Japanese pharmaceutical company what turned out to be a highly lucrative patent for a vitamin D derivative found to be effective in treating osteoporosis in women eating a very low-fat diet. Given the generally high-fat diet of most Americans, and hence, the relatively small projected U.S. market for the derivative, no U.S. pharmaceutical companies were interested in the technology. The Japanese diet, in contrast, made for a large potential domestic market for the derivative, which made the patent attractive to the Japanese firm (Wiley, 1993).

Wiley's comments, as well as those made by other university research administrators, suggest that university technology licensing offices generally turn to foreign licensees as a last resort when no prospective U.S. licensee can be found.[22]

Industrial Liaison Programs

Industrial liaison programs (ILPs) charge membership fees to companies in return for providing them with general access to the results of university research, to researchers, and to laboratories in specified fields. As part of its 1992 survey of 35 leading U.S. research universities, GAO gathered information on the growth of industrial liaison programs. Thirty of these institutions had at least one industrial liaison program. Carnegie Mellon University alone accounted for 59 of 278 such programs that were identified.

Of the 30 universities with ILPs, 24 had a total of 499 foreign companies enrolled in at least 1 industrial liaison program.[23] Nine of the 24 host institutions reported holding more than $10,000 in stock through endowments in at least one of the participating foreign companies. Eighteen of the universities surveyed provide liaison program members, whether domestic or foreign, with access to the results of federally funded research before those results are made generally available, while the other 12 institutions do not. Three institutions—MIT, Stanford, and the University of California at Berkeley, which accounted for 290, or 58 percent, of all foreign liaison program participants—do not provide advance access to research results (U.S. General Accounting Office, 1992).[24]

Only a few of the universities surveyed reported that they distinguish between U.S. and foreign companies when reviewing and approving requests to join their liaison programs, allowing members to participate in program activities, or assessing membership fees. Both the University of California at Berkeley and MIT require significantly greater participation fees from foreign companies than they do from U.S.-owned firms.[25] The universities of Michigan, Washington, and Wisconsin, as well as Columbia University, place certain restrictions on foreign participation in at least one of their industrial liaison programs (U.S. General Accounting Office, 1992).

University-Industry Research Centers[26]

University-industry research centers (UIRCs) represent a third channel through which foreign companies participate in U.S. university-based science and engineering research. During the 1970s and 1980s, increased support from state and federal governments fueled a rapid proliferation in the number of UIRCs. These seed or matching funds encouraged research universities to institutionalize more formal R&D relationships with private companies. The most aggressive federal sponsor of UIRCs during the 1980s was the National Science Foundation (NSF), which helped establish a raft of university-based centers including Engineering Research Centers, Science and Technology Centers, State/University/Industry Cooperative Research Centers, Industry/University/Cooperative Research Centers, Materials Research Centers, and Supercomputer Centers.[27]

Data gathered by Cohen et al. (1994) from over 1,000 UIRCs based at more than 200 U.S. university campuses indicate that on average, foreign firms accounted for roughly 12 percent of all companies involved in nearly 470 centers reporting at least some foreign participation (Table 4.6). Among the 17 technology areas identified, the level of foreign involvement exceeded 12 percent in five areas: biotechnology, pharmaceuticals, biomedicine, chemicals, and agriculture and food.

For the most part, the policy statements and actions of state governments appear to support foreign corporate involvement in local research universities.[28] In many if not most instances, however, the federal government restricts or places conditions on foreign participation in the centers it supports. For instance, the NSF does not allow foreign governments to participate in the Engineering Research Centers it funds. However, foreign-owned firms "are not excluded, as long as the Center can demonstrate that a quid pro quo relationship exists, where information exchange is substantially equal in both directions." In fiscal 1994, NSF classified 9.5 percent of total industrial participation in these centers as foreign. Foreign researchers may work in the centers and center researchers may spend time in labs abroad. Some centers have opted for more restrictive policies on membership for foreign firms, however.[29]

Stalson (1989) found that the strongest industry opposition to involvement in

TABLE 4.6 Foreign Company Involvement in U.S. University-Industry Research Centers as Percent of Total Industry Participation, by Technology Area, 1992

Technology Area	Percent Foreign Involvement
Biotechnology	17.4
Pharmaceuticals	16.9
Biomedicine	16.8
Chemicals	15.7
Agriculture and food	13.7
Scientific instruments	11.6
Advanced materials	10.2
Aerospace	9.5
Energy	9.5
Transportation	9.4
Environmental technology and waste management	9.3
Industrial automation and robotics	8.8
Computer software	8.5
Semiconductor electronics	7.7
Telecommunications	6.2
Computer hardware	6.1
Other technology areas	9.2

SOURCE: Wesley Cohen, Carnegie Mellon University, unpublished data.

the university-industry centers came from firms in sensitive, competitive areas or in fields where the United States was believed to have a strong technological lead. For example, some U.S. companies involved in semiconductor and microelectronics research, magnetics technology, and materials science voiced concern about foreign companies also participating in these centers.

Industrial Technology Parks

Industrial technology parks established near prominent U.S. research universities have provided another avenue for foreign access to U.S. R&D. Some states have established formal parks, such as North Carolina's Research Triangle Park (a major center for biotechnology research), to promote state or regional economic development. Other de facto technology parks have been developed near major American research universities by firms seeking to exploit the "dense externalities" or "spillovers" that come from daily interaction with university researchers or researchers working for other companies. Dalton and Serapio (1995) have documented how foreign corporate R&D facilities are clustered around major U.S. research universities, such as MIT, Princeton, Stanford, and the University of California at Berkeley (Chapter 3, Figure 3.6).

Data on the scope and nature of foreign company research activities in the Princeton and Research Triangle Park cases indicate that the R&D investments appear to be both quantitatively and qualitatively significant, at least for some of the major foreign firms. For example, although the U.S. R&D laboratories of most Japanese electronics companies are focused on highly applied research and have relatively small research staffs and budgets, the NEC Research Institute in Princeton is a notable exception. As of fiscal 1994, it employed 135 people, including 78 permanent and 26 visiting technical personnel. The institute had an operating budget of approximately $20 million, and its staff was engaged in basic computer and physical sciences research. Siemens Research Corporation, also in Princeton, had a staff of 145 with an annual budget also in the range of $20 million.[30] Research efforts at Siemens have been focused on software engineering, imagery, learning systems, and optical data processing. At Research Triangle Park, Glaxo, a British chemical and pharmaceutical company, Rhone-Poulenc and Reichold Chemicals, French and Japanese chemical companies, and Ciba-Geigy, a Swiss pharmaceutical firm, collectively employ nearly 1,700 researchers (Dalton and Serapio, 1995; Serapio and Dalton, 1994).

Other Forms of Foreign Corporate Participation in U.S. Academic R&D

Beyond the more institutionalized interaction of foreign companies and university-based researchers, a variety of relationships has developed in which university faculty act as independent professionals—often consultants, advisors, or board members. In general, American universities do not collect data on such interactions. However, a 1990 MIT survey of its faculty's consulting contacts found that foreign companies accounted for less than one-quarter of all such encounters (Massachusetts Institute of Technology, 1991).

In several celebrated instances, foreign-owned companies have hired away U.S. university-based researchers. For example, when NEC set up its research laboratory in Princeton, it hired prominent researchers from the University of California at Berkeley, MIT, AT&T Bell Laboratories, and other top U.S. research institutions to lead its basic research effort in various areas of the computer and physical sciences (Business Week, 1992).

Foreign companies have also made unrestricted gifts, such as endowed science and engineering chairs, and have given funds for physical infrastructure to U.S. research universities. For instance, as of 1991, 30 of the 215 endowed chairs at MIT were funded by foreign-owned corporations. Here again, however, no national data are available.

The Special Case of Japanese Involvement in U.S. Research Universities

While limited, existing data suggest that many Japanese-owned companies pursue more aggressively closer interactions with the U.S. academic research community than do their European or U.S. counterparts. The special interest of Japanese firms in the U.S. academic research enterprise is confirmed in a recent survey of over 240 leading European, Japanese, and U.S. R&D-intensive companies that measured the intensity of these firms' use of universities (mostly U.S. research universities) for four defined purposes: collaborative research, gleaning innovative ideas, determining technology trends, and training company personnel (Figure 4.5). Roberts (1995a) observes that Japanese companies draw upon the assets of research universities for all four purposes more intensively than do either European- or U.S.-owned companies.[31] One major exception may be U.S. academic research in biotechnology, which, according to Dibner et al. (1992), draws significantly more intensive interaction from the large European pharmaceuticals and chemicals companies than it does from the smaller Japanese drug firms.

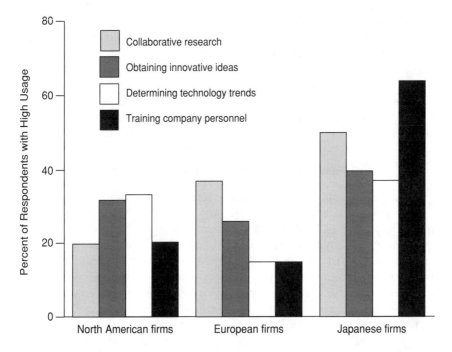

FIGURE 4.5 Use of university resources by North American, European, and Japanese companies, by type of activity, 1992. NOTE: Of 244 companies sampled, useable responses were received from 95 firms (39 percent), of which 46 were from the United States (42 percent response), 27 from Europe (34 percent), and 22 from Japan (40 percent). Most of the university resources cited by survey respondents were located in the United States. SOURCE: Roberts (1995a).

FOREIGN PARTICIPATION IN U.S. FEDERAL LABORATORY R&D

Like the nation's academic research enterprise, the nation's federal laboratory system has experienced growing foreign participation during the past decade. The more than 700 federal laboratories had a combined budget for fiscal 1993 of $23.4 billion. This total includes intramural agency laboratories as well as federally funded research and development centers (FFRDCs). FFRDCs and many intramural laboratories are government-owned, contractor-operated facilities managed by universities (e.g., Los Alamos, Lincoln Laboratory), university consortia (e.g., Brookhaven, Fermilab), industrial contractors operating on a not-for-profit basis (e.g., Oak Ridge National Laboratory and Sandia National Laboratory), or independent nonprofit organizations (e.g., MITRE Corporation, Draper Laboratory, RAND). Other intramural agency laboratories are government-owned and government-operated, such as those at the National Institutes of Health, National Institute of Standards and Technology, Naval Research Laboratory, Naval Surface Weapons Center, and certain facilities at the National Aeronautics and Space Administration.

Federal laboratories are diverse in size, character, and mission. Most are single-office facilities employing a small number of researchers; a small percentage are large organizations that employ thousands of scientists and engineers. Collectively, these laboratories employ roughly 120,000 scientists and engineers nationwide. In 1993, these institutions performed approximately 18 percent of all U.S. basic research, 16 percent of all applied research, and 13 percent of all technology development work (National Science Board, 1993).

A History of Foreign Involvement

With the exception of laboratories performing classified research, U.S. federal laboratories have traditionally been open to foreign researchers. During the past 4 decades, the U.S. government has entered into agreements with foreign governments that have allowed thousands of non-U.S. researchers to work at federal laboratories. During the 1960s and 1970s, the responsibilities of the federal laboratory system grew to include the construction and operation of major user facilities, such as particle and photon accelerators, environmental research parks, and materials laboratories. These new facilities opened the laboratory system increasingly to U.S. and foreign researchers from industry and academe.

Since 1980, growing concern about the nation's international competitiveness has led the federal government to take a number of steps designed to increase the extent to which federal laboratories support the activities of U.S. industry. These have included the creation of offices of technology transfer in the federal laboratories, changes in patenting and royalty mechanisms that allow companies to acquire exclusive licenses and permit federal laboratory researchers to receive a percentage of royalties from commercialized technology, and reimbursement schemes that allow private companies to conduct proprietary research at federal user facilities, such as the synchrotron light source at Brookhaven National Laboratory. Growing numbers of domestic and foreign visiting researchers have been drawn to the federal laboratories, as these facilities have moved into the business of technology transfer and technical support to U.S. industry.

By the mid 1980s, visiting researchers accounted for a significant share of the work conducted at federal laboratories. In its study of foreign participation in 50 federal research laboratories, GAO (1988b) reported that in addition to permanent laboratory employees, 4,657 U.S. and 3,597 foreign visiting researchers conducted R&D at these laboratories in fiscal 1986. Fifty percent of the visiting U.S. and 57 percent of the visiting foreign researchers were affiliated with universities and other nonprofit organizations. There were more Japanese, 758 (13.4 percent of the total pool of visiting foreign scientists), conducting research at the 50 federal laboratories than any other nationality. There were 448 researchers from the United Kingdom and 438 from the People's Republic of China.

From 1988 to 1991, the Department of Energy's (DOE) 10 multiprogram laboratories, operating with an annual budget of $6.2 billion and a total staff of roughly 52,300, hosted 11,000 visiting foreign scientists and engineers.[32] Approximately one-third of the visitors came from Japan. Two DOE laboratories, Lawrence Livermore National Laboratory and Los Alamos National Laboratory (LANL), hosted half of all foreign visiting researchers during the 3-year period (National Research Council, 1994a).

From 1988 to 1990, LANL hosted 4,000 foreign visitors, 700 of them Japanese. The primary focus of foreign visiting researchers' activity at LANL has been basic research. Japanese visitors to LANL have been characterized by the laboratory's administrators as "more strategic"—that is, more focused in their approach and better prepared to identify and pursue research and technologies of potential commercial importance—than other visiting foreign scientists. In addition to their interest in basic research, the Japanese scientists have also followed closely U.S. advances in the modeling of computer software codes and in laser sciences, particularly photolithography (National Research Council, 1994a).

In 1993, NIH, with a total resident technical staff of approximately 16,000, hosted approximately 1,700 foreign visiting researchers as part of its visiting fellows, visiting associates, and visiting scientists programs. As participants in these programs, foreign researchers generally spend 2 years or longer at NIH engaged almost exclusively in basic research. Stipends and salaries are provided by the agency. In order to participate, visiting researchers must agree to certain intellectual property rights provisions. Together, Japanese and Chinese scientists accounted for over one-third of participants in the program (Table 4.7). Although NIH lacks complete data on the institutional affiliation of foreign visitors, the agency estimates that only 4 percent of visiting researchers from Japan were from private industry.[33]

In its 1988 survey, GAO found that research administrators and managers at

TABLE 4.7   Participants in NIH Visiting Scientist
Programs, Top 10 Countries, Fiscal 1993

Country	Number[a]
Japan	325
China	287
Italy	131
Korea	105
India	94
Russia	92
United Kingdom	86
France	77
Germany	77
Israel	75

[a]U.S. permanent residents not included in count.

SOURCE: National Institutes of Health, unpublished data.

federal laboratories supported the open exchange of information with foreign researchers in basic scientific fields. However, in fields with commercial potential,
research managers and administrators at NIST (then the National Bureau of Standards), Langley Research Center, Oak Ridge National Laboratory, and Sandia
stated that they gave preferential access to U.S. researchers and organizations and
carefully reviewed requests for access by foreign researchers and organizations
(U.S. General Accounting Office, 1988b).

Foreign Corporate Participation in Federal Laboratories

In recent years, several federal laboratories have also entered into formal
relationships with foreign-owned companies as part of broader efforts to collaborate more with U.S.-based industry in areas of precompetitive, commercially relevant R&D. Since the late 1980s, for example, several federal labs have signed
cooperative research and development agreements (CRADAs) with foreign companies.[34] Between March 1988 and January 1995, NIST negotiated over 500
CRADAs, 34 of them with foreign companies. Over the same period, NIH entered into 237 CRADAs, 26 of which were with foreign companies, 6 of these
Japanese. Argonne National Laboratory and Oak Ridge National Laboratory have
negotiated 92 and 108 CRADAs, respectively, and each has 2 CRADAs with
foreign companies.[35]

Federal laboratories that wish to grant exclusive licenses for their technology to or engage in CRADAs with private organizations "must give preference to
business units located in the United States that agree that products embodying
inventions made under the [CRADA] or produced through the use of such inven-

tion will be manufactured substantially in the United States." In addition to this economic performance requirement, federal laboratory directors must consider whether the home governments of would-be foreign participants "permit and encourage United States agencies, organizations, or other persons to enter into cooperative research and development agreements and licensing arrangements on a comparable basis; . . . have policies to protect the United States intellectual property rights; and, for classified or sensitive research, whether the foreign government has adopted adequate measures to prevent the transfer of strategic technologies to destinations prohibited under U.S. national security export controls."[36]

Implementation of the "substantial U.S. manufacturing" requirement has been approached differently by different agencies. NIST, for example, allows its eight laboratory directors considerable discretion in the negotiation of CRADAs, including authority to decide whether the participation of a U.S. multinational company or foreign-controlled firm complies with the letter and spirit of the law. If a laboratory director considers a CRADA proposal to be particularly sensitive, he or she can request direction from the NIST Director.[37]

In contrast, DOE, whose 10 multiprogram laboratories had entered into over 1,200 CRADAs as of early 1995, allows less discretion to its contractor-operated labs in the negotiation of CRADAs in general and in the implementation of performance requirements in particular. Exercising a higher degree of centralized control, the DOE initially developed strict guidelines for compliance with the "substantial U.S. manufacturing requirement" (referred to as the U.S. Competitiveness Article within the modular CRADA), extending its scope to include all intellectual property generated under a CRADA, including subject inventions, patents, copyrights, trademarks, protected CRADA data, and mask works. Furthermore, these early DOE guidelines stipulated that such intellectual property should be practiced only in the United States.

Both large and small U.S. companies expressed concern about the highly restrictive nature of DOE's initial set of guidelines, which they believed would weaken their ability to compete globally. Required to manufacture some products abroad in order to meet foreign content laws, provide just-in-time delivery services, and maintain competitive freight charges, and unwilling to accept wholesale liens on CRADA-related intellectual property, the big three U.S. automakers and the nation's leading computer manufacturers insisted that the competitiveness article be waived or modified in the DOE CRADA agreements.[38] Several major U.S. multinational companies have indicated that delays in the CRADA negotiation process related to the U.S. competitiveness article discouraged them from concluding CRADAs with DOE.

In 1993, DOE took steps to streamline the CRADA negotiation process in response to criticisms that its procedures were too bureaucratic and time-consuming. In the process, the agency also added some flexibility to the U.S. competitiveness article by defining a process and general criteria by which a would-be CRADA participant could satisfy the performance requirement without acceding to the highly restrictive "sample language" or the all-inclusive definition of intellectual property.[39] However, in order to take advantage of these alternative eligibility guidelines, DOE still must approve the company's eligibility before the firm and laboratory can proceed with their joint work statement (U.S. Department of Energy, 1993). In short, this requirement continues to impose significant delays on the CRADA negotiation process for firms that will not accept the "sample language."

Subsequent to the introduction of performance and reciprocity requirements for foreign-controlled firms into CRADA regulations, the federal government has extended similar requirements to cover a range of financial-assistance agreements, such as contract research, joint ventures, and research grants, between federal laboratories and private companies.[40] Most noteworthy in this regard is the Energy Policy Act of 1992, which includes more detailed economic performance requirements for participating firms as well as more extensive reciprocity requirements for foreign-controlled firms.[41] With regard to the latter, DOE is obligated to determine whether the prospective foreign participant's home government: allows U.S.-owned companies opportunities, comparable to those afforded to any other company, to participate in any government-sponsored joint ventures similar to those authorized under the act; affords U.S.-owned companies local investment opportunities comparable to those afforded foreign firms in the United States; and affords adequate and effective protection for the intellectual property of the U.S.-owned companies.

Several large U.S.-owned companies have criticized DOE for lax and inconsistent enforcement of the eligibility requirements set forth in the Energy Policy Act of 1992. General Electric cited both the performance requirements and the reciprocity provisions of section 2306 of the act when it objected to DOE plans to include the European-based company Asea Brown Boveri in a program launched in 1993 to develop advanced gas turbine concepts under a cost-sharing agreement with the agency.[42] Similarly, AlliedSignal Incorporated, also citing section 2306, has objected to Oak Ridge National Laboratory's decision to include a Japanese company, Kyocera, in an advanced ceramics research project.[43]

FOREIGN PARTICIPATION IN RECENT FEDERAL INDUSTRIAL TECHNOLOGY INITIATIVES

Federally funded industrial R&D programs and consortia, such as the Department of Commerce's Advanced Technology Program (ATP), the Technology Reinvestment Project (TRP), administered by the Advanced Research Projects Agency (ARPA), the Semiconductor Manufacturing Technology Research Corporation (SEMATECH), and the U.S. Display Consortium (USDC), also have received considerable attention with regard to foreign corporate participation. These initiatives are among the most high-profile elements of recent efforts by the federal government to expand its support of industrially relevant civilian technology development and application (Advanced Research Projects Agency, 1993; Committee on Science, Engineering and Public Policy, 1992; National Academy of Engineering, 1993).

The ATP was established under the 1988 Trade Act to fund R&D in businesses, especially small and medium-sized companies. The goal of ATP is to help firms develop generic, precompetitive technology that will stimulate high-risk, high-potential products, processes, and technologies. Eligibility requirements for foreign firms wishing to participate in the program are set forth in the 1991 Technology Administration Authorization Act and are identical to those of the 1992 Energy Policy Act.[44] The Commerce Department decides whether a foreign-owned company is eligible to participate in the program on a case-by-case basis. Since the program's inception in 1990, 15 of 413 participating organizations in ATP have been foreign owned.[45]

Thus far, ATP administrators have not found it difficult to implement the eligibility requirements for foreign-owned firms (U.S. General Accounting Office, 1994a). However, it is generally acknowledged that the uncertainties surrounding the certification process, particularly those related to reciprocity, tend to discourage foreign-owned firms from applying for ATP funds. It is noteworthy that while foreign-owned firms represented only 3 percent of organizations competing for ATP funds in 1994, half of these companies received ATP awards compared with only 7 percent of all other applicant organizations.[46]

The TRP was launched in March 1993 with a budget of $472 million "to stimulate the transition to a growing, integrated, national industrial capability" through the support of technology development and deployment activities of U.S companies. The TRP, managed by ARPA in cooperation with five other federal agencies, elicited more than 2,800 proposals during its first phase. As of October 1994, the program had funded on a cost-sharing basis 212 projects involving 1,631 organizations, only five of which were foreign firms. Two of those, Mitsui Engineering and Shipbuilding (Japan) and Kvaerner Masa Marine (Canada), are involved in the TRP project designed to help Bath Iron Works Corporation of Maine diversify and modernize its shipbuilding operations to compete more effectively in the global commercial shipbuilding market.[47] Foreign firms seeking to participate in a TRP consortium must meet eligibility requirements that are basically the same as those for the ATP.[48] However, regardless of the nationalities of the countries participating, only U.S.-owned firms may submit proposals.

Unlike the ATP and the TRP, most of the publicly subsidized industry-led R&D consortia established in the United States during the past decade have not permitted foreign membership, although some nevertheless involve foreign firms. One such example is SEMATECH, a consortium of 14 U.S. semiconductor manufacturers founded in 1987 to provide U.S. manufacturers with the capability to achieve world leadership in semiconductor manufacturing technology by 1993. Since 1988, DOD has provided half of SEMATECH's $200 million annual operating budget.[49] Membership in the consortium is restricted to U.S.-owned companies. However, SEMATECH has entered into technical alliances with its European counterpart, the Joint European Semiconductor Submicron Initiative (JESSI). Furthermore, most of the U.S. companies participating in the consortium are extensively involved in various types of commercial and technical alliances with foreign firms.[50]

The U.S. Display Consortium (USDC), another industry-led, public-private partnership, was launched in mid-1993 with $20 million in public funds "to organize the U.S. manufacturing expertise to develop the U.S. infrastructure required to support a world-class manufacturing capability for high definition displays in the United States." To achieve this, the USDC brings together 13 flat-panel display manufacturers and developers, 52 flat-panel display equipment and materials suppliers, the flat-panel display user community, and the U.S. government. Membership in the consortium is currently limited to U.S.-owned firms.[51]

THE IMPLICATIONS OF FOREIGN PARTICIPATION IN PUBLICLY FUNDED U.S. R&D

There are three major concerns about foreign participation in publicly funded U.S R&D. The first is that foreign students, researchers, and companies take away more technology, know-how and, most importantly, economic value (jobs and profits) from their involvement in U.S. publicly funded R&D than they give back to the United States. The second is that other nations' publicly funded R&D, conducted outside the United States, is not as accessible to U.S. citizens, particularly U.S.-owned firms, as is U.S. publicly funded R&D to foreign entities. The third is that foreign governments, or more specifically, foreign taxpayers, may not be carrying their fair share of the global basic research burden. The following discussion addresses in turn each of these concerns and their associated implications.

Is the Quid Pro Quo Adequate?

There is no quantitative way to determine whether or not the United States receives benefits commensurate with those derived by foreign students, researchers, and corporations from their access to and participation in U.S. publicly funded research. It is possible, however, to review the costs and benefits of different types of foreign R&D involvement, both to foreign nationals, those who carry out publicly funded U.S. research, and U.S. citizens. Such an analysis suggests that some forms of foreign participation yield a more adequate quid pro quo than others.

Foreign Graduate Students, Postdoctoral Researchers, and
Long-Term Visiting Researchers

Clearly, foreign students, postdoctoral researchers, and other long-term visiting researchers derive many benefits from their involvement in publicly funded

U.S. research at universities and federal laboratories. They receive what many consider to be the world's finest advanced training in science and engineering, much of it subsidized directly or indirectly by U.S. taxpayers.[52] In the process, they are given access to cutting-edge research and knowledge in many fields. In some cases, such as university-industry research centers and federal laboratories involved in CRADAs, they also have access to the proprietary research of U.S.-owned firms. Many of these foreign researchers or newly minted Ph.D.'s return eventually to their home country and take with them the skills and specialized knowledge acquired in the United States—skills and knowledge likely to be employed by the foreign competitors of many U.S.-owned companies.

Although difficult to quantify, the nation's heavy reliance on foreign-born graduate students, postdoctoral researchers, and faculty may entail certain liabilities. Some argue, for instance, that the large presence of foreign faculty and teaching assistants in U.S. engineering programs may contribute to cultural tension and language barriers that discourage U.S.-born students, particularly women and ethnic minorities,[53] from pursuing engineering degrees. Others contend that foreign students are taking slots in graduate schools and jobs in the U.S. workforce that otherwise would go to Americans. Still others believe that the availability of abundant foreign talent may be allowing U.S. universities and the nation's educational establishment generally to avoid addressing fundamental problems in the U.S. educational system.[54]

While some of these arguments are more compelling than others, the committee remains convinced that foreign students and long-term visiting researchers are an indispensable asset to U.S. university and federal laboratory research. As key members of U.S. science and engineering departments, foreign graduate students and postdoctoral researchers represent the underpinning of many advanced research projects. Without them, laboratories would have difficulty raising research support from government, industry, and internal sources. These research programs, in turn, induce high-quality faculty to stay.

Numbers alone confirm the important role of foreign postdoctoral researchers and long-term visiting researchers in the work of federal laboratories. In the DOE multiprogram labs, for example, there is on average one foreign visiting scientist or engineer for every five members of the resident technical staff. Similarly, the NIH hosts about one long-term foreign visiting researcher for every eight members of its resident staff. Foreign postdoctoral researchers and long-term visiting researchers have made numerous intellectual contributions that have strengthened U.S. university-based research. These investigators come from both companies and nonprofit institutions. Some examples include Tokyo Electric Power researchers' work in MIT's power engineering laboratory; Japanese construction company researchers' contributions to civil engineering research at MIT, Purdue, and Stanford (Stalson, 1989); the contributions of French, Canadian, German, and Japanese researchers—from academe, industry, and government—to research at the Center for Ultrafast Optical Science at the University of Michigan, Ann Arbor (U.S. Congress, House, 1993); and the critical role of Japanese scientists and engineers in the research program of the Kent State University's Liquid Crystal Institute.[55]

Furthermore, laboratory administrators attest to the significant intellectual contributions made by many of their foreign visiting researchers. In response to a 1988 GAO survey, a majority of the federal laboratory directors contacted concluded that overall "the federal laboratories and the United States benefitted more than foreign researchers and their countries through the collaboration on research and development" (U.S. General Accounting Office, 1988b). More recently, at a National Research Council workshop on Japanese participation in U.S. federal laboratories, an administrator at Sandia National Laboratory observed that "(f)oreign visitors, Japanese, Germans, and others . . . combine interest in what is being done at Sandia with competence in the field and provide a stimulus which encourages Sandia researchers to innovate" (National Research Council, 1994a). At the same workshop, a representative from Pacific Northwest Laboratory noted that "[c]ompared to American companies, the Japanese send better-trained, better-educated people to the lab, and they are more proactive in seeking access to the lab."

Once they graduate, foreign-born students may continue to benefit their host institutions. If foreign alumni stay on as faculty, they are often able to use their ties to their home countries to attract the next generation of foreign talent and to help lure research projects and other funds from firms and government agencies. If they leave the university for positions in U.S. or foreign industry, they are likely in the future to turn to their former graduate institutions to hire graduates, contract research, or seek technical assistance. Finally, like U.S.-born alumni, foreign graduates provide funds for endowed chairs, scholarships, and new or renovated facilities, and they encourage their employers to do likewise.[56]

U.S. industry also derives many benefits from the presence of foreign science and engineering students and faculty. Currently, more than half of foreign engineering graduate students enter and remain part of the U.S. engineering workforce for at least 2 years after graduation (Finn et al., 1995; National Science Foundation, 1993a). As of 1989, more than 10 percent of all doctoral-level engineers employed in the United States were foreign nationals (Figure 4.6). U.S. companies may also derive indirect benefits from repatriated foreign alumni. It is claimed, for example, that the entire energy establishment of South Korea is run by graduates of Rensselaer Polytechnic Institute and MIT and that all senior civil engineering experts in the People's Republic of China are Cornell graduates. Presumably, these individuals' educational experience in the United States would make them more inclined to call on U.S. firms when considering sources for foreign equipment and technology (Stalson, 1989).

The benefits reaped by U.S. industry and the U.S. economy as a whole from the inflow of foreign talent, however, are greater than numbers alone suggest.

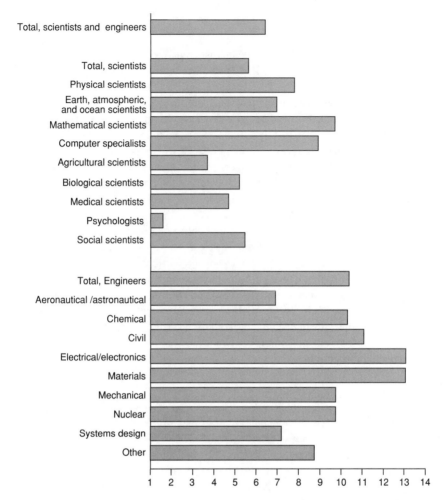

FIGURE 4.6 Non-U.S. citizens as a percent of employed Ph.D. scientists and engineers in the United States, total and by field, 1989. SOURCE: National Science Foundation (1993a).

Foreign-born graduates of U.S. universities constitute a large pool of elite technical talent with special knowledge of their nation's or region's cultures, languages, political economies, and markets—knowledge that is particularly valuable to U.S. firms as economic competition becomes increasingly global.

In conclusion, the committee is convinced that the participation of foreign graduate students, postdoctoral researchers, and other long-term visiting researchers in U.S. academic and federal laboratory research has yielded significant net benefits to the U.S. economy and national innovation system.

Short-Term Visiting Researchers

In contrast, the committee believes that short-term foreign visiting researchers—those whose stay in the United States lasts between 3 months and 1 year—are likely to take away from U.S. research universities and federal laboratories more than they contribute to them. There are few data on the number of short-term visitors to U.S. universities and federal laboratories, and the committee knows of no systematic effort to prove or disprove the more "extractive" character of foreign short-term visiting researchers. However, committee members who have hosted foreign visiting researchers at their institutions note that those individuals climb a very steep learning curve during the first 10 to 12 months in their host laboratories. They are therefore less likely to make significant contributions to the work of the host lab if their tenure is less than a year. Presumably, steep learning curves also diminish the ability of short-term visitors to extract intellectual assets from their host institutions. However, anecdotal evidence suggests that some short-term foreign visitors have been particularly aggressive in collecting and transmitting back to their home institutions information about their U.S. host organization's research activities (National Research Council, 1994a). Moreover, the fact that each foreign visiting researcher has access to the work and talents of multiple resident U.S. researchers bespeaks an inherent imbalance in the flow of ideas and information between visitors and their host institutions in any individual transaction.

Foreign Corporate Participation in Publicly Funded U.S. R&D

Foreign-owned firms have benefitted from participating in publicly supported U.S. R&D in several ways. They have gained access to many of the world's leading researchers in various fields of science and engineering and have been able to assess and acquire intellectual property and human capital outputs of U.S. public R&D activities. To a certain extent, involvement in publicly funded research has also provided those companies another window on the R&D activities of U.S.-owned firms engaged in collaborative research at university research centers or federal laboratories. Although it is impossible to place an economic value on these benefits, the committee believes they are greater than the current scope of foreign corporate participation—measured in terms of research sponsored, research personnel exchanged, and technology licenses acquired—suggests.

Through their participation in the research activities of U.S. universities and federal laboratories, foreign corporations undoubtedly extract more intellectual property from the United States than they would in the absence of such ties. It is equally certain, in the view of the committee, that in some cases, foreign-owned firms and their stakeholders have benefitted at the expense of American firms and stakeholders.

At the same time, the committee firmly believes that the flow of knowledge and technology between foreign firms and U.S. universities and federal laboratories is not unidirectional and that foreign firms, through their participation in U.S. research, return economic value to U.S. citizens in many different ways. Numerous case examples confirm that foreign-owned firms have contributed material support as well as intellectual resources to U.S. research universities and federal laboratories. This has enhanced the productivity and quality of these institutions' research efforts, thereby strengthening the nation's overall research infrastructure.[57]

Furthermore, whether foreign companies receive more from U.S. universities and federal laboratories than they contribute to these institutions says very little about the impact of foreign involvement in this research on the welfare of Americans. There is some evidence suggesting that the foreign-owned companies with the most extensive ties to U.S. publicly funded research institutions also tend to have significant U.S.-based manufacturing and R&D operations.[58] These operations employ U.S. citizens, buy from U.S.-based suppliers and equipment vendors, import as well as generate technology and know-how applied within the U.S. economy, and pay U.S. taxes.

Even if foreign companies commercialize abroad intellectual property licensed from U.S. publicly funded research institutions, it should not be assumed automatically that their gain represents a loss for the United States. In some instances, foreign firms have acquired or licensed technology generated with U.S. public funds and gone on to develop and commercialize the technology overseas.[59] Yet, as noted, foreign-based licensees have also enabled publicly funded research institutions to earn revenues on technology that otherwise would not have been commercialized. Moreover, by commercializing this otherwise unexploited technology, foreign firms have in some cases helped supply U.S. citizens with better or cheaper goods or services.[60]

As far as the transfer of codified technology is concerned, those who oversee the technology licensing offices of U.S. universities and federal laboratories suggest that foreign-owned companies are for the most part "customers of last resort" for U.S. government-subsidized intellectual property (U.S. General Accounting Office, 1988b; Wiley, 1993). That is, these companies license technology that no U.S.-owned company is willing to invest in.

In addition to their preference for dealing with U.S.-based firms, U.S. research universities and federal laboratories, in the committee's judgment, have generally made good-faith efforts to comply with federally mandated economic performance requirements. There have been several well-publicized instances in which publicly supported U.S. R&D institutions have negotiated R&D cooperation or licensing agreements with foreign firms that do not appear to be in the best interests of the United States. The committee believes that these cases are the exception rather than the rule.[61]

Increased fiscal austerity at the federal level, defense downsizing, and growing pressure on publicly funded research institutions to contribute to national and regional economic development have made research universities and federal laboratories aware of the need to demonstrate their service to the nation's economic interests. Moreover, these publicly funded institutions and their foreign corporate customers or patrons appear equally aware of the public-relations hazards associated with involving foreign firms in publicly supported research. As a result, they exercise considerable care to avoid even the appearance of impropriety.[62] Indeed, the negative fall-out from the few high-visibility cases has, in the committee's opinion, discouraged foreign corporate involvement in U.S. government-subsidized R&D.

At the same time, the manner in which some federal agencies have enforced the performance requirements embodied in recent technology transfer legislation suggests they may be overreaching in their efforts to keep the economic benefits of public R&D spending within the United States. Some agencies have developed economic performance criteria and procedures to enforce them that in the committee's view, are fundamentally at odds with the competitive R&D and technology management practices of multinational companies, strongly discourage foreign corporate involvement, and are at times in conflict with the core missions of the agencies themselves. In order to engage U.S.-owned multinational companies in CRADAs and other forms of collaborative R&D, some agencies have, on a case-by-case basis, made a more liberal interpretation of what constitutes an adequate economic quid pro quo. Nevertheless, extensive restrictions—invoked in the name of U.S. economic interests—on private-sector use of publicly subsidized intellectual property continue to discourage leading U.S.-owned high-technology companies from collaborating with federal laboratories.

With respect to foreign-owned firms, the interpretation and enforcement of economic performance requirements by various federal agencies appear to be particularly vulnerable to political and legal challenges from without. Hence, these requirements serve to discourage the involvement of foreign-owned firms that might otherwise seek to participate in publicly funded U.S. R&D. Given the growth of technical competence overseas and the prominent role of U.S.- and foreign-owned multinational companies in areas of R&D and technology of direct relevance to the core missions of U.S. federal agencies, the committee believes it is not unreasonable to question whether economic performance requirements as currently administered truly serve the nation's interests.

Reciprocal Access to Publicly Funded Foreign R&D

Reciprocal access describes, in a comparative way, the access U.S. and foreign citizens have to one another's R&D enterprises. In part because the costs and benefits to the United States in this area are difficult to quantify, reciprocal, or "equitable," access is viewed by many U.S. policymakers as an important indirect measure of whether foreign participation in the U.S. R&D enterprise is an asset or a liability. Not only does a lack of reciprocal access offend the American public's sense of fairness, it may also reduce the ability of U.S.-owned firms to compete internationally. Inspired by this reasoning, U.S. lawmakers have made reciprocal access a prerequisite for foreign corporate participation in many areas of publicly funded U.S. R&D.[63]

Several recent surveys suggest that U.S. government, academic, and industrial researchers have had few problems accessing research capabilities and activities within academic and government-operated laboratories abroad. For example, an informal survey (National Science Foundation, 1990b) of U.S. companies with foreign R&D operations in 1990 found that all sponsored university-based research in their host countries. None of the firms noted any problems establishing relationships with universities in Europe, Canada, South America, or Australia. Of 26 officials interviewed, three said their efforts to tap Japanese university research met with some government resistance.[64] At the same time, others have found that U.S. and European companies invest considerably less effort drawing on the research capabilities of U.S. research universities than do their Japanese competitors (Roberts, 1995a).

A 1988 GAO survey found that research managers and administrators at eight federal laboratories did not have "difficulty getting access to foreign laboratories and that, except for some isolated instances, foreign researchers have readily exchanged information with federal laboratory researchers" (U.S. General Accounting Office, 1988b). In 1989, researchers at NIST reported that they had good access to Japanese national laboratories, including those of the Ministry for International Trade and Industry (MITI) and Nippon Telephone and Telegraph (NTT) (National Research Council, 1989a).

What little information exists concerning access by U.S. industry-based researchers to foreign government laboratories suggests that at least for intramural research activities, accessibility has not been a problem. As noted by a National Research Council report on U.S. access to Japanese government laboratories, the principle concern may be inadequate exploitation of foreign laboratories by U.S. researchers, not lack of access (1989a). To address this concern, the National Science Foundation and other federal agencies have initiated programs designed to encourage U.S.-based researchers from academe, industry, and government to spend time working in foreign research institutions.[65]

Access by U.S.-owned companies to government-funded industrial R&D consortia in Europe appears to be fairly comparable to access by foreign-owned firms to consortia in the United States. Participation in European Community research and development (EC R&D) programs, for example, is open to all legal entities established and regularly carrying out research within member countries. Moreover, all contractors taking part in community-funded R&D are obligated to exploit the results of that work "in conformity with the interests of the community."[66] As of 1993, 25 U.S.-owned companies had participated in 53 projects (roughly 5 percent of all projects) of the community's largest research program, the European Strategic Programme for Research and Development in Information Technology. At least 1 U.S. company is participating in each of the 14 other EC R&D programs.[67] The policies of EC member states regarding foreign participation in national R&D programs appear to be consistent, at least on paper, with those of the EC. These policies require that corporate participants be established in the sponsoring country and exploit resulting intellectual property in a manner consistent with the sponsoring nation's interests.[68]

In Japan, access by foreign firms to publicly funded industrial R&D programs appears more tightly regulated than it is in the United States or in the European Community. Much more than its American or European counterparts, the Japanese government uses privately owned industrial consortia to plan, execute, and supervise most of the nation's investment in industrially relevant R&D. For the most part, U.S. and European Community R&D programs award extramural grants and contracts through relatively transparent and competitive selection processes. That is, firms, universities, and other nonprofit research organizations compete for funding by submitting proposals that are then evaluated for their relative merit by panels of experts. In contrast, the development and implementation of publicly funded industrial R&D programs in Japan is characterized by a more closed and arguably more strategic process of project and participant selection. Leading Japanese companies in a particular technology area negotiate the establishment and funding of particular research programs with MITI or other government agencies (Hane, 1993; Heaton, 1988).

In Japan, foreign firms are generally not directly involved in the planning of a particular research program, but some, including U.S. companies, have been invited specifically to participate in certain initiatives because of the particular expertise they bring to the table. For example, MITI invited Motorola to participate in the research consortium on micromachine technology, Texas Instruments was asked to join the MITI program on atomic manipulation, and IBM joined an agency-supported research program on fuzzy logic.[69] However, as suggested by repeated unsuccessful attempts by the U.S. company AlliedSignal Inc. to join a MITI-sponsored research program on advanced structural ceramics, the allocation of public research contracts and grants in Japan is not decided through a transparent competitive process solely on the relative technical and economic merits of the research proposals submitted.[70]

There is little doubt that international asymmetries of access to publicly funded research persist and impose costs (however difficult to measure) on U.S. citizens. The committee is not convinced, however, that recent U.S. government attempts to redress these asymmetries through the introduction of reciprocity requirements in federal R&D legislation are a constructive response. Indeed, reciprocity requirements, in concept as well as implementation, appear to be fraught with many more liabilities and hazards for the United States than are economic performance requirements.

First, conditioning the nondiscriminatory treatment of foreign-owned firms on their home governments' compliance with U.S. laws contradicts a longstanding commitment of the United States to the unconditional "national treatment" of multinational enterprises, a principle of international economic intercourse that the United States—with good reason—has long urged other nations to abide by.[71] Indeed, there is some evidence the inclusion of reciprocity requirements in ostensibly "domestic" legislation has encouraged at least a few major U.S. trading partners to consider introducing similar rules.[72]

Second, the process of assessing whether a particular firm's home country is in compliance with each of the various reciprocity requirements is cumbersome, time consuming, and very difficult to administer. Enforcement is made all the more difficult by the fact that federal agencies are called upon to render judgments in areas of policy where it is often difficult to determine what constitutes "comparable investment opportunities" or "adequate protection of U.S. intellectual property." The vagueness of these requirements has made it possible for some U.S.-owned companies to challenge both the eligibility of particular foreign firms to participate in the U.S. R&D enterprise as well as the enforcement processes of some federal agencies. The committee believes that these challenges have had a chilling effect on the interest of foreign-owned firms (as well as of federal R&D administrators) in participating federally funded R&D initiatives.

Given the differences in the structure and scale of publicly funded R&D activities among countries, the value to the United States of having reciprocal access will vary. In Japan, for instance, a much smaller share of leading-edge basic or generic research is reportedly conducted within publicly funded institutions than is true in the United States. Such asymmetries shift the debate for some from reciprocal access to the broader issue of international burdensharing in basic research.

International Burden Sharing in Basic Research

In terms of its scale, scope, accessibility, and productivity, U.S. basic research is globally preeminent. It is clear that foreign companies and countries draw more heavily on the results of publicly funded U.S. basic research than the United States or U.S. companies do on the research output of publicly funded research abroad. Nonetheless, international comparisons of R&D expenditures confirm that most of America's important trading partners invest as much if not more of their gross national product in basic research than does the United States (Table 4.8).

Japan is an important exception to this general trend, spending a smaller share of its gross domestic product and nearly half as much per capita on basic research as the United States (Irvine et al., 1990). Given Japanese companies' success in accessing U.S. basic research, the relatively low level of Japanese basic research spending has been particularly disturbing to many observers, who see it as evidence of Japanese free riding on the basic research output of others. This negative perception is compounded by the widely held view that much of

TABLE 4.8   Government Expenditures on Academic and Academically
Related Research as a Percentage of GDP and Per Capita, 1987

			Expenditure as a percentage of GDP (1987)	Expenditures per capita (1987 $[a])
	General university funds	United Kingdom	0.211	26.1
		Germany	0.261	34.7
		France	0.135	17.2
		Netherlands	0.329	40.3
		United States	0.070	12.7
		Japan	0.156	20.6
Academic research	Separately budgeted research	United Kingdom	0.083	10.3
		Germany	0.090	11.9
		France	0.140	17.9
		Netherlands	0.106	13.0
		United States	0.223	40.6
		Japan	0.055	7.3
	Subtotal	United Kingdom	0.295	36.4
		Germany	0.351	46.7
		France	0.275	35.0
		Netherlands	0.435	53.3
		United States	0.293	53.3
		Japan	0.212	27.9
Academically related research		United Kingdom	0.103	12.7
		Germany	0.145	19.3
		France	0.178	22.7
		Netherlands	0.098	12.0
		United States	0.043	7.9
		Japan	0.021	2.7
Total		United Kingdom	0.398	49.1
		Germany	0.496	66.0
		France	0.453	57.7
		Netherlands	0.532	65.3
		United States	0.336	61.1
		Japan	0.232	30.6

[a]Spending in national currencies converted to U.S. dollars using OECD 'purchasing power parities' for 1987 calculated in early 1989.

SOURCE: Irvine et al. (1990).

what the Japanese classify as basic research is, in fact, more application oriented and proprietary in character than similar research conducted by other advanced industrial economies. Moreover, many believe that the most important basic research in Japan takes place within closed corporate laboratories rather than in the more open and accessible publicly supported research institutions (Hicks, 1994; Hicks and Hirooka, 1992).

SUMMARY

The participation of foreign individuals and institutions in publicly funded R&D activity in the United States appears to be extensive and growing. Government surveys of the number of foreign graduate students, postdoctoral researchers, and other visiting researchers at U.S. universities and federal laboratories document a significant increase in the level of foreign involvement since the mid-1970s. At the same time, meaningful data on the scope, growth, and nature of foreign institutions' involvement in publicly funded U.S. R&D are fragmentary, dated, and scarce.

Available information suggests that foreign institutions account for a very small share (less than 2 percent) of total sponsored research at U.S. universities and federal laboratories, which is concentrated in a small number of U.S. institutions. As of the mid-1980s, Japanese institutions sponsored more U.S. university-based R&D than firms of any other nationality. During this period, most foreign-sponsored research at U.S. universities was funded by not-for-profit institutions and was focused mostly in agriculture, medicine, and geology. Only fragmentary data exist with which to assess the current magnitude, disciplinary focus, and national shares of foreign-sponsored research at individual U.S. universities and federal laboratories. However, limited survey data and anecdotal evidence indicate that Japanese companies are more diligent than their U.S. or European counterparts with regard to accessing, monitoring, and drawing upon the research capabilities of these publicly funded institutions. Foreign participation has been minimal in recently established, federally supported industrial R&D initiatives, such as the Department of Commerce's Advanced Technology Program.

As with U.S. privately funded R&D, the involvement of foreign nationals in R&D sponsored by the federal government carries both risks and opportunities for the United States. The committee believes that the extensive presence of foreign graduate students, postdoctoral researchers, and other long-term foreign visiting researchers at U.S. universities and federal laboratories has, on balance, yielded significant benefits to the U.S. economy and its innovation system. In contrast, the committee believes that short-term visiting researchers have contributed much less to the work of U.S. research universities and federal laboratories, both overall and relative to what the researchers themselves take away.

Although the committee could identify various costs and benefits of foreign institutional involvement in U.S. publicly supported research institutions, it was unable to determine the economic impact of this involvement. Through their participation in the research activities of U.S. universities and federal laboratories, foreign corporate participants undoubtedly extract more knowledge and intellectual property from the United States than they would in the absence of such ties. Likewise, the committee does not doubt that access to U.S. publicly funded R&D activities and institutions has brought extensive benefits to foreign-owned firms and their stakeholders abroad, in some cases at the expense of American firms and their American stakeholders.

Nevertheless, there is also considerable evidence to confirm that foreign firms have contributed significant material support, technology, and intellectual resources to research universities and federal laboratories. Indeed, many if not most foreign-owned companies that have extensive ties to U.S. publicly funded research institutions appear to be good corporate citizens. For instance, they establish U.S.-based manufacturing and R&D operations that employ Americans, pay U.S. taxes, buy from U.S.-based suppliers and vendors, and import as well as develop technology and know-how that is then applied in this country.

U.S. research universities and federal laboratories, in the committee's judgment, have generally made good-faith efforts to comply with federally mandated economic performance requirements for foreign company participation in U.S. publicly funded research. Foreign-owned companies are for the most part "customers of last resort" for U.S. government-subsidized intellectual property. However, the highly restrictive and somewhat inconsistent enforcement of these requirements by some federal agencies has raised questions about how well these requirements serve agency missions specifically and national interests more generally in the increasingly global economy. Aside from this general bias against multinational companies (both U.S. and foreign-owned), the performance requirements and their underlying political-economic logic serve as a disincentive to potential foreign-owned participants in publicly funded U.S. R&D activity.

With regard to mandated reciprocity requirements, it appears that federal agencies have yet to develop effective and credible procedures for establishing compliance or noncompliance. Indeed, in conception as well as implementation, reciprocity requirements appear to be fraught with significant short- and long-term liabilities and hazards for the United States.

U.S. government, academic, and industrial researchers seem to have few problems accessing publicly funded research capabilities and activities in academic and government-operated laboratories abroad. Furthermore, access by U.S.-owned companies to government-funded industrial research consortia in Europe appears to be comparable to that extended foreign-owned firms in the United States. Japan, however, has restricted foreign participation in its publicly funded industrial R&D consortia to a greater extent than either the United States or the European Community through its closed, strategic process of project and participant selection.

Given differences in the organization, scale, and sophistication of publicly funded R&D activities among countries, the value to Americans of greater access to publicly funded foreign R&D is not clear. Nevertheless, lack of reciprocal access may have damaging results. In some cases, it may disadvantage U.S.-owned firms in international competition, with negative consequences for their U.S.-based stakeholders. But its greatest cost to the nation may be the extent to which it offends the American public's sense of fairness, thereby undermining public support for efforts to negotiate remedies to these asymmetries in international forums.

International comparisons of R&D expenditures confirm that most of America's advanced industrialized trading partners invest as much if not more of their gross national product in basic research than does the United States. Japan, despite recent efforts to expand its basic research capabilities, spends a smaller share of its gross domestic product and only about half as much per capita in this area compared with the United States. The committee believes strongly that the federal government should continue to encourage Japan to assume a role in the global basic research community that is commensurate with its industrial, technological, economic, and diplomatic standing in the world.

NOTES

1. In 1994, public funds accounted for 36.1 percent of all R&D dollars invested in the United States—57.6 percent of all basic research funding, 36.6 percent of all applied research funding, and 29.7 percent of the nation's total investment in technology development (National Science Foundation, 1995b).

Data on the scope, composition, nature, and growth of foreign participation in U.S. publicly funded research is more scarce and fragmentary than those on foreign involvement in U.S. privately funded R&D. Accordingly, it is more difficult to assess its importance and consequences for the U.S. innovation system and national economy than foreign participation in U.S. privately funded R&D activity.

2. U.S. affiliates of foreign-owned firms employed 104,500 U.S. residents in R&D activity in 1992 (U.S. Department of Commerce, 1995).

3. For a discussion of the reasons foreign firms become involved in U.S. academic research, see National Science Board (1993), Serapio (1994), Stalson (1989), Massachusetts Institute of Technology (1991), and U.S. Congress, House (1993).

It is instructive to compare the findings of the above-cited studies with those of a National Science Foundation (NSF) report (1990b), which among other things reported on reasons why U.S. firms invest in academic research abroad. Based on informal inquiries to 21 U.S. multinational companies, accounting for more than half of U.S. overseas industrial R&D in 1988, NSF found that the principal reason these firms sponsored research at foreign universities was "to benefit from the work of individual scientists and engineers who are leading, world-renowned experts in their respective fields." The desire to foster goodwill and promote the company's reputation within the scientific community as well as the desire to take advantage of tax laws also were cited as important incentives.

4. These data probably overestimate the share of foreign-born engineering faculty, according to several experts, due to problems with the survey methods used and a lack of information on emigration of foreign-born Ph.D's.

5. The University of Texas at Austin reported 181 international scholars in science and engineer-

ing fields for fiscal 1993, roughly 10 percent funded by foreign companies; correspondence from Dale Klein, University of Texas at Austin, to Proctor Reid, NAE, March 17, 1995.

6. Remarks by J. William Doane at the National Academy of Engineering workshop on the flat panel display industry, Committee on Technological Innovation in Small Business, December 7, 1993; correspondence from Doane to Proctor Reid, NAE, March 31, 1995.

7. The U.S. General Accounting Office defined foreign sources as foreign governments and individuals, nonprofit organizations headquartered in a foreign country, businesses headquartered in a foreign country, U.S. subsidiaries of foreign corporations, and joint-venture businesses in which the foreign partner has a controlling interest (U.S. General Accounting Office, 1988a).

8. In 1990, the National Science Foundation Division of Science Resources Studies conducted an informal telephone inquiry into fiscal 1988 levels of foreign funding of U.S. academic research. Division staff contacted essentially the same population of universities that the General Accounting Office had surveyed in 1988.

9. The data collected by the NAE via an informal telephone inquiry looked at foreign-sponsored research as a share of total sponsored research (not total R&D expenditures) at the institutions canvassed. Not all of the institutions approached were able to distinguish readily between research sponsored by foreign organizations and that sponsored by U.S. organizations. Moreover, tracking and accounting procedures with regard to sponsored research appear to vary significantly among institutions.

Representatives from several institutions contacted by the NAE noted that the volume of foreign awards received can fluctuate, in some cases significantly, from one year to the next. Nevertheless, multiyear data provided by several of the top 20 research universities show that the foreign share of total sponsored research averaged over 3 to 5 fiscal years (FY) was very close to its present share for the single-FY estimate provided in Table 4.2 for FY 1993 or FY 1994. For example, the foreign share of total sponsored research at the University of Minnesota (FY 1992–94), Stanford and Penn State (FY 1989–93), and the University of Illinois-Urbana (FY 1990–94) averaged 0.5 percent or less. At the University of California at Berkeley, the foreign share averaged 1.7 percent for the 5-year period, FY 1989–93.

10. This is not to say that the only, or even the most important, reason foreign-owned firms participate in U.S. university-based research is to acquire commercially valuable intellectual property. Available data suggest that much of the financial and other material "research" support provided to U.S. universities by foreign-owned companies takes the form of outright gifts and grants for which no specific deliverables other than "goodwill" are promised in return. Nevertheless, the fact that a growing number of foreign-owned companies are availing themselves of the relatively free access to the intellectual assets and research activities resident at U.S. universities has led many American observers to question whether the nation loses more than it gains from foreign corporate participation in the U.S. academic research enterprise.

11. For example, during the 1991–1992 academic year, Berkeley's College of Engineering hosted 17 visiting industrial fellows from Japanese companies that had provided between $2 and $3 million in research support, mostly in the form of grants or gifts. The fellows' salaries and expenses were paid by their companies. Those sent are typically engineers with M.S. degrees and 5 to 10 years experience in the company's R&D laboratory. (Personal communication between David Hodges, University of California at Berkeley, and William Spencer, SEMATECH, January 20, 1992.)

12. In 1989, Helena Stalson prepared a draft report for the National Academy of Engineering, "Foreign Participation in Engineering Research at U.S. Universities," which was based on interviews conducted at the following eight universities: Carnegie Mellon, Columbia, Cornell, Massachusetts Institute of Technology, Princeton, Rensselaer Polytechnic Institute, University of Illinois (Urbana), and University of Wisconsin (Madison).

13. Correspondence from Marion Lentz, UC Berkeley, to Proctor Reid, NAE, June 14, 1994.

14. The agreement signed by Massachusetts General Hospital and Shiseido Co. Ltd. in August 1989 provides for Shiseido to spend up to $9 million a year over 10 years to support a 100-person skin research center at the hospital's Charlestown Navy Yard facilities in return for rights to commercial-

ize any discoveries the center makes. (See "Dollars for Science" in the September 10, 1989, Boston Globe.) In 1989, Shiseido established two U.S.-based research centers, the Cutaneous Biology Research Center and Shiseido America Technocenter (Dalton and Serapio, 1995).

15. As of 1993, Ciba-Geigy had nine U.S. research facilities working in areas of biotechnology, pharmaceuticals, advanced components, chromatography, resins and plastics, and plant development (Dalton and Serapio, 1995).

16. See Gibbons (1992), Healy (1993), and National Institutes of Health (1994a,b). As of 1993, Sandoz Pharmaceutical employed roughly 180 R&D professionals at its research and manufacturing facility in East Hanover, N.J. The Swiss parent company also had seven other U.S.-based research facilities (Dalton and Serapio, 1995).

17. In 1993, the University of California at San Francisco (UCSF) and Daiichi Pharmaceuticals entered into an agreement to establish a center to study atherosclerosis. In exchange for providing $20 million in research funding over 5 years, Daiichi received first rights to negotiate for exclusive licenses to any drugs developed at the center as well as the right to delay publication of research results until it decided whether or not to apply for a patent. It is noteworthy that UCSF requires foreign sponsors of university research to pay all direct and indirect costs of research for which they are awarded patent rights (Helm, 1994).

18. In her testimony before the House Subcommittee on Regulation, Business Opportunities and Energy of the Committee on Small Business on March 11, 1993, former NIH Director Bernadine Healy noted how the Scripps-Sandoz agreement illustrated potential contradictions in U.S. policy concerning the Bayh-Dole Act and agency implementing regulations. "These global first refusal rights may seem to conflict with some of the policy behind Bayh-Dole, such as the preference for collaboration with small business and the promotion of free competition and enterprise. However, the grant of these global rights may not conflict with the U.S. Department of Commerce regulations implementing Bayh-Dole [37 CFR § 401.1(a)] [which] provide for: '. . . the rights of research organizations to accept supplemental funding from other sources for the purpose of expediting or more comprehensively accomplishing the research objectives of the government sponsored project.' Similarly, [37 CFR § 401.7] states that the small-business preference:

> . . . is not intended, for example, to prevent nonprofit organizations from providing larger firms with a right of first refusal or other options in inventions that relate to research being supported under long-term or other arrangements with larger companies.

Thus, the Scripps-Sandoz agreement illustrates a potential contradiction between what some view as the policy underlying the Bayh-Dole Act and the regulations implementing it.

"The Bayh-Dole Act articulates multiple policies and objectives which may prove difficult to reconcile. For example, an action by a nonprofit organization, while clearly advancing one objective of the Act, such as promoting collaborations between commercial and nonprofit organizations, might not advance—and may, in fact, appear to undermine—another objective of the Act, like promoting free competition and enterprise. Needless to say, application of the objectives of the Bayh-Dole Act requires a balancing of statutory objectives in the overall best interests of the American public. That is the challenge for NIH and other agencies that support research. It would be foolhardy and irresponsible for federal agencies to champion open competition at the expense of denying the institutions it supports an opportunity to seek additional research funding. To restrain collaborations between federal grantees and industry simply because the competitive advantage of a given collaboration may not be readily apparent, while simultaneously undermining the best opportunities to rapidly commercialize inventions, would also be unwise. In short, we must achieve a balance, remembering that the general intent of the legislation is to promote product development—not commercial monitoring." (Healy, 1993).

19. For an informative discussion of the origins and consequences of Bayh-Dole, see Wisconsin BioIssues (1994).

20. The 18 foreign companies granted exclusive licenses included 4 French firms, 3 British companies, 2 Swiss companies, and 1 Canadian, 1 Israeli, 1 Finnish, and 1 Japanese company. Five licenses were awarded to one or more unidentified foreign-owned pharmaceutical company(ies). At

least five of the foreign firms of known nationality have affiliates of parent companies with manufacturing or R&D facilities in the United States (U.S. General Accounting Office, unpublished data).

21. Correspondence from Joel Moses, MIT, to Proctor Reid, NAE, June 14, 1994; correspondence from Jean Fort, UCSD, to Proctor Reid, NAE, April 3, 1995; correspondence from Homer Neal, University of Michigan, to Proctor Reid, NAE, April 4, 1995; correspondence from Robert Nerem, Georgia Institute of Technology, to Proctor Reid, NAE, February 7, 1995.

22. See, for example, the testimony of Susan D. Wray, director, Office of Patent, Copyright and Technology Licensing, University of Florida at Gainesville in U.S. Congress, House (1993).

23. Since a foreign firm could participate in more than one university's industrial liaison program, the number of foreign firms participating is probably less than the 499 reported (U.S. General Accounting Office, 1992, p. 17).

24. It should be noted that neither the National Science Foundation nor the National Institutes of Health guidelines for universities and other recipients of federal research support address the issue of whether industrial liaison program members should be given advance access to research results.

25. Foreign participants in the University of California at Berkeley's industrial liaison programs pay fees twice as high as those submitted by U.S.-owned firms. MIT charges foreign-owned firms roughly 30 percent more than it does U.S.-owned firms.

26. This section draws heavily on *University-Industry Research Centers in the United States* by Cohen, Florida, and Goe (1994).

27. Seed money for these centers has been provided to a select group of universities by the sponsoring federal agency with the expectation that the host institutions will raise matching funds from industry, state and local governments, and internally.

28. See, for example, discussion of the efforts by state governments to attract foreign direct investment and associated economic activity to their jurisdictions in Feller (1994) and Kayne (1992).

29. Data are from the NSF ERC Database. Proctor Reid, NAE, phone conversation with Lynn Preston, Engineering Education and Centers Division, NSF, December 1, 1995.

Stalson's (1989) found that foreign participation in ERCs and other university-industry research centers at the eight universities she surveyed was relatively modest with only limited participation from European firms in basic chemical and power engineering research. Moreover, it appeared that a number of European industrial commitments to these centers were "inherited" when European firms acquired participating U.S. firms.

30. Remarks by William Gear, President, NEC Research Institute, and Knut Merten, President and CEO, Siemens Corporate Research, at the NAE roundtable on foreign participation in U.S. research and development, November 9, 1993.

31. These findings, in turn, are consistent with the tendency of Japanese companies to acquire externally developed technology by way of licenses. See Chapter 3, pp. 56, 66-67.

32. The 10 multiprogram labs of DOE are: Argonne National Lab, Brookhaven National Lab, Idaho National Engineering Lab, Lawrence Berkeley Lab, Lawrence Livermore National Lab, Los Alamos National Lab, Oak Ridge National Lab, National Renewable Energy Lab, Pacific Northwest Lab, and Sandia National Laboratories (National Research Council, 1994a, p. 90).

33. National Research Council (1994a) and unpublished data provided to the study committee by the National Institutes of Health.

34. The 1986 Federal Technology Transfer Act authorized CRADAs between government-operated laboratories and industry. Under a CRADA, a private organization provides personnel, equipment, and/or financing for a specified R&D activity that complements the mission of its federal laboratory partner. CRADAs include provisions for the allocation of rights to intellectual property resulting from the cooperative research. In 1987, Executive Order 12591 directed agencies to delegate authority for entering into CRADAs to their respective laboratories, and contained guidelines for the granting of intellectual property rights under these agreements. In 1989, the National Competitiveness Technology Transfer Act extended authority for negotiating CRADAs to contractor-operated government laboratories. See Committee on Science, Engineering, and Public Policy (1992).

35. Correspondence from Wanda Bullock, NIH, to Proctor Reid, NAE, April 4, 1995; correspondence from Robert Petit, ORNL, to Proctor Reid, NAE, April 10, 1995; correspondence from Stephen Lake, ANL, to Proctor Reid, NAE, April 10, 1995.

36. See the Stevenson-Wydler Technology Innovation Act of 1980 (P.L. 96-480) as amended by the Technology Transfer Act of 1986 (P.L. 99-502) and the Advanced Technology Program Act of 1989 (P.L. 101-189), and Executive Order 12591. For further discussion of the reciprocity provisions of these and other recents acts of law, see Schwartz and Caplan (1993).

37. Proctor Reid, NAE, phone discussions, March 8, 9, and 31, 1995, with David Edgerly and Bruce Mattson, NIST, Office of Technology Services. NIST is currently reviewing its implementation of the economic performance requirements of the Bayh-Dole Act and CRADA legislation.

38. The automobile industry's "umbrella" CRADA with DOE stipulates that the R&D will be done in the United States and that manufacturing for the first 2 to 3 years will be done predominantly in the United States and will continue in the United States where practical thereafter.

39 In 1993, DOE modified its modular CRADA agreement to offer would-be private sector participants the option of either accepting the "sample U.S. competitiveness language *in toto*" or agreeing "to provide specific economic benefit to the U.S. economy under one or more criteria [eight in total] of the U.S. competitiveness work sheet." The sample U.S. competitiveness language states:

> In exchange for the benefits received under this CRADA, the Parties therefore agree to the following:
>
> A. Products embodying Intellectual Property developed under this CRADA shall be substantially manufactured in the United States;
>
> B. Processes, services, and improvements thereof which are covered by intellectual Property developed under this CRADA shall be incorporated into the Participant's manufacturing facilities in the United States either prior to or simultaneously with implementation outside the United States. Such processes, services, and improvements, when implemented outside the U.S., shall not result in reduction of the use of the same processes, services, or improvements in the United States; and
>
> C. In the event that it is not feasible to meet the requirements of A. and B., a plan for providing net benefit to the U.S. economy is attached in Document B [the U.S. competitiveness work sheet].

If a would-be participant chooses option C, it "must furnish a description of specific economic or other benefits to the U.S. economy which are related to the commercial use by Participant(s) of the technology being funded under the CRADA and which are commensurate with the Government's contribution to the proposed work." The benefits criteria set out in the U.S. competitiveness work sheet include:

1. Direct or indirect investment in U.S.-based plant and equipment.

2. Creation of new and/or higher-quality U.S.-based jobs.

3. Enhancement of the domestic skills base.

4. Further domestic development of the technology.

5. Significant reinvestment of profits in the domestic economy.

6. Positive impact on the U.S. balance of payments in terms of product and service exports as well as foreign licensing royalties and receipts.

7. Appropriate recognition of U.S. taxpayer support for the technology (e.g., a quid pro quo commensurate with the economic benefit that would be domestically derived by the U.S. taxpayer from U.S.-based manufacture).

8. Cross-licensing, sublicensing, and reassignment provisions in licenses that seek to maximize the benefits to the U.S. taxpayer." (U.S. Department of Energy, 1993, pp. 56-57, 86.)

Whereas a DOE laboratory can move directly to receive approval of the CRADA joint work statement from its regional operations office if the would-be participants accepts the sample U.S. competitiveness language, the laboratory must receive approval first from its operations office or DOE headquarters of the participant's alternative statement of specific economic benefits to the U.S. economy before it can proceed with the joint work statement. (U.S. Department of Energy, 1993).

In the DOE modular CRADA, intellectual property is defined as "patents, trademarks, copyrights, mask works, protected CRADA information [generated information which is marked as being protected CRADA information by a party to the CRADA] and other forms of comparable property rights protected by Federal Law and other foreign counterparts." With the permission of their regional operations office, DOE laboratories may work with a more narrow definition of intellectual property that includes only patents, trademarks, copyrights, and mask works.

40. See, for example, the Energy Policy Act of 1992 (42 U.S.C. §13525), and the Technology Administration Authorization Act (15 U.S.C. §278n) in the American Technology Preeminence Act of 1991 P.L. 102-245.

41. For a company to be eligible to receive financial assistance under the Act, the DOE secretary must find "that the company's participation in the Program would be in the economic interest of the United States, as evidenced by investments in the United States in research, development, and manufacturing (including, for example, the manufacture of major component or subassemblies in the United States); significant contributions to employment in the United States; and agreement with respect to any technology arising from assistance provided under this section to promote the manufacture within the United States of products resulting from that technology (taking into account the goals of promoting the competitiveness of United States industry), and to procure parts and materials from competitive suppliers." 42 U.S.C. §13525 Energy Policy Act of 1992, Sec. 2306 Limits on Participation by Companies.

42. "General Electric has circulated a paper implying that the Swedish-Swiss ABB should not be allowed to participate [in the advanced gas turbine programme] because its home governments do not protect intellectual property rights . . . The paper also suggests that if ABB were involved in the programme, it would use the fruits of the research not to create employment in the U.S. but to strengthen its technological capacity in Europe." (Financial Times, 1994)

43. AlliedSignal Corp. protested Oak Ridge National Laboratory's selection of a Japanese and a French firm in a conservation procurement for advanced ceramic manufacturing technology. However, DOE refused to obtain information to make a finding under Section 2306. "Lack of DOE action and inconsistent application of the law has been the subject of Congressional correspondence from Senate and House authorization and appropriations committees." (Correspondence from Maxine Savitz, AlliedSignal Corp., to Proctor Reid, NAE, June 2, 1994; Inside Energy, 1994.)

In response to criticism that it lacked a clear and consistent implementation strategy for these eligibility requirements, DOE submitted a statement of policy guidance for public comment in February 1995. (Federal Register, 1995)

44. The Technology Administration Authorization Act of 1991 includes "buy American" provisions (15 U.S.C. §278n) that prohibit the use of funds authorized under the legislation to procure components manufactured in a foreign country whose government unfairly maintains a procurement policy discriminating against U.S. products or services.

45. Telephone discussion between Connie Chang, Advanced Technology Program, NIST, and Proctor Reid, NAE, February 24, 1995.

46. Ibid.

47. Two U.S.-based ocean carriers, American Automar Inc. and Great American Lines Inc., are also participants in the Bath Iron Works TRP. The Japanese and Canadian participants will transfer commercial shipbuilding technology to Bath. (Defense News, 1993; Journal of Commerce, 1993)

48. "ARPA Technology Reinvestment Project, section 2.2.2. 'Guidelines for Assembling a Team of Eligible Participants.' In general, an 'eligible firm' as defined by legislation is a company or other business entity that conducts a significant level of its research, development, engineering, and manufacturing activities in the United States. A firm not meeting this test may still be an 'eligible firm' if its majority ownership or control is by United States citizens. In addition, a foreign-owned firm may be an 'eligible firm' if its parent company is incorporated in a country whose government encourages the participation of U.S.-owned firms in research and development consortia to which that government provides funding, if that government also affords adequate and effective protection for the intellectual property rights of companies incorporated in the United States. Determination of eligibility of firms in this last category [foreign-owned firms] will be made by the Secretary of Commerce as

mandated by 10 U.S.C. 2491(9). No prior certification of eligibility will be issued or accepted, and the burden of establishing eligibility will ultimately rest on the proposer." (Advanced Research Projects Agency, 1993)

49. William Spencer, executive director of SEMATECH, announced on October 5, 1994, that SEMATECH would no longer seek a DOD subsidy. (Corcoran, 1994)

50. See Committee on Science, Engineering, and Public Policy (1992); Issues in Science and Technology (1994); testimony by S. Richard Deininger, Director of SEMATECH's National Resource Program, before the NAE study committee, November 9, 1993; and Grindley et al. (1994).

51. The issue of foreign participation in the U.S. Display Consortium, like in SEMATECH, is primarily a political one. Both consortia represent a public-private response to an onslaught of foreign competition. As such, it is politically very difficult to open them up to foreign participation, even though there may be some technological advantages to doing so. Note that the Microelectronics and Computer Technology Corporation, a privately funded consortium, is trying to expand its funding and technology base by recruiting foreign-owned firms. Proctor Reid, NAE, phone discussion with Peter Mills, CEO, U.S. Display Consortium, February 1994.

52. For data on sources of funding for foreign doctoral candidates in science and engineering, see National Science Foundation, 1993a, Table A-21, pp. 94-96.

53. These are the very subgroups targeted by the National Research Council (1988) study as the greatest potential source of U.S.-born engineers in the coming decades.

54. See "Foreign Nationals Change the Face of U.S. Science," Science (261), 1993, pp. 1769-1775.

55. See note 6, above.

56. To be sure, contributions by foreign alumni to U.S. universities are a small fraction of those by U.S.-born alumni. Considering the countries of origin of the majority of foreign-born engineering students and faculty—the People's Republic of China, Korea, and India—this should come as no surprise. Nevertheless, there are numerous examples of foreign alumni generosity. For example, in gratitude for kindness shown by a professor in the mid-1950s, Gordon Wu of Hong Kong has endowed a $1.5 million Sollenberger chair at Princeton University, having earlier financed construction of a Gordon Wu Hall at the university. The Mogami Geotechnical Laboratory at Cornell University has been endowed by a former student and Japanese national who now teaches at Kyoto University (Stalson, 1989).

57. See the comments of Dr. Gerard Mourou, director of the National Science Foundation's Center for Ultrafast Optical Science at the University of Michigan, on the contributions of two large foreign sponsors, Fujitsu and Thomson, to the center's basic and long-term research program (U.S. Congress, House, 1993, pp.102-103); testimony of John Wiley, University of Wisconsin, before the NAE study committee, November 9, 1993 (Wiley, 1993); and the comments of federal laboratory representatives in U.S. General Accounting Office (1988b) and National Research Council (1994a).

58. Of the 17 foreign-owned firms involved in industrial affiliate programs at the Georgia Institute of Technology, 16 are known to have U.S.-based manufacturing and R&D operations (Correspondence from Robert Nerem, Georgia Institute of Technology, to Proctor Reid, NAE, January 1995). Of 102 foreign-owned members of Stanford University's industrial liaison programs, 34 have U.S.-based manufacturing and/or R&D facilities (Correspondence from Marianne Meredith, Stanford, to Proctor Reid, NAE, April 7, 1995).

59. In at least two instances, foreign companies have replicated technologies developed by U.S. federal laboratories, thereby denying U.S.-owned firms opportunities to exploit first-mover advantages. The two examples cited most often in this context include the KEVA code (developed by Los Alamos National Laboratory), used to model the workings of the internal combustion engine, and the laminar-flow clean room concept (developed by Sandia National Laboratory), used in microelectronics manufacturing. (National Research Council, 1994a)

60. See, for example, p. 107 above, Wiley (1993), and U.S. Congress, House (1993).

61. Some observers have questioned whether most university technology licensing offices are

adequately funded and staffed to negotiate effectively with corporate partners—U.S. or foreign—in the best interest of the United States. In testimony before the House Subcommittee on Science on October 28, 1993, Robin Frank Risser, CEO of Picometrix Inc., made the following observation regarding his company's participation in the University of Michigan's Center for Ultra-Fast Optical Science:

> Our biggest area of concern surrounds background technology which might have been available for exclusive licensing by Fujitsu had USL and Picometrix not paid particular attention to this area. I believe this to be a problem area. University researchers often operate in an environment where there are significant barriers to constructively reducing inventions to practice by filing patent applications. Patent budgets at the University of Michigan are small compared to the amount of research. As a result, it is usually difficult to patent many background discoveries prior to entering into a research contract with a foreign company. Since foreign companies usually obtain options for exclusive licenses on patents "conceived or reduced to practice" during the term of the agreement, this means that they could reach back to obtain exclusive rights to background technology that they did not really fund. In my opinion, this occurrence could be substantially reduced if patent budgets were substantially increased, faculty were better educated, and other barriers to patenting were reduced. Perhaps requiring that a percentage of federally funded research and development be set aside for foreign and domestic patents is appropriate. (U.S. Congress, House, 1993, pp. 60-61)

62. See, for example, Stalson (1989), Massachusetts Institute of Technology (1991), U.S. House of Representatives (1993).

63. See discussion on pp. 114-117 and notes 36 and 40, above.

64. Although U.S.-industry contacts with foreign universities are widespread, actual U.S. corporate funding of foreign university research is small compared to industrial R&D spending. Companies supported foreign university research at about the same rate that they support R&D in U.S. universities (i.e., roughly 1 percent of total company-funded R&D, or, by NSF's (1990b) estimates, $50 million to $100 million per year).

The U.S. companies surveyed indicated that the principal rationale for establishing linkages with foreign universities was to benefit from the work of world-renowned scientists and engineers. Other reasons given included fostering good will and promoting the company's reputation in the host country's scientific community.

65. See, for example, the program announcement for NSF's (1995c) Division of International Programs as well as the U.S.-Japan Manufacturing Fellowship Program administered by the U.S. Department of Commerce, which was launched during the final year of the Bush Administration. U.S. Department of Commerce (1993b).

66. Correspondence from Helen Donoghue, Second Secretary, Science and Technology, Delegation of the European Communities, Washington, D.C., to Proctor Reid, NAE, May 18, 1994.

67. Ibid.

68. Very little information is available on the specific requirements individual European nations impose on would-be foreign participants in their national R&D programs. For information regarding the policies of several OECD countries, see Organization for Economic Cooperation and Development (1992b). In late 1993 and early 1994, the U.S. Department of State conducted a survey of U.S. access to publicly funded research abroad as part of an ad hoc interagency working group chaired by the Council of Economic Advisors. The findings of the survey confirm that the formal policies of individual EC member states with respect to international access to national R&D programs are, for the most part, consistent with those of the European Community proper. However, some survey respondents indicated that, in some cases, national practices vis-à-vis foreign-owned firms were more restrictive than their formal policies would suggest. Proctor Reid, NAE, discussions with Anthony Rock and Gary Couey, U.S. Department of State, March 14, 1995.

69. The High-Speed Civil Transport "Piper" project was designed from the outset to include foreign collaborators (National Research Council, 1994b).

70. See note 42, above.

71. The rationale for extending national treatment to multinational firms is essentially the same as that underlying the U.S. commitment to free trade and free investment: They offer the most effective

route to economic growth and rising living standards for all nations. Moreover, the United States remains the world's largest source of foreign direct investment. U.S.-owned multinationals account for a majority of U.S. exports and depend increasingly on foreign markets.

The U.S. commitment to the principle of national treatment is manifested in bilateral and multilateral investment treaties it has negotiated with other countries, and the federal government's official negotiating position within the Organization for Economic Cooperation and Development (OECD), General Agreement on Tariffs and Trade (GATT), and most recently, the Asian-Pacific Economic Cooperation Forum. The United States and its trading partners have negotiated exceptions to national treatment in areas concerning national security and public order. Investment treaties and OECD code have also listed specific excluded sectors; these vary somewhat from one agreement/ treaty to another. Despite these inconsistencies and exceptions, the U.S. commitment to national treatment has been strong and has clearly contributed to a movement in this direction at the international level.

Federal R&D programs that condition national treatment on foreign-government (non-foreign-owned firm) compliance with/or application of U.S. laws and standards undermine U.S. efforts to push national treatment in international forums. As recent developments in the EC suggest, U.S. moves toward reciprocity in this and other areas of so-called domestic policy may encourage other nations to introduce similar requirements. The consequences of this for the United States in the long term, if not more immediately, could be costly (Graham and Krugman, 1995).

72. While there has been legislation put forward in the European Parliament that would introduce similar reciprocity "conditional national treatment" requirements in EC programs, it has not yet become law. See European Parliament (1994).

5

Findings and Recommendations

In the decades immediately following World War II, the United States occupied a position of global technological and industrial preeminence. There was little question that Americans would reap most of the economic and technological benefits generated by public and private investments in R&D and in other types of technologically innovative activity. The American public generally viewed the predominately one-way transfer of technology and know-how out of the United States as a way to increase both short- and long-term economic, political, and national security returns on these investments.

Recent decades have brought increasing convergence in the technological capabilities of industrialized nations as well as growing cross-penetration of national innovation systems through foreign direct investment and transnational industrial alliances. The United States remains a leader in the generation of new knowledge and technology, but its position today is better characterized as first among equals. Similarly, the technological and economic autonomy of the United States has given way to deepening international interdependence. Accompanying these trends, changes have taken place in the organization and management of R&D within the United States, and new links have been forged between different U.S.-based R&D-performing institutions.

These changes have given rise to new questions about the consequences of the growing involvement of foreign nationals in publicly and privately funded U.S.-based R&D activity. Are foreign nationals receiving more knowledge, know-how, technology, and associated economic benefits than they are contributing to the United States? Does increasing foreign participation in U.S. R&D pose a threat to the nation's military or economic security?

140

R&D AND ECONOMIC PERFORMANCE

Understanding the nature of R&D activity, technology transfer, and the ways R&D contributes to corporate and national economic performance is vital to any attempt to assess the consequences of growing foreign participation for the United States. The following observations are of particular relevance to the emerging policy debate:

• R&D activity is a critical, yet relatively small, subset of the many interlocking activities and capabilities that make up the complex process of technological innovation, the iterative process by which new knowledge and technology are generated or acquired and developed so that they may be incorporated into useful products or services;

• R&D activity yields many different economically valuable outputs. Among them are codified knowledge, know-how or techniques, highly skilled human capital, instrumentation, and technology;

• A variety of individuals and institutions may benefit from a given R&D activity. Many of the outputs of publicly and privately funded R&D are "public goods" usable by one party without diminishing their value to others and are accessible to anyone with the technical skills to absorb them. Even where R&D outputs are proprietary in nature (i.e., patents, copyrights, and trade secrets), they yield economic benefits to many entities, including customers, suppliers, and competitors, beyond those who hold title;

• There are significant barriers to the movement of scientific and technological knowledge across national boundaries and even between organizations or regional centers with technological competence in specific fields. Technology transfer—even in an era of global telecommunications—remains a "contact sport" that demands the ongoing, intensive, face-to-face interaction of individual scientists and engineers. Therefore, R&D activity continues to cluster geographically, and much of the economically valuable outputs of publicly and privately funded R&D tend to be highly localized;

• In order for a company to draw effectively on advanced technological capabilities and R&D outputs beyond its own walls, that firm generally needs to be performing R&D at a level commensurate with that of the organizations whose R&D activities it hopes to exploit; and

• Neither R&D capabilities nor ownership of technology alone are reliable indicators of the economic or competitive strength of a company or a nation. Rather, economic and competitive strength are determined by how effectively technology is used and managed in combination with other factors of production, such as labor, capital, and managerial and organizational capabilities. Similarly, the economic or other societal returns a nation may gain from a particular R&D investment depends on whether its innovation system can foster widespread diffusion and effective use of the outputs generated. These factors are, in turn, influenced by the skill level of a nation's work force, by the size, wealth, and technological sophistication of its domestic market, and, increasingly, by the ability of firms within its borders to access markets and technology abroad.

These observations suggest that the task of appropriating the many valuable outputs of U.S.-based R&D activity is significantly more complex and difficult than is generally assumed. They imply also that foreign-owned firms wishing to effectively exploit technology and knowledge generated in the United States must establish a significant, technologically sophisticated presence here to do so. Moreover, as the level of technological sophistication and extractive capabilities of foreign participants and their home countries increase, so too does the potential for reciprocal transfers of knowledge and technology into the United States. Under most circumstances, then, any country, including the United States, should welcome R&D activity within its borders regardless of the nationality of the R&D performer. If a large share of the returns to R&D investments are captured by those proximate to the R&D activity, and these returns are considered desirable, it is clearly better to have R&D performed within one's borders than beyond them.

FOREIGN PARTICIPATION IN PRIVATELY
FUNDED U.S. R&D: FINDINGS

The past decade has brought a significant increase in foreign participation in privately funded R&D in the United States. This participation has taken the form of both direct investment and intercorporate technical alliances. In 1992, U.S. affiliates of foreign-owned firms accounted for nearly a fifth of all R&D spending by U.S. high-technology companies. Affiliate shares of U.S. industrial R&D were particularly large in three manufacturing industries: industrial chemicals (47.5 percent); pharmaceuticals (42.7 percent); and audio, video, and communications equipment (33 percent). In general, foreign parent companies invest in U.S. high-technology assets in areas in which they have a strong export position or perceived competitive advantage.

No single country dominates the field of foreign investors in privately funded U.S. R&D. Roughly two-thirds of affiliate R&D spending in the United States is accounted for by companies based in Canada, the United Kingdom, Germany, Switzerland, and Japan. Since the mid-1980s, Japanese-owned affiliates have increased their share of affiliate R&D activity more rapidly than any other major investing country.

Foreign companies cite two principal motives for establishing a U.S.-based R&D presence: to help the local manufacturing affiliate and the parent company meet the demands of U.S. customers more effectively and to improve access to the scientific and technical talent in established U.S. centers of technology and innovation. Both motives are reflected in the activities and locations of a majority of affiliate facilities. Comparative surveys of U.S.- and foreign-owned multinational companies in a variety of industries suggest that both the motives for engaging in R&D in foreign markets and the type of R&D activity vary by industry as well as among firms with the same industry. However, for the most part, there is considerably less variation in motive and R&D type among companies of different nationality within the same industry.

The committee concludes that the strength and momentum of the trends that have fueled the growth of foreign involvement in privately funded U.S. R&D will continue into the next century. Regardless of what individual nations do to slow or otherwise modify these trends, global technological and economic capabilities will become increasingly distributed among an expanding population of industrialized countries, and competition and innovation in most manufacturing and service industries will become increasingly internationalized.

The Quid Pro Quo

Growing foreign involvement in the nation's industrial R&D base is accompanied by both costs and benefits. The question of whether foreign nationals take away more technology and associated economic value than they contribute to the United States cannot be definitively answered. The few quantitative measures available indicate, however, that the U.S.-based affiliates of foreign-owned firms import significantly more codified technology from their parent companies than they export to them or to unaffiliated firms abroad. Case studies show that foreign-owned companies, especially Japanese firms, have in several industries imported significant amounts of advanced production technology and methodologies into the United States. Thus, while in some cases foreign involvement in U.S.-based industrial R&D has resulted in lost opportunities for U.S.-owned firms and foregone wealth for their U.S.-based stakeholders, in many others foreign firms have created opportunities and wealth for Americans and American firms by transferring technology, know-how, capital, and other assets to the United States.

On balance, the committee believes that the growth of foreign direct investment is a positive-sum trend, one that enhances the productivity and wealth of the United States and its trading and investing partners overseas. The same finding holds for the proliferation of transnational corporate alliances. Furthermore, the committee believes that foreign participation in privately funded U.S. R&D cannot be separated meaningfully from the larger trends of which it is part.

Asymmetries of Access

Limits on American access to various non-U.S. economies and innovation systems have had a profound effect on public perceptions and federal policies related to foreign involvement in R&D in this country. Over the last 10 years, U.S. trading partners have modified their policies on foreign direct investment—

the most important avenue of access to privately funded R&D activities abroad. In doing so, they have moved significantly toward the more liberal policies of the United States. Nevertheless, the committee found that important impediments to U.S. access remain in some major economies. Arising from structural barriers, government policies, or collusive or discriminatory corporate practices, these lingering barriers have led to calls for unilateral U.S. action to force the pace of liberalization abroad. While appealing to one's sense of fairness and equity, many of these unilateral measures would pose significant risks and costs for the United States.

In the committee's judgment, many of the proposed policy changes, such as placing additional restrictions or reporting requirements on foreign direct investment in U.S. high-tech industries are unlikely to advance the short- or long-term interests of U.S. citizens. Such measures risk discouraging more "good" foreign direct investment with its many associated benefits to the United States than "bad." They also risk undercutting the United States' credibility as it negotiates the further opening of foreign markets to international trade and investment. In addition, unilateral measures by the United States—still the world's largest national economy—risk encouraging other nations to backslide in their treatment of foreign direct investment, potentially at significant cost to U.S. multinationals and their U.S.-based stakeholders.

Threats to National Security

Concerns over the risk to national security posed by foreign involvement in the U.S. research enterprise have focused on growing foreign participation in particular R&D-intensive industries, whether through investment or industrial alliances. The committee found that current national security regulations and procedures minimize the chances that militarily sensitive U.S. technology will be transferred to foreign-owned companies. These regulations and procedures, however, may not be as effective in addressing the medium-to-long-term risks of delayed or denied access to militarily critical technological capabilities posed by foreign direct investment, or mergers and acquisitions generally.

In addition, current monitoring efforts and methodologies associated with U.S. antitrust law enforcement may be inadequate to address the monopoly risks posed by mergers and acquisitions in niche defense markets, whether instigated by foreign- or U.S.-owned companies. Further complicating the situation, the federal government has no clearly defined, agreed-upon criteria or procedures for deciding whether a given company's technological capabilities have critical military implications. This makes it difficult to identify vulnerable niche sectors.

At the same time, little consideration has been given to the costs and risks to national security posed by existing procurement regulations that discourage foreign-owned firms from contracting directly with the Department of Defense or investing in existing U.S.-based defense contractors. The committee believes such risks should be accorded greater weight given the current relatively high level of U.S. dependence on foreign sources of component technology, the growing importance to the nation's military of technologies that have both civilian and military applications, and the increasing strength of foreign-owned firms in many of these dual-use technologies.

The Threat of Technological Monopolies

At the national and global levels, many high-technology industries are already highly concentrated. Consequently, at least some of the many recent mergers and acquisitions have probably diminished competition in particular civilian high-technology industries. However, there is no evidence to suggest that foreign-owned firms are any more likely to engage in anticompetitive activity in the United States than are their U.S.-owned counterparts. Growing foreign involvement in U.S. industrial R&D appears to be causing little if any damage to U.S. economic security, as measured by the ability of U.S.-based companies to access key technologies, components, and subsystems required to produce goods competitive with those made by foreign companies.

FOREIGN PARTICIPATION IN PRIVATELY FUNDED U.S. R&D: RECOMMENDATIONS

The central policy challenges facing the U.S. government with respect to foreign participation in privately funded U.S. R&D are inseparable from the nation's broader foreign economic policy agenda, particularly as it relates to foreign direct investment and international trade. As a first step toward meeting these challenges, the committee makes two closely related recommendations.

1. In the absence of clear threats to national security, the Congress should avoid legislating restrictions on foreign participation in privately funded U.S. R&D.

The committee concludes that the risks posed by growing foreign involvement in privately funded U.S. R&D do not in and of themselves warrant special regulation of foreign direct investment in the United States or of transnational corporate alliances involving U.S.-owned firms, except in the area of national military security. Moreover, the committee believes that discriminatory treatment of foreign-owned firms beyond what may be required to protect U.S. military security imposes economic costs on U.S. citizens. Such treatment discourages foreign direct investment in the United States and undermines long-standing U.S. efforts to secure national treatment of U.S.-owned companies in foreign markets.

The committee also cautions against invoking concerns about military security as justification for excluding foreign participation in the nation's industrial

R&D enterprise. The nation's military security will be served more effectively once the federal government develops more sophisticated capabilities for both assessing and addressing the risks and capitalizing on the opportunities presented by the growth of foreign involvement in the nation's dual-use industrial technology base. In particular, the committee calls upon the Department of Defense to define clearly criteria and procedures for identifying militarily critical technological assets and to broaden its portfolio of strategies for managing inevitable U.S. dependence on certain foreign technologies.

2. The federal government should continue to seek to open foreign markets to U.S. trade and investment through negotiation in bilateral and multilateral forums. The United States should hold itself and its trading partners accountable to existing international agreements and should redouble its efforts to negotiate more comprehensive, internationally enforceable rules on monopoly formation, foreign direct investment, technical standards, environmental regulation, and intellectual property rights. Above all, the United States should reaffirm its long-standing commitment to the principles of nondiscrimination (national treatment) and transparency (full disclosure of terms) in policies that influence international investment and trade flows.

The committee believes it is essential that the federal government continue to seek to reduce policy- and business practice-induced barriers that impede U.S.-owned companies' access to foreign markets and private R&D assets located abroad. The United States has long championed the worldwide opening of markets to the free flow of goods, services, investment, and technology based on internationally agreed-upon principles and rules of conduct. Thanks in large part to U.S. leadership in this area, there has been significant progress in recent years in liberalizing national foreign direct investment policies. Structural and policy-induced barriers to investment are a source of continuing friction in U.S. relations with some of its major trading partners, and negotiations to reduce these remaining barriers have been difficult and progress has been slow. Nevertheless, the committee believes that U.S. advocacy of liberal treatment of foreign direct investment through multilateral agreements continues to serve well the nation's economic interests.

The committee also urges the federal government to resist pressures to force the pace of these negotiations with aggressive unilateral actions, beyond those currently provided for in U.S. law. In the opinion of the committee, unilateral measures aimed at eliminating asymmetries of access—particularly those which contradict the principles of nondiscrimination and transparency—risk discouraging more "good" foreign investment in the United States than "bad," undercutting rather than strengthening the position of the United States in bilateral and multilateral negotiations, and inviting retaliation by U.S. trading partners all at significant cost to U.S. citizens.

FOREIGN PARTICIPATION IN PUBLICLY
FUNDED U.S. R&D: FINDINGS

During the past 15 years, participation in U.S. publicly funded R&D activities by individual foreign students and researchers as well as foreign corporations has grown sufficiently to capture the attention of the American public. National and institution-specific data on foreign graduate students, postdoctoral researchers, and long-term visiting researchers (who stay in the United States for at least 12 months) indicate that these groups participate extensively in research at U.S. universities and federal laboratories. Although no aggregate data are available on foreign researchers who work at U.S. publicly funded research facilities for short periods (fewer than 12 months), anecdotal evidence from various institutions suggests that their numbers may be significant as well.

There is little good information on the scope and nature of foreign institutional involvement in publicly funded R&D in the United States. Apparently, such support represents a relatively small share (1 to 2 percent) of total sponsored research and is concentrated in a small number of U.S. institutions. As of the late 1980s, a majority of foreign-sponsored research was funded by not-for-profit institutions and was concentrated in agriculture, medicine, and geology. However, at select U.S. research universities, such as the Massachusetts Institute of Technology and the University of Wisconsin, a majority of foreign-sponsored research is accounted for by private companies. As of 1986, Japanese institutions sponsored more U.S. university-based R&D than did those of any other nationality. More recent data indicate that Japanese-owned multinational companies rely more heavily on U.S. research universities for training company personnel and collaborative research than do their U.S. or European counterparts (Roberts, 1995a).

Foreign-owned companies that opt to participate in U.S. publicly supported R&D may do so in any number of ways, including via sponsored research, patent licensing, university industrial liaison programs, or by employing university faculty and recent graduates from science and engineering doctoral programs. A paucity of data makes it difficult to say much about the aggregate magnitude, disciplinary focus, and national shares of foreign corporate involvement. Anecdotal evidence suggests that Japanese companies may be the most diligent of all foreign-owned firms in monitoring the research activities of U.S. federal laboratories. To date, few foreign firms have participated in the recently established federal industrial R&D programs, such as the Advanced Technology Program at the Department of Commerce.

The Quid Pro Quo

The committee believes that the extensive involvement of foreign graduate students, postdoctoral researchers, and other long-term visiting researchers in publicly funded U.S. research institutions has, on balance, significantly benefited the U.S. economy and national innovation system. By contrast, the committee believes that foreign visiting researchers who stay in this country for less than 1 year gain more than they contribute from their work in U.S. research universities and federal laboratories. Evidence concerning the scope and nature of participation by these short-term visiting researchers is mostly anecdotal. The committee believes further study of this category of foreign visiting researcher is warranted.

The costs and benefits of foreign corporate involvement in U.S. government-funded research institutions are readily identifiable, but it is impossible either to quantify them or determine their net economic impact. Through their participation in the research activities of U.S. universities and federal laboratories, foreign corporations undoubtedly extract more knowledge and intellectual property from the United States than they would in the absence of such ties. It is equally certain, in the view of the committee, that foreign-owned firms and their stakeholders abroad have garnered extensive benefits, in some cases at the expense of American firms and stakeholders, through their access to U.S. publicly funded R&D activities and institutions.

At the same time, the committee firmly believes that knowledge and technology flows between foreign firms and U.S. universities and federal laboratories are far from unidirectional and that foreign firms through their R&D participation also return economic value to U.S. citizens in many different ways. Numerous examples confirm that foreign-owned firms have contributed material support as well as intellectual resources to U.S. research universities and federal laboratories, enhancing the productivity and quality of these institutions' research efforts and strengthening the nation's research infrastructure.

Furthermore, whether or not foreign companies acquire more intellectual property and knowledge from U.S. universities and federal laboratories than they bring to them says very little, in and of itself, about the impact of foreign corporate research participation on the welfare of U.S. citizens. Many if not most of the foreign-owned companies that have extensive ties to U.S. publicly funded research institutions also tend to have significant U.S.-based manufacturing and R&D operations—operations that employ U.S. citizens, buy from U.S.-based suppliers and equipment vendors, import as well as generate technology and know-how that is applied within the U.S. economy, and pay U.S. taxes.

Even if foreign companies go abroad to exploit intellectual property licensed from U.S. publicly funded research institutions, their gain does not automatically represent a loss for the United States. It is true that in some instances, foreign firms have acquired or licensed technology generated with U.S. government funds only to develop and commercialize the technology overseas. Yet, the committee also believes that many foreign-based licensees have enabled publicly supported U.S. research institutions to earn revenues on technology that otherwise would not have been commercialized. By doing so, foreign firms have in some instances supplied Americans with higher-performance or lower-cost goods or services embodying the licensed technology.

American research universities and the nation's federal laboratories, in the committee's judgment, have generally extended preferences to U.S.-based firms and made good-faith efforts to comply with the federally mandated economic performance requirements in their dealings with both U.S.- and foreign-owned companies. In general, foreign-owned firms are buyers or licensees of last resort for technology owned by U.S. universities and federal laboratories. That is, these institutions are licensing to foreign entities technology that no U.S.-owned company wants to invest in.

In a few well-publicized cases, publicly funded institutions have seemed to be unwilling or unable to negotiate deals with foreign firms (or U.S.-owned firms for that matter) that are in the best interest of the United States. However, the committee believes these to be the exception, not the norm. Indeed, most U.S. universities and federal laboratories appear to be very aware of the need to affirm their service to the nation's economic welfare. They are also cognizant of the highly volatile public relations hazards associated with foreign corporate involvement in publicly funded research, as are foreign firms themselves. The sharply critical public response to the few highly controversial cases of foreign participation in U.S. R&D has, in the committee's opinion, had a distinct chilling effect on the willingness of some foreign firms to enter into closer working relationships with publicly funded U.S. research institutions.

At the same time, the manner in which some federal agencies have implemented the performance requirements embodied in recent technology transfer legislation suggests that they may be overreaching in their efforts to contain the economic benefits of public R&D spending within the United States. Some agencies have developed economic performance criteria and procedures for implementing them that are fundamentally at odds with the competitive R&D and technology management practices of multinational companies, strongly discourage foreign corporate involvement, and are at times in conflict with the core missions of the agencies themselves. In order to engage U.S.-owned multinational companies in cooperative research and development agreements (CRADAs) and other forms of collaborative R&D, some agencies have developed procedures that allow for a broader, case-by-case interpretation of what constitutes an adequate economic quid pro quo. Nevertheless, extensive restrictions on private-sector use of publicly subsidized intellectual property, invoked in the name of U.S. economic interests, continue to discourage many leading U.S.-owned high-technology companies from collaborating with federal laboratories.

With respect to foreign-owned firms, the interpretation and implementation of economic performance requirements by various federal agencies appear to be particularly vulnerable to political and legal challenges. Thus, as currently implemented by some agencies, these requirements serve as a major disincentive to foreign-owned firms that might otherwise participate in publicly funded U.S. R&D. Given the growth of technical competence overseas and the prominent role of U.S.- and foreign-owned multinational companies in R&D and technology areas of direct relevance to the core missions of U.S. federal agencies, it is worth asking whether economic performance requirements as currently administered are serving the nation's best interests.

Asymmetries of Access

U.S. government, academic, and industrial researchers appear to have few problems accessing publicly funded research capabilities and activities within academic and government-operated laboratories abroad. Furthermore, at least on paper, access by U.S.-owned companies to government-funded industrial research consortia in Europe is apparently equal to if not greater than the access that the United States extends to foreign-owned firms in this country. Japan, however, has restricted foreign participation in its publicly funded industrial R&D consortia to a greater extent than either the United States or the European Community.

Given differences in the organization, scale, and sophistication of publicly funded R&D activities among countries, the value to Americans of reciprocal access to publicly funded R&D abroad is not always clear. In some cases, the lack of reciprocal access may hurt the international competitiveness of U.S.-owned firms with negative consequences for their U.S.-based stakeholders. However, its greatest impact may be the extent to which it offends the American sense of fairness, thereby undermining public support for efforts to negotiate remedies to these asymmetries.

In the committee's judgment, recent U.S. government efforts to address international asymmetries of access to publicly funded R&D through the introduction of reciprocity requirements have proved problematic. Indeed, even more than economic performance rules, reciprocity requirements present liabilities and hazards for the United States. First, by requiring that foreign firms' home governments comply with U.S. laws before the firms may expect nondiscriminatory treatment, the United States is violating its long-standing adherence to unconditional national treatment of multinational enterprises. Some evidence suggests that the U.S. move toward reciprocity requirements has encouraged a few major U.S. trading partners to consider imposing similar conditions. Second, multiple agencies must be involved in the process of assessing whether a particular firm's home country is in compliance with each of the various reciprocity requirements, making the process cumbersome, time consuming, and difficult to administer. Federal agencies must also make decisions in situations in which it is often difficult to determine just what constitutes "comparable investment opportunities" or "adequate protection of U.S. intellectual property." These vagaries have encouraged some U.S. companies to challenge both the eligibility of particular foreign firms to participate in U.S. R&D and the way federal agencies implement the eligibility requirements. The committee believes that these challenges, in turn, have discouraged many foreign-owned firms from even applying for access to U.S. publicly funded R&D initiatives.

International Burden-Sharing in Basic Research

The argument that basic research should be more equitably distributed among nations is directed primarily at Japan. International comparisons of R&D expenditures confirm that most of America's advanced industrialized trading partners invest as much if not more of their gross national product in basic research than does the United States. Japan, however, despite recent efforts to expand its basic research capabilities, spends a smaller share of its gross domestic product and nearly half as much per capita as the United States on basic research.

FOREIGN PARTICIPATION IN PUBLICLY FUNDED U.S. R&D: RECOMMENDATIONS

Foreign participation in R&D funded by the U.S. government is regulated by a patchwork of confusing and at times contradictory intergovernmental science and technology agreements, federal agency directives, and guidelines based on recent federal legislation. In the committee's judgment, leading U.S. research universities and federal laboratories generally have made good-faith efforts to comply with federally mandated economic performance and reciprocity requirements. Nevertheless, the committee believes that at the very least these requirements risk impeding the ability of agencies to perform their primary missions as well as diminishing the contribution of federal R&D programs to U.S. economic performance and competitiveness. At worst, these requirements risk imposing significant economic costs on the United States. Recommendations 1 through 3, directed at the federal government, are intended to minimize these risks to the United States as well as lay the foundation for more effective, mutually beneficial management of foreign participation in government-funded R&D in all industrialized countries.

Private-sector institutions that conduct or otherwise benefit from R&D activity supported by the U.S. government should recognize that concerns about foreign involvement are more than a public relations problem. The actions of a limited number of institutions have evoked legitimate worries regarding the fairness and economic logic of certain types of private-company involvement in publicly subsidized R&D. The committee does not believe that increased restrictions on foreign corporate participation are the necessary political price to pay for avoiding further public criticism. Rather, the committee calls upon universities and other performers of publicly funded research to communicate more effectively the costs and benefits of foreign participation in U.S. R&D. Recommendations 4 through 6, aimed at the performers of publicly funded U.S. R&D, outline steps these institutions might take to become more constructive participants in the public debate.

1. U.S. federal agencies charged with administering public R&D resources should be empowered and encouraged to implement with greater flexibility and discretion the economic performance requirements embodied in recent federal R&D legislation. This should be done in a manner that is consistent with the core missions of the agencies involved, the realities of competitive corporate R&D practice, and the principles of nondiscrimination (national treatment) and transparency (full disclosure of terms).

As mission agencies are called upon to contribute more directly to U.S. economic growth and competitiveness through their R&D activities, they must become more adept at balancing this new role with their core missions in a manner that is consistent with the opportunities and constraints of an increasingly interdependent world economy. Most private companies in a position to make significant technological contributions to federal agency missions or to successfully commercialize technology developed with public funds will balk at rules that limit the transfer or commercial application of publicly-subsidized intellectual property beyond U.S. borders. For that matter, the very existence of such extreme restrictions sends a signal to potential foreign participants that they need not apply.

In addition to more flexible implementation, there needs to be strong interagency policy guidance that explicitly reconciles economic performance requirements with the demands of agency core missions, the nature of multinational R&D and technology practice, and the long-standing U.S. commitment to national treatment of all companies operating in the United States.[1]

Federal policy guidance in this area should make it clear that there will be circumstances in which agency missions and the more immediate economic objectives of these requirements will not overlap and may even diverge. Such guidance should recognize that there are many direct and indirect ways—as a licensee, contractor, or collaborator—that a firm's involvement in publicly funded R&D can contribute to the economic welfare of the United States. It should acknowledge the existence of highly specialized technical competence overseas and the dominant role of multinational companies (both U.S.- and foreign-owned) in areas of R&D and technology that are critical both to the core missions of U.S. agencies and the broader economic interests of the nation. Finally, policy guidance should inform policymakers and the general public of the complex, highly case-specific calculus involved in implementing economic performance requirements and emphasize the need for flexibility, discretion, and decentralized decision-making in that process.

The committee believes that in most instances, determining whether or not licensing a technology to a foreign-owned company or including a foreign firm in a CRADA or government R&D contract advances the nation's economic interest requires the consideration of a number of highly case-specific factors. These factors are generally best understood, explained, and, if need be, justified by the institutions performing the R&D. Therefore, to the extent possible, federal agencies should devolve responsibility for implementing economic performance requirement to these "front-line" institutions, which would remain accountable to their respective sponsor agencies and should be prepared to justify their decisions within the context of the agencies' policy guidance. Such an approach would be far superior, in the committee's judgment, to the current situation, in which some agencies have attempted to reduce general statutory language regarding "substantial manufacturing presence" and "national economic interest" to highly detailed regulations.

Ultimately, strong federal policy guidance is a prerequisite to more flexible and discretionary implementation of statutory economic performance requirements. Such guidance would provide federal agencies and front-line R&D-performing institutions with the authority and legitimacy they need to implement the requirement. In the process, it would provide those responsible for assessing compliance with some shelter from unwarranted political interference.

2. Congress should strike reciprocity requirements from existing laws governing federal R&D spending and exclude them from future R&D legislation. Instead, the federal government should pursue more aggressively reciprocal access to publicly and privately funded R&D activities abroad through U.S. trade and antitrust law, existing bilateral and multilateral trade and technology agreements, and the negotiation of more comprehensive bilateral and multilateral agreements.

Although the committee understands the logic that led to reciprocity requirements, it does not believe that these requirements serve U.S. interests. Admittedly, such requirements appeal to a collective sense of fair play. Moreover, the history of recent U.S. trade policy suggests that highly specific "tit-for-tat" reciprocity requirements (i.e., those that make access by foreign companies to U.S. government-supported R&D contingent upon reciprocal access by U.S.-owned firms to comparable publicly funded R&D abroad) may help force foreign governments to reduce access barriers.[2] Nevertheless, the committee considers the potential benefits of such requirements to be marginal and more than offset by their potential costs and risks.

First, nondiscriminatory, or national, treatment of multinational companies is a fundamental tenet of post–World War II U.S. foreign economic policy. It has been codified—with certain exceptions based on concerns for national security and public order—in numerous bilateral and multilateral investment treaties to which the United States is a signatory. It is also a central element of the federal government's investment policy agenda within multilateral forums, including the General Agreement on Tariffs and Trade (GATT), the Organization for Economic Cooperation and Development (OECD), and the Asian-Pacific Economic Cooperation (APEC) Forum. The committee believes this commitment has served and continues to serve U.S. national interests very effectively, even though it has yet to be embraced fully by several of the United States' major trading partners. Reciprocity requirements in federal R&D legislation make nondiscriminatory treatment of foreign-owned companies conditional on foreign-government compliance with U.S. laws in areas in which no international agreement exists. Such requirements contradict stated U.S. foreign economic policy objectives, undercut U.S. efforts to persuade other nations to move toward unconditional nondiscriminatory treatment, and even encourage U.S. trading partners to introduce into their laws similar reciprocity requirements.

Second, implementation of these requirements is cumbersome and time consuming, involving the cooperation of multiple federal agencies that must render judgments in areas of policy where compliance is extremely difficult to define. The absence of international standards or rules to measure the compliance of foreign host countries with reciprocity requirements has encouraged some U.S.-owned companies and members of Congress to challenge the eligibility of particular foreign firms (as well as the implementation processes of some federal agencies). The committee believes that these challenges have had a chilling effect on the interest of foreign-owned firms that might otherwise have sought to participate in federally funded R&D initiatives. No doubt they have also served as a political "shot across the bow" for federal agencies and their mission laboratories in their dealings with foreign-owned companies. To the extent that reciprocity requirements discourage foreign-owned firms from applying to participate in federal R&D programs, they deny agencies access to potentially valuable information contained in the proposals of would-be foreign applicants. Of course, any potential technical and economic contributions these firms might make to the United States are also lost.

Finally, the committee believes that there are more promising approaches for increasing U.S. access to publicly and privately funded R&D in other nations. These include greater insistence on mutual accountability in existing or renegotiated bilateral science and technology agreements, negotiation of new rules at the multilateral level (such as within the OECD, GATT, APEC, and the North American Free Trade Agreement), and more rigorous enforcement of existing U.S. trade laws and international trade and investment agreements or treaties.[3]

To strengthen the hand of U.S. negotiators at the international level as well as facilitate enforcement of existing international agreements concerning mutual access to government-funded R&D, the committee also recommends that Congress charge an agency of the federal government with monitoring and periodically reporting on U.S. access to government-sponsored R&D abroad.[4]

> *3. The federal government should continue to seek more equitable international sharing of the basic research burden through moral suasion, the negotiation of bilateral science and technology agreements, the development of government-to-government international research consortia, and other mechanisms that foster international R&D collaboration.*

The committee believes strongly that U.S. citizens and foreign citizens would benefit from having other wealthy nations, Japan in particular, carry their fair share of the global burden of basic research. Therefore, the federal government should continue to encourage Japan and other nations to assume a role within the global basic research community that is truly commensurate with their industrial, technological, economic, and diplomatic standing in the world. To facilitate this process, the U.S. government should expand its support of international public-and-private-sector collaboration in areas of basic and precompetitive applied research through bilateral science and technology agreements and through international research programs, such as the Human Genome Project and the Intelligent Manufacturing Systems Initiative.

The committee believes it is essential that the federal government continue to work to enhance U.S. access to both publicly and privately funded basic research abroad through bilateral and multilateral negotiation and cooperation. At the same time, the committee believes that the federal government should acknowledge the existence and legitimacy of differences in the structure, organization, and comparative advantage of national R&D systems, and it should not expect other nations to reshape their innovation systems to fit the American model. For example, U.S. access to privately funded basic research in Japan would be improved if the United States could negotiate a reduction in barriers to U.S. foreign direct investment in Japan. However, the committee does not believe that the U.S. government should expect Japanese corporations to open their laboratories to U.S. researchers as a quid pro quo for Japanese access to U.S. publicly supported basic research activities.

In spite of the internationalization of industry and R&D, the United States continues to derive important competitive advantages from its large investment in basic research. In the eyes of the committee, these advantages would exist whether or not foreign companies and countries took advantage of the U.S. investment in basic research. The committee believes that the strength of the U.S. basic research enterprise is closely linked to its openness and permeability. Therefore, any efforts to restrict or artificially increase the cost of access by foreign companies and foreign governments to this resource might damage the research enterprise in the process and should be avoided.

4. The National Academies' Government-University-Industry Research Roundtable (GUIRR) should take the lead in promoting the exchange of information and "good practices" among the nation's leading research universities concerning relations with foreign-owned firms, foreign governments, and other foreign institutions.

Recognizing the diversity of institutions that constitute the nation's academic research enterprise, the committee believes that the GUIRR should move aggressively to identify and highlight examples of good practice with regard to university relationships with foreign entities and to develop channels for U.S. research universities to share with each other their experiences working with such entities. Building on this process, the GUIRR might formulate guidelines for good practice concerning industrial liaison programs, contract research, standards of conduct for foreign researchers in U.S. publicly supported research institutions, and other measures to ensure reciprocal access for U.S. researchers to the laboratories and know-how of the foreign sponsoring organizations.

> *5. All institutions that perform federally funded R&D should have procedures in place to manage effectively intellectual property resulting from publicly funded R&D. To assist U.S. universities and the federal government in this regard, the National Academies' Government-University-Industry Research Roundtable (GUIRR) should work with the Association of University Technology Managers (AUTM) and other appropriate organizations to develop and disseminate to the nation's academic research enterprise good practices and general guidelines related to the management of intellectual property.*

While most of the major research universities appear to have established adequate capabilities for insuring compliance with the requirements of the 1980 Bayh-Dole Act, universities with more modest research activities may not be devoting sufficient resources to this task. In the committee's judgment, collaboration among the GUIRR, AUTM, and other appropriate organizations to develop and disseminate to the nation's research universities good practices and general guidelines addressing this concern would be a useful step.

> *6. U.S. research universities and federal laboratories should expand their efforts to establish quid-pro-quo relationships with all foreign institutions that perform R&D. Among other things, this might include the increased exchange of engineering and scientific personnel.*

CHANGING PERCEPTIONS AND THEIR IMPLICATIONS

Given trends in the global economy, the openness of the U.S. economy, and the comparative strengths of the U.S. innovation system, the committee considers it inevitable that foreign participation in U.S.-based R&D activity will grow in the coming decades, as will U.S. involvement in the markets and R&D systems of its trading partners. Furthermore, these trends will continue to produce costs and risks as well as benefits and opportunities for the United States. In this environment, effective policy responses from U.S. public- and private-sector players will be needed if the interests of U.S. citizens are to be defended and advanced. Nevertheless, the committee believes that efforts to stop, reverse, or otherwise significantly impede these trends are unlikely to succeed in the long term and are very likely to impose unacceptably high costs on U.S. citizens.

It is the sense of the committee that many of the circumstances that have focused the attention of the public and of policymakers on the costs, risks, and asymmetries of foreign R&D participation during the past decade are changing in ways likely to foster a more balanced response in the coming decade. In particular, the widespread perception of the mid- to late 1980s that many U.S.-owned companies were far less effective at harnessing the output of U.S. research for commercial advantage than were their foreign competitors is giving way to cautious optimism regarding the continuously improving technology management and competitive capabilities of U.S.-owned firms across a range of industries. Although still in their infancy, recent federal, state, and university initiatives designed to foster collaborative R&D and more effective use and diffusion of industrially relevant technology and know-how throughout the U.S. economy have also contributed to a more positive outlook on the nation's industrial future.

Admittedly, new concerns are emerging regarding the tepid growth of U.S. industrial R&D, the contraction of industry-based basic and long-term applied research, and the implications of defense conversion for the nation's R&D system. However, the committee believes that these concerns, unlike the recent preoccupation with the nation's weaknesses in technology commercialization and use, are likely to have a more balanced and constructive influence on the way the American public looks upon foreign participation in publicly and privately funded U.S. R&D.

NOTES

1. In response to a request by the National Institutes of Health (NIH) for guidance on these issues raised by the Bayh-Dole Act of 1980, an ad hoc consultant panel to the Advisory Committee to the Director of NIH made the following observations and recommendations:

> The [Bayh-Dole] Act permits agencies to grant waivers to its explicit U.S. manufacturing requirement. The Panel recognizes that grantees are obligated to require their exclusive licensees to agree that any products embodying licensed inventions that will be used or sold in the United States must be substantially manufactured in the United States. However, other economic benefits should be regarded when considering waivers of the U.S. manufacturing requirement. The Panel urges NIH officials to continue to implement a flexible policy for fulfilling this part of the law, since in the biomedical area it is not always feasible to manufacture substantially in the United States. Moreover, important public health and other economic benefits could be lost if product development is delayed because of rigid enforcement of this provision. The Panel adds that because national boundaries are increasingly ignored as science and science-based industries become more global in focus, it is becoming increasingly difficult to distinguish foreign and domestic entities. Moreover, these distinctions can be muddled further when a so-called U.S. corporation chooses to manufacture certain products in offshore facilities or when a foreign corporation manufactures its products at a U.S. subsidiary.

> Because grantees are more familiar with the licensed technology capabilities of the licensee and the market for a particular product, they are far better suited than NIH to undertake the primary responsibility of overseeing the utilization requirement of the Act or ensuring that federally supported research is being licensed and made available and useful to the public. The Panel indicates that the use and active enforcement of performance benchmark and diligence requirements would greatly enhance grantees' capabilities to meet this oversight responsibility. (National Institutes of Health, 1994b)

In the spring of 1994, NIH (1994a) issued a "Final Report and Analysis of Selected Sponsored Research Agreements" as part of its efforts to develop guidelines to assist universities that receive NIH funding in their relationship with private industry. In November 1994, NIH published its statement of policy guidance in the Federal Register (1994).

An ad hoc committee of the Advisory Panel to the National Institute of Standards and Technology (NIST) is currently reviewing the institute's policies concerning relationships with private industry, including implementation of mandated economic performance requirements. (Phone conversation between Bruce Mattson, NIST, and Proctor Reid, NAE, March 31, 1995)

2. By contrast, the recent history of U.S. foreign economic policy offers precious little evidence to suggest that more broad-based "linked" reciprocity requirements (e.g., those that make a foreign-owned firm's participation contingent upon the equivalent treatment of U.S.-owned firms by its home government in broader areas of foreign economic policy, such as intellectual property rights or investment) will yield any advantage whatsoever for the United States in its effort to achieve greater access to publicly funded R&D activities abroad.

For an instructive review of arguments both for and against reciprocity see Bayard and Elliott (1994), which assesses all section 301 cases brought and concluded under U.S. trade law between 1975 and 1993. See also Chapter 3, note 43.

3. See, for example, the National Research Council (1995) proposals for achieving greater reciprocity between the United States and Japan in the exchange of defense-related technology.

4. Since late 1993, the State Department has been examining U.S. access to publicly funded research abroad as part of an ad hoc interagency working group chaired by the Council of Economic Advisors that is evaluating U.S. policy governing foreign access to U.S. publicly funded research. Conceivably, the working group could periodically evaluate the status of U.S. access to publicly funded R&D overseas.

References

Advanced Research Projects Agency. 1993. Program Information Package for Defense Technology Conversion, Reinvestment, and Transition Assistance. Arlington, Va.: Technology Reinvestment Project.

Alic, J. A., L. M. Branscomb, H. Brooks, A. B. Carter, and G. L. Epstein. 1992. Beyond Spinoff: Military and Commercial Technologies in a Changing World. Boston, Mass.: Harvard Business School Press.

American Association for the Advancement of Science. 1995. Senate appropriations committee reports S&T appropriations. Science and Technology in Congress. October. Washington, D.C.: Center for Science, Technology and Congress.

Bayard, T. O., and K. A. Elliott. 1994. Reciprocity and Retaliation in U.S. Trade Policy. Washington, D.C.: Institute for International Economics.

Beltz, C. A., ed. 1995. The Foreign Investment Debate: Opening Markets Abroad or Closing Markets at Home? Washington, D.C.: The American Enterprise Institute Press.

Brooks, H. B. 1993. Research Universities and the Social Contract for Science. Pp. 202–234 in Empowering Technology: Implementing a U.S. Strategy, L. M. Branscomb, ed. Cambridge, Mass.: The MIT Press.

Brooks, H. B. 1994. The relationship between science and technology. Research Policy 23:477–486.

Business Week. 1992. Pure research compliments of Japan. July 13:136–137.

Cheng, J. L. C., and D. S. Bolon. 1993. The management of multinational R&D: A neglected topic in international business research. Journal of International Business Studies, First Quarter:1–18.

Chesnais, F. 1988. Technical co-operation agreements between firms. STI Review:51–119.

Christelow, D. B. 1989. U.S.-Japan joint venture: Who gains? Challenge (November-December):29–38.

Cline, W.R. 1982. "Reciprocity": A New Approach to World Trade Policy? Washington, D.C.: Institute for International Economics.

Coalition for Open Trade. 1994. Dealing with Japan: Responding to Private Practices in Restraint of Trade: An Assessment of Policy Tools.

Cohen, W., R. Florida, and W. R. Goe. 1994. University-Industry Research Centers in the United States. Center for Economic Development, Carnegie Mellon University.

Committee on Science, Engineering, and Public Policy. 1992. The Government Role in Civilian Technology: Building a New Alliance. Washington, D.C.: National Academy Press.

Competitiveness Policy Council. 1993. Reports of the Subcouncils. March. Washington, D.C.

Corcoran, E. 1994. Chip research consortium to drop U.S. subsidy: Decision to rely on corporate funding reflects industry's comeback. Washington Post (October 5):F2.

Council on Competitiveness. 1991. Gaining New Ground: Technology Priorities for America's Future. Washington, D.C.

Council on Competitiveness. 1993. Roadmap for Results: Trade Policy, Technology and American Competitiveness. Washington, D.C.

Cusumano, M., and A. Takeishi. 1991. Supplier relations and management: A survey of Japanese, Japanese-transplant, and U.S. auto plants. Strategic Management Journal 12(8):563-588.

Dalton, D. H., and P. A. Genther. 1991. The Role of Corporate Linkages in U.S.-Japan Technology Transfer 1991. Washington, D.C.: U.S. Department of Commerce.

Dalton, D. H., and M. G. Serapio, Jr. 1993. U.S. Research Facilities of Foreign Companies. U.S. Department of Commerce. Springfield, Va.: National Technical Information Service.

Dalton, D. H., and M. G. Serapio, Jr. 1995. Globalizing Industrial Research and Development. Office of Technology Policy. Washington, D.C.: U.S. Department of Commerce.

Dasgupta, P., and P. A. David. 1992. Toward a New Economics of Science. CEPR Publ. No. 320. Center for Economic Policy Research, Stanford University, Stanford, Calif.

David, P. A., D. C. Mowery, and W. E. Steinmuller. 1992. Analyzing the economic payoffs from basic research. Economics of Innovation and New Technology 2:73–90.

Defense News. November 29, 1993. Buzz Fitzgerald: chief executive officer, Bath Iron Works.

Defense Science Board. 1990. Foreign Ownership and Control of U.S. Industry. Washington, D.C.: Defense Science Board.

Dertouzos, M. L., R. K. Lester, R. M. Solow, and the MIT Commission on Industrial Productivity. 1989. Made in America: Regaining the Productive Edge. Cambridge, Mass.: The MIT Press.

Dibner, M. D., G. N. Stock, and N. P. Greif. 1992. Away from home: U.S. sites of European and Japanese biotech R&D. Biotechnology 10(December):1535–1538.

Directory of American Research and Technology: Organizations Active in Product Development for Business. 1994. 29th ed. New Providence, N.J.: R. R. Bowker.

Ergas, H. 1987. Does technology policy matter? Pp. 191–245 in Technology and Global Industry: Companies and Nations in the World Economy, H. Brooks and B. Guile, eds. Washington, D.C.: National Academy Press.

European Parliament. 1994. Report on the State of the European Electronics Industry. Committee on Economic and Monetary Affairs and Industrial Policy. January 5.

Federal Register. 1994. Developing Sponsored Research Agreements: Considerations for Recipients of NIH Research Grants and Contracts. Federal Register 59(215):55674–55678. November 8.

Federal Register. 1995. Part VII: Department of Energy. 10 CFR Part 600. Financial Assistance Rules: Eligibility Determination for Certain Financial Assistance Programs; Proposed Rule. Federal Register 60(36):10296–10302. February 23.

Feller, I. 1994. The University as an Instrument of State and Regional Economic Development: The Rhetoric and Reality of the U.S. Experience. Paper presented at the CEPR/AAAS conference on University Goals, Institutional Mechanisms, and the "Industrial Transferability" of Research, March 18–20. Stanford University.

Financial Times. May 6, 1994. Dispute over ABB bid for energy grant.

Finn, M. G., L. A. Pennington, and K. H. Anderson. 1995. Foreign Nationals Who Receive Science or Engineering Ph.D.s from U.S. Universities: Stay Rates and Characteristics of Stayers. Oak Ridge Institute for Science and Education.

Florida, R. 1995a. Foreign Direct Investment and the Economy. Pp. 63–118 in The Foreign Investment Debate: Opening Markets Abroad or Closing Markets at Home, C.A. Beltz, ed. Washington, D.C: The American Enterprise Institute Press.

Florida, R. 1995b. Technology policy for a global economy. Issues in Science and Technology (Spring 1995):49–56.

Florida, R., and M. Kenney. 1992. Restructuring in place: Japanese investment, production, organization, and the geography of steel. Economic Geography 68(2):146-173.

Florida, R., and M. Kenney. 1993. The Globalization of Innovation: The Economic Geography of Japanese R&D in the United States. Working Paper 93–55. H. John Heinz III School of Public Policy and Management, Carnegie Mellon University.

Fusfeld, H. I. 1994. Industry's Future: Changing Patterns of Industrial Research. Washington, D.C.: American Chemical Society.

Gaster, R. 1992. Protectionism with purpose: Guiding foreign investment. Foreign Policy 88(Fall):91–106.

Gaster, R., and C. V. Prestowitz, Jr. 1994. Shrinking the Atlantic: Europe and the American Economy. Washington, D.C.: Economic Strategy Institute and North Atlantic Research, Inc.

Gibbons, A. 1992. Biotechnology—Scripps signs a deal with Sandoz. Science 258(5088) (December 4):1570.

Glickman, N. J., and D. P. Woodward. 1989. The New Competitors: How Foreign Investors Are Changing the U.S. Economy. New York: Basic Books, Inc.

Godfrey, J. M. 1991. Institutional Linkages Between U.S. and Foreign Universities and Research Centers. Final Report. Arlington, Va.: SRI International.

Gomory, R. E. 1989. From the "Ladder of Science" to the product development cycle. Harvard Business Review 67(6):99–105.

Government-University-Industry Research Roundtable. 1989. Science and Technology in the Academic Enterprise: Status, Trends, and Issues. A Discussion Paper. October. Washington, D.C.: National Academy Press.

Graham, E. M. 1992. Japanese control of R&D activities in the United States: Is this cause for concern? Pp. 189–206 in Japan's Growing Technological Capability: Implications for the U.S. Economy, T. S. Arrison, C. F. Bergsten, E. M. Graham, and M. C. Harris, eds. Office of Japan Affairs. Washington, D.C.: National Academy Press.

Graham, E. M., and P. R. Krugman. 1991. Foreign Direct Investment in the United States. 2nd ed. Washington, D.C.: Institute for International Economics.

Graham, E. M., and P. R. Krugman. 1995. Foreign Direct Investment in the United States. 3rd ed. Washington, D.C.: Institute for International Economics.

Grindley, P., D. C. Mowery, and B. Silverman. 1994. SEMATECH and collaborative research: Lessons in the design of high-technology consortia. Journal of Policy Analysis and Management 13(4):723–758.

Hagedoorn, J., and J. Schakenraad. 1993. Strategic technological partnering and international corporate strategies. Pp. 60–86 in European Competitiveness, Kirsty S. Hughes, ed. New York: Cambridge University Press.

Hakanson, L., and U. Zander. 1988. International management of R&D: The Swedish experience. R&D Management 18:217–226.

Hane, G. J. 1993. The real lessons of Japanese research consortia. Issues in Science and Technology (Winter 1993–94):56–62.

Healy, B. 1993. Testimony before the Subcommittee on Regulation, Business Opportunities and Energy of the Committee on Small Business, on March 11. U.S. House of Representatives, Washington, D.C.

Heaton, G. R., Jr. 1988. The truth about Japan's cooperative R&D. Issues in Science and Technology (Fall):32–40.

Helm, L. 1994. Foreign firms with deep pockets test U.S. labs. Los Angeles Times, November 6.

Herbert, E. 1989. Japanese R&D in the United States. Research•Technology Management (November-December):11–20.

Hexner, E. 1945. International Cartels. Durham, N.C.: University of North Carolina Press.

Hicks, D. 1994. Institutional Mechanisms Governing University-Industry Research Cooperation in Japan. Paper presented at the CEPR/AAAS conference on University Goals, Institutional Mechanisms, and the "Industrial Transferability" of Research, March 18–20. Stanford University, Stanford, Calif.

Hicks, D., and M. Hirooka. 1992. Science in Japanese Companies. Japanese Journal of Science and Technology Studies (1):109–140.

Hladik, K. J. 1985. International Joint Ventures: An Economic Analysis of U.S.-Foreign Business Partnerships. Lexington, Mass.: Lexington Books.

Hladik, K. J., and L. Linden. 1989. Is an international joint venture in R&D for you? Research•Technology Management 32(4):11–13.

Imai, K. 1990. Japan's National System of Innovation. Paper presented at the International Conference on "Science and Technology Policy Research—What Should Be Done? What Can be Done?" February 2–4, 1990. Tokyo, Japan.

Inside Energy. May 9, 1994. Foreign eligibility for DOE R&D mulled.

Institute for Defense Analysis. 1990. Dependence of the U.S. Defense Systems on Foreign Technologies. Alexandria, Va.

Irvine, J., B. R. Martin, and P. A. Isard. 1990. Investing in the Future: An International Comparison of Government Funding of Academic and Related Research. Great Britain: Billing & Sons Ltd.

Issues in Science and Technology. 1994. SEMATECH's evolving role: An interview with William J. Spencer. (Winter 1993–94):63–68.

Jaffe, A. B., M. Trajtenberg, and R. Henderson. 1993. Geographic localization of knowledge spillovers as evidenced by patent citations. Quarterly Journal of Economics 108(3):577–598.

Jaikumar, R. 1989. Japanese flexible manufacturing systems: Impact on the United States. Pp. 113–143 in Japan and the World Economy, vol. 1.

Japan Economic Institute. 1991. The structure of Japan's imports: Causes and consequences. JEI Report No. 22A(June 14):1–13. Washington, D.C.

Journal of Commerce. December 16, 1993. Maine yard gets U.S. aid in designing cargo vessels.

Kash, D. E. 1989. Perpetual Innovation: The New World of Competition. New York: Basic Books.

Kash, D. E., and R. W. Rycroft. 1992. Two Streams of Technological Innovation: Implications for Policy. Working Paper 92:5. George Mason University, Fairfax, Va.

Kayne, J. 1992. Investing in America's Economic Future: States and Industrial Incentives. Washington, D.C.: National Governors' Association.

Keck, O. 1993. The national system for technical innovation in Germany. In National Innovation Systems: A Comparative Analysis, Richard R. Nelson, ed. New York: Oxford University Press.

Kenney, M., and R. Florida. 1991. How Japanese industry is rebuilding the rust belt. Technology Review (February/March):25–33.

Kenney, M., and R. Florida. 1993a. Beyond Mass Production: The Japanese System and Its Transfer to the U.S. New York: Oxford University Press.

Kenney, M., and R. Florida. 1993b. The organization and geography of Japanese R&D: Results from a survey of Japanese electronics and biotechnology firms. Research Policy 23:305–323.

Kline, S. J. 1990. Models of Innovation and Their Policy Consequences. Report INN-4B. Stanford, Calif.: Stanford University.

Kline, S. J., and N. Rosenberg. 1986. An Overview of Innovation. Pp. 275–305 in Positive Sum Strategy, R. Landau and N. Rosenberg, eds. Washington, D.C.: National Academy Press.

Kodama, F. 1991. Analyzing Japanese High Technologies: The Techno-Paradigm Shift. London: Pinter Publishers.

Koprowski, G. 1991. Japanese snare small space firms. Washington Technology, July 25.

Krugman, P., ed. 1991. Trade With Japan: Has the Door Opened Wider? Chicago: The University of Chicago Press.

Kümmerle, W. 1993a. Praxisorientierte Grundlagenforschung im dienst japanischer wettbewerbsstrategie. Forschung und Technik 129:24.

Kümmerle, W. 1993b. The Silent Logic - Japanese Enterprises are Establishing Global Research Networks. Paper. Berlin: Science Center Berlin.

Lawrence, R. Z. 1991a. Efficient or Exclusionist? The Import Behavior of Japanese Corporate Groups. Brookings Papers on Economic Activity, No. 1.

Lawrence, R. Z. 1991b. How open is Japan? Pp. 9–37 in Trade With Japan: Has the Door Opened Wider?, P. Krugman, ed. Chicago: The University of Chicago Press.

Lundvall, B.-Å, ed. 1992. National Systems of Innovation: Towards a Theory of Innovation and Interactive Learning. London: Pinter Publishers.

Lynn, L. H. 1988. Multinational joint ventures in the steel industry. Pp. 267–300 in International Collaborative Ventures in U.S. Manufacturing, D. C. Mowery, ed. Cambridge, Mass.: Ballinger Publishing Co.

Mansfield, E. 1986. Microeconomics of Technological Innovation. Pp. 307–325 in Positive Sum Strategy. National Academy of Engineering. Washington, D.C.: National Academy Press.

Mansfield, E. 1988a. Industrial innovation in Japan and the United States. Science 241(September 30):1769–1774.

Mansfield, E. 1988b. Industrial R&D in Japan and the United States: A comparative study. American Economic Review 78(2):223–228.

Mansfield, E., D. Teece, and A. Romeo. 1979. Overseas research and development by U.S.-based firms. Economics 46:187–196.

Massachusetts Institute of Technology. 1991. The International Relationships of MIT in a Technologically Competitive World. Cambridge, Mass.: Massachusetts Institute of Technology.

McKinsey Global Institute. 1993. Manufacturing Productivity. Washington, D.C.: McKinsey Global Institute.

Ministry of International Trade and Industry. 1992. Issues and Trends in Industrial/Scientific Technology: Towards Techno-Globalism. BI-80. Tokyo, Japan.

Moran, T. H. 1990. The globalization of America's defense industries: Managing the threat of foreign dependence. International Security 15(1)(Summer):57–99.

Moran, T. H. 1993. American Economic Policy and National Security. New York: Council on Foreign Relations.

Mowery, D. C., ed. 1988a. International Collaborative Ventures in U.S. Manufacturing. Cambridge, Mass.: Ballinger Publishing Co.

Mowery, D. C. 1988b. Joint ventures in the U.S. commercial aircraft industry. Pp. 71–110 in International Collaborative Ventures in U.S. Manufacturing, D. C. Mowery, ed. Cambridge, Mass.: Ballinger Publishing Co.

Mowery, D. C. 1991. Public Policy Influences on the Formation of International Joint Ventures. Paper. Haas School of Business, University of California, Berkeley. January.

Mowery, D. C., and N. Rosenberg. 1993. The U.S. national innovation system. Pp. 29–75 in National Innovation Systems: A Comparative Analysis, R. R. Nelson, ed. New York: Oxford University Press.

Mowery, D. C., and D. J. Teece. 1993. Japan's growing capabilities in industrial technology: Implications for U.S. managers and policymakers. California Management Review 35(2):9–34.

National Academy of Engineering. 1993. Mastering a New Role: Shaping Technology Policy for National Economic Development. Washington, D.C.: National Academy Press.

National Critical Technologies Panel. 1993. Report of the National Critical Technologies Panel. Washington, D.C.: U.S. Government Printing Office.

National Defense University. 1987. U.S. Industrial Base Dependence/Vulnerability. Report of the Mobilization Concept Development Center.

National Institutes of Health. 1994a. Final Report and Analysis of Selected Sponsored Research Agreements. Prepared by the Office of Science Policy and Technology Transfer and the Office of the General Counsel, NIH. Bethesda, Md.: National Institutes of Health.

National Institutes of Health. 1994b. Panel Report of the Forum on Sponsored Research Agreements: Perspectives, Outlook, and Policy Development. Bethesda, Md.: National Institutes of Health.

National Research Council. 1976. Technology Transfer from Foreign Direct Investment in the United States. Springfield, Va.: National Technical Information Service.

National Research Council. 1988. Foreign and Foreign-Born Engineers in the United States: Infusing Talent, Raising Issues. Office of Scientific and Engineering Personnel. Washington, D.C.: National Academy Press.

National Research Council. 1989a. Learning the R&D System: National Laboratories and Other Non-Academic, Non-Industrial Organizations in Japan and the United States. Office of Japan Affairs. Washington, D.C.: National Academy Press.

National Research Council. 1989b. The Working Environment for Research in U.S. and Japanese Universities: Contrasts and Commonalities. Office of Japan Affairs. Washington, D.C.: National Academy Press.

National Research Council. 1990. Learning the R&D System: Industrial R&D in Japan and the United States. Office of Japan Affairs. Washington, D.C.: National Academy Press.

National Research Council. 1992a. Japanese Investment and Technology Transfer: An Exploration of its Impact. Report of a Workshop. Office of Japan Affairs. Washington, D.C.: National Academy Press.

National Research Council. 1992b. U.S.-Japan Strategic Alliances in the Semiconductor Industry: Technology Transfer, Competition, and Public Policy. Office of Japan Affairs. Washington, D.C.: National Academy Press.

National Research Council. 1992c. U.S.-Japan Technology Linkages in Biotechnology: Challenges for the 1990s. Office of Japan Affairs. Washington, D.C.: National Academy Press.

National Research Council. 1994a. Foreign Company Access to U.S. National Laboratories. Report of a Workshop held December 16, 1993. Committee on Japan, Office of International Affairs. Unpublished.

National Research Council. 1994b. High-Stakes Aviation: U.S.-Japan Technology Linkages in Transport Aircraft. Office of Japan Affairs. Washington, D.C.: National Academy Press.

National Research Council. 1995. Maximizing U.S. Interests in S&T Relations with Japan. Office of Japan Affairs. Washington, D.C.: National Academy Press.

National Science Board. 1987. Science and Engineering Indicators—1987. Washington, D.C.: U.S. Government Printing Office.

National Science Board. 1989. Science and Engineering Indicators—1989. Washington, D.C.: U.S. Government Printing Office.

National Science Board. 1990. Foreign Involvement in Scientific Research at U.S. Universities. Washington, D.C.: National Science Foundation.

National Science Board. 1991. Science and Engineering Indicators—1991. Washington, D.C.: U.S. Government Printing Office.

National Science Board. 1993. Science and Engineering Indicators—1993. Washington, D.C.: U.S. Government Printing Office.

National Science Board. 1995. Science and Engineering Indicators—1995. Washington, D.C.: U.S. Government Printing Office. Forthcoming.

National Science Foundation. 1990a. National Patterns of R&D Resources: 1990. Final Report by J. E. Jankowski, Jr. NSF 90-316. Washington, D.C.: National Science Foundation.

National Science Foundation. 1990b. Special Report on Foreign Involvement in U.S. Academic Research. Science Resource Services. January 30. Unpublished.

National Science Foundation. 1990c. Special Report on U.S. Industrial Support of Research at Foreign Universities. Science Resource Services. Unpublished.

National Science Foundation. 1991. Survey of Direct U.S. Private Capital Investment in Research and Development Facilities in Japan, NSF 91-312, A Report Prepared for the National Science Foundation under Grant No. SRS-8912547. Washington, D.C.

National Science Foundation. 1992. National Patterns of R&D Resources: 1992. Final Report by J. E. Jankowski, Jr. NSF 92-330. Washington, D.C.: National Science Foundation.

National Science Foundation. 1993. Foreign Participation in U.S. Academic Science and Engineering: 1991. NSF 93-302. Washington, D.C.: National Science Foundation.

National Science Foundation. 1994. Research and Development in Industry: 1991. NSF 94-322. Arlington, Va.: National Science Foundation.

National Science Foundation. 1995a. National Patterns of R&D Resources: 1994. Final Report by J. E. Jankowski, Jr. NSF 95-304. Arlington, Va.: National Science Foundation.

National Science Foundation. 1995b. National Patterns of R&D Resources: 1995. Data Update. Unpublished.

National Science Foundation. 1995c. International Opportunities for Scientists and Engineers. NSF 95-88. Arlington, Va.: National Science Foundation.

National Science Foundation. 1996. Selected Data on R&D in Industry: 1993. Arlington, Va.: National Science Foundation. Forthcoming.

Nelson, R. R. 1989. What is private and what is public about technology? Science, Technology, and Human Values 14(Summer):229–241.

Nelson, R. R. 1992. National innovation systems: A retrospective on a study. Industrial and Corporate Change 1(2):347-374.

Nelson, R. R., ed. 1993. National Innovation Systems: A Comparative Analysis. New York: Oxford University Press.

Nelson, R. R., and R. Levin. 1986. The Influence of Science University Research and Technical Societies on Industrial R&D and Technical Advance. Policy Discussion Paper Series Number 3. Research Program on Technology Change, Yale University.

Nelson, R. R. and N. Rosenberg. 1993. Technical innovation and national systems. Pp. 3–21 in National Innovation Systems: A Comparative Analysis, R. R. Nelson, ed. New York: Oxford University Press.

Noguchi, W. 1989. NEC's scenario for basic research. Trigger (November).

Office of the United States Trade Representative. 1995. 1995 National Trade Estimate Report on Foreign Trade Barriers. Washington, D.C.: Office of the United States Trade Representative.

Organization for Economic Cooperation and Development. 1992a. International Direct Investment: Policies and Trends in the 1980s. Paris: Organization for Economic Cooperation and Development.

Organization for Economic Cooperation and Development. 1992b. Summary of Country Replies: Information on Policies Linked With Globalization. DSTI/IND (93)17. Paris: Organization for Economic Cooperation and Development. June 18.

Organization for Economic Cooperation and Development. 1993. Industrial Policy in OECD Countries: Annual Review 1993. Paris: Organization for Economic Cooperation and Development.

Organization for Economic Cooperation and Development. 1994. The Performance of Foreign Affiliates in OECD Countries. Paris: Organization for Economic Cooperation and Development.

Ozawa, T. 1991. Japan in a new phase of multinationalism and industrial upgrading: Functional integration of trade, growth and FDI. Journal of World Trade 25(1):43–60.

Patel, P. 1995. Localised production of technology for global markets. Cambridge Journal of Economics 19(1):141–153.

Patel, P., and K. Pavitt. 1991. Large firms in the production of the world's technology: An important case of "non-globalisation." Journal of International Business Studies 22(1):1-21.

Patel, P., and K. Pavitt. 1994. The nature and economic importance of national innovations sytems. Pp. 9–32 in STI Review, No. 14. Paris, France: Organization for Economic Cooperation and Development.

Pavitt, K. 1991. What makes basic research economically useful? Research Policy 20:109–119.

Pearce, R. D., and S. Singh. 1992. Globalizing Research and Development. London: The Macmillan Press Ltd.

Peters, L. S. 1987. Technical Networks Between U.S. and Japanese Industry. Center for Science and Technology Policy, School of Management. Rensselaer Polytechnic Institute. March.

Peters, L. S. 1991. Technology Strategies of Japanese Subsidiaries and Joint Ventures in the United States. Pp. 221–231 in International Commercial Policy: Issues for the 1990s, M. E. Kreinin, ed. New York, N.Y.: Taylor and Francis.

Peters, L. S. 1992. Technology Management and the Research and Development Activities of Multinational Enterprises. The 1992 Annual Meeting of The Academy of International Business, Northeast USA Region. Loyola College, Baltimore, Md. June.

Peters, L. S. 1993a. Industrial Ecology, Ethical Management and the Research and Development Activities of Multinational Enterprises. Draft of paper presented at the Annual Meeting of the American Sociological Association, Miami Beach, Fla. May.

Peters, L. S. 1993b. The Multinational and Its Foreign University Connections. Draft of paper presented at the Purchase Conference on Academic Industry Relationships. May.

Peters, L. S. 1995. Strategies of foreign corporate R&D investment and sourcing in the U.S. Paper presented at conference titled "Beyond Us and Them: Foreign Ownership and U.S. Competitiveness," September 22–23, 1995.

Pisano, G. P., W. Shan, and D. J. Teece. 1988. Joint ventures and collaboration in the biotechnology industry. Pp. 183–222 in International Collaborative Ventures in U.S. Manufacturing, D. C. Mowery, ed. Cambridge, Mass.: Ballinger Publishing Co.

Press, F. 1990. Scientific and Technological Relations Between the United States and Japan: Issues and Recommendations. Report prepared for the Commission on US-Japan Relations for the Twenty First Century. Washington, D.C.

Randazzese, L. P. 1994. GCA and Domestic Lithography: Managing Procurement Incentives in SEMATECH and Vertical Consortia. RAND Project Memorandum PM-199-OSTP. Washington, D.C.: Critical Technologies Institute.

Roberts, E. B. 1995a. Benchmarking the strategic management of technology—I. Research•Technology Management (January/February):44–56.

Roberts, E. B. 1995b. Benchmarking the strategic management of technology—II. Research•Technology Management (March/April):18–26.

Rose, C. D. 1993a. Dual jobs abound in world of medical labs, business. San Diego Union-Tribune (April 7):A1, A12.

Rose, C. D. 1993b. U.S. pays for work; scientists reap profits. San Diego Union-Tribune (April 4):A1, A20.

Rosenberg, N. 1990. Why do firms do basic research (with their own money)? Research Policy 19:165–174.

Rosenberg, N., and R. R. Nelson. 1994. American universities and technical advance in industry. Research Policy 23:323–348.

Roussel, P. A., K. N. Saad, T. J. Erickson, and Arthur D. Little, Inc. 1991. Third Generation R&D: Managing the Link to Corporate Strategy. Boston, Mass.: Harvard Business School Press.

Saxonhouse, G. R. 1991. How open is Japan?: Comment. Pp. 38–46 in Trade With Japan: Has the Door Opened Wider?, P. Krugman, ed. Chicago: The University of Chicago Press.

Schmidt, S. 1993. Schools look to profit, walk ethical tightrope. San Diego Union-Tribune (April 5):A1, A8.

Schrage, M. 1990. Foreign firms are starting to go bottom fishing for U.S. technology companies. Washington Post. June 22.

Schwartz, R. S., and B. A. Caplan. 1993. Conditioning the Unconditional. New York Law Journal 210(35)(August 19):5.

Serapio, M. G., Jr. 1994. Japan-U.S. Direct R&D Investments in the Electronics Industries. Prepared by the U.S. Department of Commerce Technology Administration and The Japan-U.S. Friendship Commission. PB94-127974. Springfield, Va.: National Technical Information Service.

Serapio, M. G., Jr., and D. H. Dalton. 1994. Foreign R&D in the United States. IEEE Spectrum (November):26–30.

Spencer, L. 1991. Foreign Investment in the United States: Unencumbered Access. Washington, D.C.: Economic Strategy Institute.

Stalson, H. 1989. Foreign Participation in Engineering Research at U.S. Universities. Paper prepared for the NAE Committee on Engineering as an International Enterprise. Spring.

Steinmuller, W. E. 1988. International joint ventures in the integrated circuit industry. Pp. 111–145 in International Collaborative Ventures in U.S. Manufacturing, D. C. Mowery, ed. Cambridge, Mass.: Ballinger Publishing Co.

Stocking, G. W., and M. W. Watkins. 1946. Cartels in Action. New York: Twentieth Century Fund.

The Analytic Sciences Corporation. 1990. Foreign Vulnerability of Critical Industries. Arlington, Va.

Tolchin, S. J. 1993. Halting the erosion of America's critical assets. Issues in Science and Technology (Spring):65–72.

Tyson, L. D'A. 1992. Who's Bashing Whom?: Trade Conflict in High-Technology Industries. Washington, D.C.: Institute for International Economics.

U.S. Congress, House. 1989. Is Science for Sale? Conflicts of Interest vs. the Public Interest. Hearing before the Human Resources and Intergovernmental Relations Subcommittee of the Committee on Government Operations. June 13.

U.S. Congress, House. 1993. Access by Foreign Companies to U.S. Universities. Hearing before the Subcommittee on Science of the Committee on Science, Space and Technology. October 28.

U.S. Congress, Office of Technology Assessment. 1993. Multinationals and the National Interest: Playing by Different Rules. OTA-ITE-569. Washington, D.C.: U.S. Government Printing Office.

U.S. Congress, Office of Technology Assessment. 1994. Multinationals and the U.S. Technology Base: Final Report of the Multinationals Project. Washington, D.C.: U.S. Government Printing Office.

U.S. Department of Commerce. 1967. Technological Innovation: Its Environment and Management. Washington, D.C.: U.S. Government Printing Office.

U.S. Department of Commerce. 1990. Emerging Technologies: A Survey of Technical and Economic Opportunities. Washington, D.C.: U.S. Department of Commerce.

U.S. Department of Commerce. 1991. Foreign Direct Investment in the United States: Review and Analysis of Current Developments. Washington, D.C.: U.S. Government Printing Office.

U.S. Department of Commerce. 1993a. Foreign Direct Investment in the United States: An Update: Review and Analysis of Current Developments. Washington, D.C.: U.S. Government Printing Office.

U.S. Department of Commerce. 1993b. The U.S.-Japan Manufacturing Fellowship 1993–1994. Technology Administration. Washington, D.C. January 5.

U.S. Department of Commerce. 1994a. Foreign Direct Investment in the United States: 1992 Benchmark Survey, Preliminary Results. Bureau of Economic Analysis. Washington, D.C.: U.S. Government Printing Office.

U.S. Department of Commerce. 1994b. Survey of Current Business. Economics and Statistics Administration, Bureau of Economic Analysis. Vol. 74, No. 7. Washington, D.C.: U.S. Government Printing Office.

U.S. Department of Commerce. 1995a. Foreign Direct Investment in the United States: 1992 Benchmark Survey, Final Results. Bureau of Economic Analysis. Washington, D.C.: U.S. Government Printing Office.

U.S. Department of Commerce. 1995b. Statistical Abstract of the United States, 1995. Washington, D.C.: U.S. Government Printing Office.

U.S. Department of Energy. 1993. DOE-Approved CRADA Language and Guidance. Washington, D.C.: U.S. Department of Energy.

U.S. General Accounting Office. 1988a. R&D Funding: Foreign Sponsorship of U.S. University Research. GAO/RCED-88–89BR. Washington, D.C.: U.S. General Accounting Office.

U.S. General Accounting Office. 1988b. Technology Transfer: U.S. and Foreign Participation in R&D at Federal Laboratories. GAO/RCED-88-203BR. Washington, D.C.: U.S. General Accounting Office.

U.S. General Accounting Office. 1990a. Foreign Investment: Analyzing National Security Concerns. GAO/NSIAD-90–94. Washington, D.C.: U.S. General Accounting Office.

U.S. General Accounting Office. 1990b. Foreign Investment: Concerns in the Banking, Petroleum, Chemicals, and Biotechnology Sectors. GAO/NSIAD-90–129. Washington, D.C.: U.S. General Accounting Office.

U.S. General Accounting Office. 1991a. Diffusing Innovation: Implementing the Technology Transfer Act of 1986. GAO/PEMD-91-23. Washington, D.C.: U.S. General Accounting Office.

U.S. General Accounting Office. 1991b. International Trade: U.S. Business Access to Certain Foreign State-of-the-Art Technology. GAO/NSIAD-91–278. Washington, D.C.: U.S. General Accounting Office.

U.S. General Accounting Office. 1992. University Research: Controlling Inappropriate Access to Federally Funded Research Results. GAO/RCED-92–104. Washington, D.C.: U.S. General Accounting Office.

U.S. General Accounting Office. 1994a. Advanced Technology: Proposal Review Process and Treatment of Foreign-Owned Businesses. GAO/RCED-94–81. Washington, D.C.: U.S. General Accounting Office.

U.S. General Accounting Office. 1994b. Industrial Base: Assessing the Risk of DOD's Foreign Dependence. GAO/NSIAD-94–104. Washington, D.C.: U.S. General Accounting Office.

U.S. General Accounting Office. 1995. National Laboratories: Are Their R&D Activities Related to Commercial Product Development? GAO/PEMD-95–2. Washington, D.C.: U.S. Government Printing Office.

Voisey, C. J. 1992. Issues in the Internationalization of Research and Development in High Technology Companies. M.S. thesis. The Alfred P. Sloan School of Management, Massachusetts Institute of Technology, Cambridge, Mass.

Vonortas, N. S. 1989. The Changing Economic Context: Strategic Alliances Among Multinationals. Troy, N.Y.: Center for Science and Technology Policy, Rensselaer Polytechnic Institute.

Weinig, S. 1990. Oh, to be sold to the Japanese. Across the Board 27(5):34–38.

Westney, D. E. 1993. Cross-Pacific internationalization of R&D by U.S. and Japanese firms. R&D Management 23(2):171–181.

Wiley, J. D. 1993. Foreign Participation in U.S. Research and Development. Paper presented at 9 November workshop at the National Academy of Engineering, Washington, D.C. Unpublished.

Wisconsin BioIssues. 1994. Bayh-Dole, tech transfer and the public good: An interview with Howard Bremer. University of Wisconsin, Madison. March.

Wolff, M. F. 1994. Meet your competition: Data from the IRI R&D survey. Research• Technology Management (January-February):18–24.

Womack, J. P. 1988. Multinational joint ventures in motor vehicles. Pp. 301–347 in International Collaborative Ventures in U.S. Manufacturing, D. C. Mowery, ed. Cambridge, Mass.: Ballinger Publishing Co.

Womack, J. P., D. T. Jones, and D. Roos. 1990. The Machine that Changed the World. New York: Macmillan Publishing Company.

Committee and Staff Biographies

PETER BEARDMORE is director of the Chemical and Physical Sciences Laboratory at the Ford Motor Company. In this position, he is responsible for a wide range of research activities, including polymeric catalyst development and the application of modern analytical techniques. Before joining Ford in 1966, Dr. Beardmore spent 3 years at the Massachusetts Institute of Technology and 2 years in the nuclear power industry, during which time his research focused primarily on the deformation and fracture of metals, polymers, and composites. He is a recognized international authority on composite materials and has published over 83 technical articles. Dr. Beardmore is a member and fellow of the American Society for Metals, and the Engineering Society of Detroit, and is a member of the National Academy of Engineering and the Metallurgical Society of AIME. He received his B.Met. (First Class Honors) in metallurgy from the University of Sheffield and a Ph.D. in metallurgy from the University of Liverpool, both in England.

SAMUEL H. FULLER is vice president of research at Digital Equipment Corporation, where he is responsible for the company's corporate research programs. These include DEC's research laboratories in Massachusetts and California, joint research with universities, and DEC's participation in industrial research consortia. Dr. Fuller joined DEC in 1978 as engineering manager for the VAX Architecture group. In 1983, he was appointed vice president, research. He has been instrumental in initiating work in local area networks, high performance workstations, and new computer architectures. Prior to coming to DEC, Dr. Fuller was an associate professor of computer science and electrical engineering at Carnegie

Mellon University. While at CMU, he was involved in the design and performance evaluation of several experimental, multiprocessor computer systems. Dr. Fuller is a member of the board of directors of Analog Devices, MCC, and the Corporation for National Research Initiatives. He also serves as a member of the advisory councils of several universities. Dr. Fuller received his B.S.E. from the University of Michigan and his M.S. and Ph.D. from Stanford University. He is a member of the National Academy of Engineering and is a fellow of the Institute of Electrical and Electronics Engineers.

JOHN E. GRAY is a director of several technology companies, the chairman of three others, and vice chairman of the Atlantic Council of the United States, a nonprofit policy research institution dealing with global issues affecting U.S. interests. His experience includes serving as CEO of companies engaged in consulting, engineering, development, operations, and maintenance in energy and environmental fields in the United States, Europe, and Japan. He received a B.S. in chemical engineering from the University of Rhode Island and is a member of the National Academy of Engineering.

KARL E. MARTERSTECK is president of San Jose, California-based ArrayComm, Inc., a company devoted to enhancing the performance of personal wireless telecommunications systems. Prior to assuming his present position in July 1995, Mr. Martersteck spent 36 years with AT&T, primarily at AT&T Bell Labs, where he most recently was vice president, AT&T architecture. In that position, he led work to identify opportunities and define applications of new technologies for AT&T products and services. Previously, Mr. Martersteck directed the design and development of various digital switching systems, primarily the 5ESS Digital Switch, which has become the AT&T flagship switching product and is widely deployed throughout the world. From 1964 to 1973, Mr. Martersteck was at Bellcomm, Inc., an AT&T subsidiary, where he headed systems engineering and mission planning work for the Apollo lunar landing and Skylab projects of NASA. Early in his Bell Labs career, Mr. Martersteck did pioneering work on silicon integrated circuits. Mr. Martersteck received a B.S. in physics from the University of Notre Dame and an M.S. in electrical engineering from New York University. He is a member of the National Academy of Engineering, a fellow of the Institute of Electrical and Electronics Engineers, and a board member of the International Engineering Consortium.

JOEL MOSES is provost and Dugald C. Jackson professor of computer science and engineering at the Massachusetts Institute of Technology. Prior to assuming the provost's position in June 1995, Dr. Moses was dean of the MIT School of Engineering, from 1991 to 1995, and head of the department of electrical engineering and computer science, from 1981 to 1989. A member of the MIT faculty since 1967, he is recognized for developing MACSYMA, one of the largest computer systems for symbolic algebraic manipulation. His interests include the organization of large complex systems, competitiveness, product realization, software production, telecommunications systems, and knowledge-based systems. Dr. Moses received a B.A. and M.A. from Columbia University and his Ph.D. in mathematics from MIT. He is a member of the National Academy of Engineering, a fellow of the American Academy of Arts and Sciences, and a fellow of the Institute of Electrical and Electronics Engineers. He received an American Society for Engineering Education Centennial Award in 1993.

THOMAS J. MURRIN is dean of Duquesne University's A. J. Palumbo School of Business Administration. Prior to assuming that post in 1991, Dr. Murrin served for 18 months as deputy secretary of the U.S. Department of Commerce. At Duquesne, he has helped develop innovative teaching and research programs, particularly in the area of global competitiveness and economic growth. Dr. Murrin was the first chairman of both the Board of Overseers of the Commerce Department's Malcolm Baldrige National Quality Award and the Defense Department's Defense Manufacturing Board. He is a member of the National Academy of Engineering and was a member of the President's Commission on Industrial Competitiveness and was chairman of the Board of Governors of the Aerospace Industries Association. Dr. Murrin received his B.S. in physics from Fordham University and an honorary Doctor of Management Science from Duquesne University. He was awarded an Honorary Doctorate of Humane Letters from his alma mater in 1995.

ROBERT M. NEREM is director of the newly established Institute for Bioengineering and Bioscience at Georgia Institute of Technology, where he is also the Parker H. Petit Professor. Dr. Nerem received his Ph.D. in 1964 from Ohio State University and joined the faculty there in the department of aeronautical and astronautical engineering. He was later promoted to professor and then served as associate dean for research in the graduate school. From 1979 to 1986, he was professor and chairman of the department of mechanical engineering at the University of Houston. Dr. Nerem, the author of 100 refereed journal articles, joined Georgia Tech in 1987. Dr. Nerem is a fellow of the American Association for the Advancement of Science, the Council of Arteriosclerosis of the American Heart Association, the American Physical Society, and the American Society of Mechanical Engineers. He currently serves as technical editor of the ASME *Journal of Biomechanical Engineering*. He is a member of the National Academy of Engineering, the Institute of Medicine, and is a foreign member of the Polish Academy of Sciences. Dr. Nerem's research interests are in bioengineering, including biofluid mechanics, cardiovascular devices, cellular engineering, vascular biology, and tissue engineering.

C. KUMAR N. PATEL is vice chancellor for research at the University of California, Los Angeles. Prior to joining UCLA in 1993, he was the executive director, research, in the Materials Science, Engineering and Academic Affairs Division at AT&T Bell Laboratories. Dr. Patel joined Bell Labs in 1961, where he carried out research in the field of gas lasers, nonlinear optics, molecular spectroscopy, pollution detection, and laser surgery. His current research interests include spectroscopy of highly transparent liquids and solids, and surgical and medical applications of carbon dioxide lasers. He is the recipient of many awards and honors, including the Medal of Honor of the Institute of Electrical and Electronics Engineers, the Frederic Ives Medal of the Optical Society of America, and the William T. Ennor Manufacturing Technology Award of the American Society of Mechanical Engineers. Dr. Patel is a member of the National Academy of Engineering and the National Academy of Sciences, a foreign fellow of the Indian National Science Academy and The Institution of Electronics and Telecommunications Engineers, and an associate fellow of the Third World Academy of Sciences. Dr. Patel received his B.E. in telecommunications from the College of Engineering in Poona, India, and his M.S. and Ph.D. in electrical engineering from Stanford University.

EDWIN P. PRZYBYLOWICZ is director of the Chester F. Carlton Center for Imaging Science at the Rochester Institute of Technology. Dr. Przybylowicz began his career at Eastman Kodak Co., where he was first a research chemist and later held positions of increasing technical and managerial responsibilities before being named director of research and elected a senior vice president in 1985. He retired from Kodak in 1991 but remains active in a number of initiatives intended to help commercialize technology and stimulate closer working relationships between industry and academia. Dr. Przybylowicz is a commissioner of the U.S.-Polish Joint Fund for Cooperation in Science and Engineering and has cochaired international conferences on technology commercialization. He has published 2 books and over 20 technical articles in the field of chemistry and photography, and he holds 4 patents in related fields. Dr. Przybylowicz received his B.S. in chemistry from the University of Michigan and his Ph.D. in analytical chemistry from MIT. He is a member of the National Academy of Engineering.

MAXINE L. SAVITZ is general manager of AlliedSignal Ceramic Components. She was formerly the deputy assistant secretary for conservation at the Department of Energy, where she received the President's Meritorious Rank Award in 1980 and the department's Outstanding Service Medal in 1981. Dr. Savitz is a member of the Secretary of Energy's Advisory Board, Defense Science Board, Visiting Committee on Advanced Technology for National Institute of Standards and Technology, and Council of the National Academy of Engineering. She received her B.A. from Bryn Mawr College, her Ph.D. from MIT, and completed a postdoctoral fellowship at the University of California at Berkeley.

ALAN SCHRIESHEIM (*chair*) is a research and engineering executive whose experience spans the innovation chain from pioneering science to engineering in both industry and government. He is director and chief executive officer at Argonne National Laboratory and is professor of chemistry at the University of Chicago. He joined Argonne in 1983, becoming the first director of a nonweapons national laboratory to be recruited from industry. From 1956 to 1983, he held a number of technical management positions at Exxon Research and Engineering, including director of corporate research and general manager of engineering technology. Before joining Exxon, Dr. Schriesheim was affiliated with the National Bureau of Standards. He holds a B.S. in physical organic chemistry from Polytechnic University in Brooklyn and a Ph.D. in chemistry from The Pennsylvania State University. Dr. Schriesheim is the author or coauthor of over 70 papers and holds 22 U.S. patents. He is a member of the National Academy of Engineering, the National Research Council, the American Chemical Society, Phi Lambda Upsilon, and Sigma X. He is on the board of two publicly held companies: Rohm and Haas, and Heico.

CHANG-LIN TIEN is the seventh chancellor of the University of California, Berkeley, and the first Asian-American to head a major research university in the United States. A faculty member in Berkeley's mechanical engineering department since 1959, Dr. Tien has been chair of the department, vice chancellor for research, and currently holds the A. Martin Berlin Chair Professorship in mechanical engineering. From 1988 to 1990, he served as executive vice chancellor and UCI distinguished professor at the University of California, Irvine. Dr. Tien is internationally recognized for his scholarly contributions in the field of heat transfer. He was born in Wuhan, China, and educated in Shanghai and Taiwan, where his family fled after World War II. Dr. Tien completed his undergraduate education at National Taiwan University and came to the United States in 1956. He earned an M.A. at the University of Louisville and a second M.A. and a Ph.D. at Princeton University in 1959. He currently serves on the board of the Carnegie Foundation for the Advancement of Teaching, the Asia Foundation, and Wells Fargo Bank, and has just completed a term on the Board of Trustees at Princeton University. Dr. Tien is a member of the National Academy of Engineering.

Study Director

PROCTOR P. REID is a senior program officer with the National Academy of Engineering (NAE) in Washington, D.C., where he directs a multiyear program of policy research on technology, trade, and economic growth. Since joining the NAE as a postdoctoral fellow in 1988, he has directed multiple NAE committee studies that have resulted in published reports. These have included *National Interests in an Age of Global Technology* (1991), *Mastering a New Role: Shaping Technology Policy for National Economic Performance* (1993), and a forthcoming report on technology transfer in Germany and the United States. In addition to his work with the Academy, Reid is a professorial lecturer in European studies at the Johns Hopkins University, Paul Nitze School of Advanced International Studies, where he received his Ph.D. in international relations in 1989. Before joining the NAE, he was an instructor in political economy at Oberlin College (1986–1987) and worked as a consultant to the National Research Council (1988) and the Organization for Economic Cooperation and Development (1984–1985).

APPENDIXES

Agenda

Roundtable on Foreign Participation in U.S. Research and Development: Economic Asset or Liability?

Room 250, National Academies Building
2101 Constitution Avenue, N.W.
Washington, D.C.
November 8-9, 1993

Monday, November 8

6:00 p.m. Reception and Dinner, Executive Dining Room

Welcome and opening remarks
> **Robert M. White**, President, National Academy of Engineering
> **Alan Schriesheim**, Committee Chairman, Argonne National
> Laboratory

8:00   Adjourn

Tuesday, November 9

7:45 a.m. Continental Breakfast (in meeting room 250)

8:15   Chairman's overview of issues raised
> **Alan Schriesheim**

Each speaker has been asked to make brief remarks—15 to 20 minutes—drawing on their personal experiences with these issues and on the unique perspective provided by their institutional affiliation.

8:30   **David Goldston**, Committee on Science, Space and Technology,
            U.S. House of Representatives

9:15   **Governor Richard F. Celeste**, Celeste & Sabety Ltd.

10:15   BREAK

10:30   **Robert Charpie**, Chairman, Ampersand Ventures
            (venture capitalist)

11:15   **Geza Feketekuty**, Senior Policy Advisor, Office of the
            U.S. Trade Representative, and Chairman, OECD
            Trade Committee

12:00 p.m. Working lunch in the meeting room

1:15   **C. William Gear**, President, NEC Research Institute, Princeton
            Knut Merten, President & CEO, Siemens Corporate Research, Inc.

2:45   **C. Richard Deininger**, Director, National Resource Program,
            SEMATECH

3:30   BREAK

3:45   **John Wiley**, Dean of Graduate Studies and Vice President
            for Research, University of Wisconsin, Madison

4:30   Summary of issues and roundtable discussion
            NAE Committee Members

5:15   Closing remarks
            Alan Schriesheim, Chairman

5:30   ADJOURN

Participants

Roundtable on Foreign Participation in U.S. Research and Development: Economic Asset or Liability?

November 8-9, 1993

Reid Adler
Special Assistant for Technology
   Transfer Policy
National Institutes of Health

Thomas Arrison
Research Associate
Office of Japan Affairs
National Research Council

Joseph Asbury
Deputy to the Laboratory Director and
   Director of the Strategic Planning Group
Argonne National Laboratory

John Campbell
Assistant Executive Director
Office of International Affairs
National Research Council

Richard F. Celeste
Celeste & Sabety Ltd.

Robert A. Charpie
Chairman
Ampersand Ventures

Donald Crafts
Acting Director, Office of International
   Investment
U.S. Department of the Treasury

C. Richard Deininger
Director, National Resource Program
SEMATECH

John D. Donahue
Assistant Secretary of Labor for Policy
U.S. Department of Labor

Geza Feketekuty
Senior Policy Advisor
Office of the U.S. Trade Representative

Kenneth S. Flamm
Principal Deputy Assistant Secretary of
   Defense and Special Assistant to the
   USDA

Alexander Flax
Senior Fellow
National Academy of Engineering

C. William Gear
President
NEC Research Institute

Howard J. Gobstein
Vice President
Association of American Universities

David Goldston
Committee on Science, Space and
  Technology
U.S. House of Representatives

John E. Gray
Vice Chairman
Atlantic Council of the United States

Elton Kaufmann
Associate Director of the Strategic
  Planning Group
Argonne National Laboratory

Karl E. Martersteck
Vice President, AT&T Architecture
AT&T Bell Laboratories

Knut Merten
President and CEO
Siemens Corporate Research, Inc.

William G. Morin
Director, Technology Policy
National Association of Manufacturers

Joel Moses
Dean of Engineering
Massachusetts Institute of Technology

James Murphy
Senior Policy Advisor
Office of the U.S. Trade Representative

Robert M. Nerem
Parker H. Petit Professor for Engineering
  in Science
Georgia Institute of Technology

Alan Schriesheim
Director and CEO
Argonne National Laboratory

Paul Reagan
House Committee on Science, Space
  and Technology

James J. Verrant
Senior Vice President
AlliedSignal Aerospace

Pat Vroom
Director of Technology Planning
Siemens Corporate Research, Inc.

Robert M. White
President
National Academy of Engineering

John D. Wiley
Dean of Graduate Studies and
  Vice President for Research
University of Wisconsin, Madison

John S. Wilson
Board on Science, Technology and
  Economic Policy
National Research Council

NAE Staff

Bruce Guile
Director, Program Office

Penny Gibbs
Administrative Assistant

Index

A

Access issues. *See also* National security
asymmetries, 6, 9–10, 17, 25–26, 36, 39–
40, 70–74, 82, 91, 126, 143–144,
146, 150
costs of access barriers, 71, 73–74, 126
militarily important components and
subsystems, 40, 144, 145
as motivation for foreign investment, 84
n.5
privately funded foreign R&D, 6, 70–74,
82, 143–144, 146
publicly funded foreign R&D, 124–127,
130, 138 n.68, 150, 158 n.4
reciprocity requirements, 10, 11, 73, 89
n.43, 116, 117, 126, 130, 135 n.36,
150, 151, 153–154, 158 n.2
self-imposed barriers to, 72–73
transparency of public policies, 7–8, 126,
146, 152
Adobe Systems, 87 n.29
Advanced materials, 44, 57, 58, 80
Advanced Technology Program, *See* U.S.
Department of Commerce
Aerospace industry, 80
Affiliates of foreign-owned firms in U.S.
See also companies by country

applied research, 54, 64
basic reasearch by, 54–55, 64–65
by country, 62, 142
defined, 13 n.4
economic performance requirements, 10,
11, 60, 64, 73, 77, 114–115, 116,
123–124, 130, 149–150, 151–153
employment, 49–50, 55–56, 86 n.21, 131
n.2
expenditures for R&D, 3–4, 17, 39, 42–
48, 60, 81, 83 n.2, 85 n.9
freestanding R&D facilities, 48–53, 56,
85 n.14, 86 nn.16, 21
by industry, 61–62, 142
intrafirm trade, 89 n.41
objectives and motivations for R&D
activities, 50, 54–56, 63–64, 81, 84
n.4, 87 n.25, 142–143
organization and character of R&D
activities, 22–25, 36, 41, 48–56,
60–70, 81, 143
reciprocity requirements, 10, 11, 130,
150, 153–154
R&D intensity of activities, 60–64, 81
technology flows, 66, 81, 143
technology stripping, 70
types of R&D activities, 48–56, 64–65
value of R&D, 64–66

Affiliates, U.S.-owned, 65, 131 n.3, 138
    n.64. *See also* Foreign direct
    investment by U.S. Companies,
    multinational corporations, U.S.
Aircraft industry, 67
AlliedSignal Incorporated, 116, 126, 136
    n.43
American Microsystems, 87 n.29
Antitrust issues, 6, 57, 73, 76, 77, 87 n.27,
    144, 153. *See also* Monopolies
Applied research
    by affiliates of foreign firms in U.S., 54,
        64
    defined, 29
    and economic development, 33, 34
    outputs of, 30, 31, 38 n.9
    by U.S.-owned affiliates abroad, 65
Argonne National Laboratory, 114
Asea Brown Boveri, 116
Asian-Pacific Economic Cooperation Forum,
    73, 153
Association of University Technology
    Managers (AUTM), 12, 156
AT&T, 87 n.29, 110
Australia, 80, 125
Automation, 44
Automotive industry, 48–49, 50, 51, 55, 56,
    58, 60, 61, 62, 67, 69, 84 n.4, 85
    n.12, 86 n.21, 135 n.38

B

Basic research
    by affiliates of foreign firms in U.S., 54–
        55, 64–65
    defined, 29
    and economic development, 33–34
    funding, 31, 131 n.1
    industry trends, 13, 24
    international equity issues, 10, 11–12, 25,
        127–129, 131, 151, 154–155
    by Japan, 12, 86 n.21, 87 n.29, 104, 110,
        127–129, 131, 150, 154–155
    links with applied research, 33
    outputs of, 30, 37 n.1
    at universities, 91, 104, 110
    U.S. capabilities and comparative
        strength in, 90–91
    by U.S.-owned affiliates abroad, 65
Bath Iron Works Corporation of Maine, 117,
    136 n.47

Bayh-Dole Act of 1980, 106, 133 n.18, 156,
    157–158 n.1
Belgium, 65
Biotechnology, 44, 48, 49, 50, 51, 55, 56,
    58, 59, 64, 65, 67, 69, 80, 86 n.19,
    87 n.28, 111
Bureau of the Census, Survey of Industrial
    Research and Development, 83

C

Canada
    foreign direct investment in, 22
    high-tech production and exports, 20
    R&D spending by foreign-owned
        companies in, 22
Canadian-owned companies
    acquisitions of U.S. high-technology
        companies by, 80
    affiliates in U.S., 42–45, 46, 48, 49
    expenditures for R&D in U.S., 4, 19, 22,
        42, 43, 45, 46, 81
    involvement in U.S. university research,
        100, 103
    patenting activities, 65, 106
    and publicly funded U.S. research, 117
Canon, 48, 49, 54, 86 n.18, 89 n.45
Carnegie-Mellon University, 107
Chemical industry, 15, 43–47, 48, 50, 51,
    56, 58, 60–63, 66, 81, 142
Ciba-Geigy, 105, 110, 133 n.15
Cold War, 23
Columbia University, 108
Committee on Foreign Investment in the
    United States, 75, 76, 88 n.37
Communications industry, 43, 44, 45, 46, 47,
    50, 51, 60, 61, 62, 63, 80, 81, 87
    n.28, 142
Computer and office equipment industry, 21,
    43–45, 46, 47, 48, 50, 51, 57, 60–
    63, 80
Cornell University, 98, 103, 120, 137 n.56
Council of Economic Advisors, 158 n.4
Cooperative Research and Development
    Agreements (CRADAs). *See* Federal
    laboratories

D

Daichii Pharmaceuticals, 105, 133 n.17
Defense Investigative Service, 75, 77

Defense Production Act, 76, 77
Doane, Jay William, 95
DuPont, 84–85 n.7

E

Economic performance. *See also*
    Monopolies; U.S. competitiveness
basic research and, 33–34
R&D and, 2–3, 32–35, 78–80, 141–142
requirements for foreign affiliates, 10,
    11, 60, 64, 73, 77, 114–115, 116,
    123–124, 130, 149–150, 151–153
Electronics industry, 44, 45, 46, 47, 48, 50,
    51, 55, 56, 57, 59–63, 65, 67, 80,
    86 n.21, 88 n.34
Employment in U.S. by foreign-owned
    affiliates, 42, 49–50, 55–56, 86
    n.21, 131 n.2
Energy Policy Act of 1992, 116, 117
Engineering Research Centers, 108, 134 n.25
Environmental regulation, 56, 146
European Community
    U.S. access to R&D in, 10, 125–
    126, 138 n.68, 150
European-owned companies
    expenditures for R&D in U.S., 4, 42, 45,
    46
    freestanding R&D facilities in U.S., 48,
    49–50, 56
    history of investments in U.S., 15–16, 88
    n.34
    international technology flows and, 67
    involvement in university research in
    U.S., 101, 125
    patenting activities, 65, 106
    R&D intensity of U.S. activities, 62
    technical alliances involving, 57
    value of R&D investments in U.S., 65
European Strategic Programme for Research
    and Development in Information
    Technology, 125–126
Expenditures for R&D
    defense technologies, 23
    domestic, 42
    by industry, 4, 5, 42, 43, 45, 46, 47, 81
    international comparisons, 4, 10, 19–20,
    22, 42, 45, 46, 81, 128
    privately funded R&D, 47
    publicly funded R&D, 23
    rates of return, 33, 34, 38 n.6

R&D intensities, 60–64, 81
university research in U.S., 95–99, 103,
    128
U.S. affiliates of foreign-owned firms, 3–
    4, 17, 39, 42–48, 60, 81, 83 n.2, 85
    n.9
Export Administration Act of 1979, 75, 76

F

Fairchild Space Company, 104
Federal laboratories. *See also various*
    federal agencies and individual
    federal laboratories
budget, 112
Cooperative Research and Development
    Agreements (CRADAs), 114–116,
    119, 134 n.34, 135–136 n.39, 149,
    152
economic performance requirements,
    114–115
federally funded research and
    development centers, 212
foreign corporate participation in, 114–
    116, 122–124
history of foreign involvement in, 112–
    114
intellectual property rights at, 113, 114–
    115
intramural agency laboratories, 112
national security issues, 115
visiting researchers, 8, 10, 113–114,
    118–122, 147, 148
Federal Technology Transfer Act of 1986,
    134 n.34, 135 n.36
Finland, 65
Food and kindred products, 45, 48, 49, 50,
    51
Foreign direct investment by U.S.
    companies, 21, 41, 65. *See also*
    Affiliates, U.S.-owned;
    Multinational corporations, U.S.
Foreign direct investment in the U.S. *See*
    also Affiliates of foreign-owned
    firms in U.S.; International
    corporate alliances; various
    countries
barriers to, 71
benefits of, 57–58, 118–121, 129
data on, 17
defined, 13 n.3, 27 n.1, 84 n.7

economic concerns, 39–40, 58
history of, 15–16, 112–114
international negotiations regarding, 71
motivations for, 4, 40–41
national security concerns, 6–7, 74–78, 82–83, 144–146
quid-pro-quo relationships, 5–6, 59–70, 102
surveys of, 83–84 n.2
trends, 3–4, 16, 21, 39, 42–56, 81
France
foreign direct investment in, 22
high-tech production and exports, 20
R&D spending by foreign-owned companies in, 22
French-owned companies
acquisitions of high-technology companies in U.S., 80
affiliate companies in U.S., 43–46, 51, 62
expenditures for R&D in U.S., 4, 19, 22, 42, 45, 46, 128
freestanding R&D facilities in U.S., 51
patenting activities, 20, 65
R&D intensity of U.S. activities, 61, 62
involvement in university research in U.S., 103, 104, 110, 128

G

General Agreement on Tariffs and Trade, Uruguay Round, 71, 73, 139 n.71, 153
General Electric, 87 n.29, 116, 136 n.42
Georgia Institute of Technology, 100, 106, 137 n.58
German-owned companies
acquisitions of high-technology companies in U.S., 80
affiliate companies in U.S., 43–46, 51, 61, 62, 81
expenditures for R&D in U.S., 4, 19, 22, 42, 43, 45, 46, 81, 128
freestanding R&D facilities in U.S., 51
international technology flows and, 66, 67, 68
involvement in university research in U.S., 97, 101, 103, 104, 128
patenting activities, 20, 65
R&D intensity of U.S. activities, 61, 62
Germany
foreign direct investment in, 22, 71–73

high-tech production and exports, 20
R&D spending by foreign-owned companies in, 22
U.S. access to R&D in, 26, 71–72
Glaxo, 110
Government-University-Industry Research Roundtable, 12, 155–156
Grumman, 87 n.29

H

Harvard University, 97, 98, 99, 100, 103, 105
Hewlett Packard, 87 n.29
High-Speed Civil Transport "Piper" project, 138 n.69
High-technology industries. See also Industrial R&D; Military technology
defined, 13–14 n.5, 27–28 n.7
direct foreign investment in, 40, 42, 144
foreign ownership of companies by technology field, 44, 79–80
spending for R&D, 4, 42
start-up companies, 79
High-technology products, 14 n.5, 27–28 n.7
Hitachi Chemical Company, 104
Hughes, 87 n.29
Human Genome Project, 12, 155

I

IBM, 126
Industrial liaison programs, See Universities and university research
Industrial R&D. See also Privately funded R&D; individual industries
internationalization of, 41
surveys of, 83–84 n.2
technology parks, 109–110
trends, 13, 27 n.3, 157
and U.S. competitiveness, 19, 157
Industry/University Cooperative Research Centers, 108
Information technology, 57, 58
Innovation, technological, 30, 32, 34, 38 n.5, 141. See also Communications industry; Computer and office equipment industry; National innovation systems
Instrumentation industry, 43, 45, 46, 47, 49, 50, 51, 57, 60, 61, 62, 63

Intellectual property
  defined, 135–136 n.8
  distribution of benefits of, 34
  management of, 12, 18–19, 31, 152, 156
  ownership issues, 30–31, 37 n.4, 104–
    106, 113, 114–116, 146, 152
Intelligent Manufacturing Systems Initiative,
    12, 155
International corporate alliances
  access issues and, 73
  economic effects, 82
  national security and, 75
  objectives of, 89 n.42
  in privately funded R&D and, 3, 56–58
  technology flows and, 67–68
  trends, 3, 39, 87 nn.26, 28
Investment. *See* Foreign direct investment
    in the U.S.
Italy, 65, 103

J

Japan
  foreign direct investment in, 22, 71–73
  high-tech production and exports, 20
  Ministry for International Trade and
    Industry, 125, 126
  R&D spending by foreign companies in,
    22
  U.S. access to R&D in, 10, 17, 19, 71–
    73, 125–127, 150, 155
Japanese-owned companies
  affiliate foreign companies in U.S., 42–
    43, 45–51, 55, 61–63, 65, 81, 86
    n.16, 142
  basic research, 12, 86 n.21, 87 n.29, 104,
    110, 127–129, 131, 150, 154–155
  competitiveness, 19, 20, 22, 26
  demand for scientists and engineers, 40–
    41, 87 n.23
  and dual-use technologies, 77
  expenditures for R&D, 4, 20, 22, 42, 45,
    46, 47, 81, 128
  and federal (U.S.) laboratory research,
    113, 114, 116
  foreign-direct investment in U.S., 71–73
  freestanding R&D facilities in U.S., 48,
    49, 50, 51, 86 n.16
  high-technology acquisitions, 78–80
  international technology flows and, 66–
    68, 81–82

involvement in university research in
    U.S., 97, 99, 100, 104, 105, 110–
    111, 125, 128, 129, 132 n.11, 147
  monopoly issues, 78–79
  patenting activities, 20, 65, 88 n.34, 106
  and publicly funded U.S. R&D, 9, 113,
    114, 116, 117, 119–120
  R&D intensity of U.S. activities, 61, 62,
    63, 88 n.34
  R&D objectives in U.S., 55–56, 59–60,
    65–66, 84 nn.4, 5, 87 n.25, 111, 147
  reverse engineering, 38 n.11
  technical alliances involving, 57
  value of R&D activities to U.S., 65–68
Johns Hopkins University, 98, 101, 103
Joint European Semiconductor Submicron
    Initiative, 118
Joint ventures, 57, 69, 75, 78, 87 n.27, *See
    also* International corporate
    alliances

K

Kent State University Liquid Crystal
    Institute, 95, 120
Kvaener Masa Marine, 117
Kyocera, 77, 116

L

Langley Research Center, 114
Lawrence Livermore National Laboratory,
    113
Licensing agreements and programs, 57, 66,
    67, 68, 88 n.36, 102–103, 106–107;
    See also Patents and patenting
Los Alamos National Laboratory, 113, 137
    n.59

M

Machinery industry, nonelectrical, 48, 50, 51
Massachusetts General Hospital, 105, 132–
    133 n.14
Massachusetts Institute of Technology, 95,
    97, 98, 99, 100–101, 102–103, 106,
    107, 108, 109, 110, 119, 120, 134
    n.25, 147
Materials Research Centers, 108
Materials Research Corporation, 74–75, 78,
    88 n.37

Matsushita, 54, 86 n.18
Metals industry, primary and fabricated, 45,
    48, 50, 51, 60, 61
Microelectronics and Computer Technology
    Corporation, 137 n.51
Military technology. *See also* National
    security
  access to components and subsystems,
    40, 144, 145
  civilian technologies and, 23–24
  identification of critical technologies, 6,
    77, 78, 144, 146
  illegal sales to U.S. adversaries, 89 n.46
  and industrial R&D, 13
  reducing risks of foreign involvement in,
    75–77, 78, 82, 144–145
  Tomahawk missile program, 77
Mitsubishi Electric, 54, 86 n.18
Mitsui Engineering and Shipbuilding, 117
Monopolies. *See also* Antitrust issues
  access to components and subsystems, 40
  competitiveness and, 6–7
  and economic security, 78–79
  international corporate alliances and, 58
  national security threats, 6, 77
  in niche defense markets, 77, 82, 144
  regulation of, 18, 146
Motorola, 126
Multinational corporations, U.S. *See also*
    Affiliates, U.S. owned; *individual*
    corporations
  direct investment abroad, 21
  transnational corporate technical
    alliances, 3, 21, 39

N

National Aeronautics and Space
    Administration, 112
National Center for Manufacturing Sciences,
    84 n.5
National Cooperative Production
    Amendments, 87 n.27
National Cooperative Research Act of 1984,
    87 n.27
National innovation systems, 1–2, 13 n.2,
    18, 25–26, 27 n.2, 141–142, 148,
    156–157
National Institute of Standards and
    Technology, 112, 114, 115, 125,
    157–158 n.1

National Institutes of Health, 105, 112, 113,
    114, 119, 134 n.24, 157 n.1
National Science Foundation, 18, 29, 83 n.2,
    108, 125, 132, 134 n.24, 138 n.65
National security issues. *See also* Military
    technology
  costs and benefits of foreign participation
    in privately funded R&D, 6, 7, 74–
    78, 82–83, 144–146
  identifying critical military technologies,
    6, 78
  monopolies and, 6, 77–78, 82, 144
  in publicly funded research, 115
  recommendations regarding, 7, 145–146
  restrictions on foreign access to U.S.
    technology, 26, 36, 115
National treatment. *See* Nondiscrimination
    policies
Naval Research Laboratory, 112
Naval Surface Weapons Center, 112
NEC, 54, 55, 86 n.18, 87 n.29, 110
Netherlands, 51, 65, 80, 103, 128
Nippon Sanso KK, 88 n.37
Nippon Telephone and Telegraph, 125
Nondiscrimination policies, 7–8, 71, 126–
    127, 138–139 n.71, 146, 150, 152,
    153–154
North American Free Trade Agreement, 71,
    73, 88 n.38
North Carolina State University, 100
Norway, 65

O

Oak Ridge National Laboratory, 114, 116,
    136 n.43
Omnibus Trade and Competitiveness Act,
    75, 76
Oregon Health Science University, 100
Oregon State University, 97, 99, 100
Organization for Economic Cooperation and
    Development, 13–14 n. 5, 20, 27–28
    n.7, 71, 73, 88 n.37, 139 n.71, 153
Organization of Petroleum Exporting
    Companies, 76

P

Pacific Northwest Laboratory, 120
Patents and patenting, U.S., 20, 64–65, 66,
    106–107

Pennsylvania State University, 98, 103, 132
    n.9
People's Republic of China, 113, 120
Perceptions of foreign participation, 12–13,
    16–17, 35–36, 104–105, 143, 156–
    157
Petroleum industry, 45, 48
Pharmaceutical industry, 43, 45, 46, 47, 48,
    49, 50, 51, 56, 59–64, 81, 85 n.9,
    87 n.28, 142
Philips, 54
Photonics and optics, 44, 50, 51
Princeton University, 109, 110
Privately funded R&D in the U.S.. *See also*
    Affiliates of foreign-owned firms;
    High-technology industries;
    Industrial R&D; *individual
    corporations*
    access issues, 6, 70–74, 82, 143–144
    affiliates of foreign-owned firms (in
        U.S.), 42–56, 60–64
    defined, 13 n.1, 27 n.4
    and economic security, 78–80, 145
    expenditures by U.S. affiliates of foreign
        firms, 42–43, 45–48, 60, 142
    foreign direct investment and, 3–7, 39–89
    international corporate alliances, 56–58,
        142
    "lost opportunities," 69–70, 81–82
    national security threats, 6, 7, 74–78, 82–
        83, 144–146
    performance requirements, 10, 11, 60,
        64, 73, 77
    political-economic logic of, 31–32
    quid-pro-quo relationships, 59–70, 143
    R&D intensity of affiliates, 60–64
    recommendations regarding, 7–8, 145–
        146
    strategies, 24
    technology flows, 66–69
    technology stripping, 70
    trends in foreign participation, 3–5, 16,
        60–64, 142–143
    types of affiliate R&D activities, 48–56
    value of affiliate R&D, 64–66
Product life cycles, 22, 41
Publicly funded R&D (U.S.). *See also*
    Federal laboratories; Universities
    and university research
    access asymmetries, 9–10, 91, 124–127,
        150, 158 n.4

basic research, 11–12, 31, 90–91, 127–
    129, 151
    criticisms of foreign participation in, 18
    defined, 27 n.4
    disciplicary focus, 9, 147
    effects of foreign involvement, 9–10,
        118–124, 137 n.56
    expenditures, 23
    industrial technology inititatives, 116–
        118
    industry cooperation in, 25, 31
    and intellectual property rights, 113,
        114–115, 152
    military-civilian technology relationships,
        23–24
    objectives of foreign researchers
        concerning, 113, 147
    political-economic logic of, 32
    quid-pro-quo relationships with foreign
        firms and foreign nationals, 9, 12,
        91, 102–103, 108, 118–124, 147–
        150
    recommendations regarding, 10–12, 151–
        156
    regulation of, 10, 18–19, 41, 84 n.5, 108,
        115–116, 123–124, 149–150, 151
    strategies, 24–25
    trends in foreign participation in, 8–9,
        16, 90–92, 129, 147
    and U.S. competitiveness, 90
Purdue University, 119

R

Recommendations
    basic research burden sharing, 11–12,
        154–155
    economic performance requirements, 10,
        11, 151–153
    intellectual property management, 12,
        156
    national security issues, 7, 145–146
    privately funded R&D, 7–8, 145–146
    publicly funded R&D, 10–12, 151–156
    reciprocity requirements, 10, 11, 150,
        153–154
    regulatory policies, 7, 146
    trade and investment policy, 11, 146,
        152, 153
    university "good practices," 155–156
Reichold Chemicals, 110

Rensselaer Polytechnic Institute, 120
Research and development. *See also*
    Privately funded R&D; Publicly
    funded R&D
    activities, 29–39
    defined, 29
    distribution of benefits, 34–35
    and economic performance, 2–3, 32–35,
        78–80, 141–142
    funding, 31
    and innovation, 32
    organization and management of, 22–25,
        36, 41
    outputs, 30–31, 37 n.3, 141
    quality of activity, 64–68
    scanning capabilities and, 88 n.35
    spillovers from, 33, 109
    taxonomy, 29–30
Research Triangle Park, 109, 110
Reverse engineering, 38
Rhone Poulenc, 110
Robotics industry, 69

S

Sandia National Laboratory, 114, 120, 137
    n.59
Sandoz Pharmaceutical, 105, 133 n.16
Science and Technology Centers, 108
Scientists and engineers
    demand for, 40–41, 87 n.23, 91–92, 94–
        95
    employment by U.S. affiliates of foreign-
        owned firms, 49–50, 55–56, 86
        n.21, 131 n.2
    non-U.S. citizens employed in U.S., 121
Scripps Research Institute, 105
Semiconductor industry, 50, 51, 57, 69, 74–
    75, 78–79, 80, 89 n.45
Semiconductor Manufacturing Technology
    Consortium (SEMATECH), 18, 25,
    28 n.9, 84 n.5, 89 n.45, 116, 117–
    118
Semi-Gas System Inc., 88 n.37
Service industries, 45, 46
Shisiedo Co. Ltd., 105, 132–133 n.14
Siemens Research Corporation, 104, 110
Slovenian J. Stefan Institute, 95
Software industry, 44, 50, 51
Sony Corporation, 74–75, 78, 88 n.37
South Korea, 44, 48, 49, 51, 67, 80, 120

Spencer, William, 28 n.9
Stanford University, 98, 103, 107, 109, 119,
    132 n.9
State/University/Industry Cooperative
    Research Centers, 108
Steel industry, 67, 69
Stevenson-Wydler Technology Innovation
    Act of 1980, 135 n.36
Summit Micro Circuit, 87 n.29
Supercomputer Centers, 108
SVG Lithography Systems, 89
Sweden, 22, 44, 51, 65
Swiss-owned companies
    acquisitions of U.S. high-technology
        firms, 80
    affiliates in U.S., 42–46, 51, 61, 62, 81
    expenditures for R&D in U.S., 4, 42, 43,
        45, 46, 81
    freestanding R&D facilities in U.S., 51
    R&D intensity of activities, 61, 62
    patenting activities, 65
    international technology flows, 66, 68
    involvement in university research in
        U.S., 105, 110

T

Taiwan, 44, 80
Technology
    defined, 37 n.2
    fusion, 22
    scanning capabilities, 88 n.35
    policies, 17–18, 41
Technology Administration Authorization
    Act, 117, 136–137 n.44
Technology/knowledge transfer. *See also*
    Intellectual property
    balance of international technology
        flows, 36, 66–69, 81, 122–123, 130,
        143, 147
    barriers to, 2–3, 35, 141, 149
    consequences of, 35–36
    importance of proximity, 35, 41, 50, 53,
        81, 141
    technological sophistication and, 35, 37,
        38 n.11, 141, 142
    technology stripping, 70
Technology Reinvestment Project, 18, 25, 28
    n.9, 84 n.5, 116, 136 n.48
Telecommunications. *See* Communications
    industry

Tektronix, 87 n.29
Texas A&M University, 97–101, 103
Texas Instruments, 126
Tokyo Electric Power, 119
Tokyo University of Agriculture and
    Technology, 95
Toshiba Corporation, 89 n.46
Trade policies, 41, 71, 73, 75, 117, 146, 152,
    153–154
Transportation equipment (nonautomotive),
    46, 47, 60, 61, 62, 63

U

U.K.-owned companies
    affiliates in U.S., 43–46, 51, 61, 62
    expenditures for R&D in U.S., 4, 22, 42,
        43–46, 81, 128
    freestanding facilities in U.S., 51
    high-technology acquisitions, 80
    international technology flows, 66, 67, 68
    involvement in university research in
        U.S., 97, 100–101, 103, 104, 110,
        128
    patenting activities, 20, 65
    R&D intensity of activities, 19, 61, 62
United Kingdom
    foreign direct investment in, 22, 72
    high-tech production and exports, 20
    R&D spending by foreign-owned firms
        in, 22
    U.S. access to R&D in, 72
    visiting researchers at U.S. federal
        laboratories, 113
Universities and university research
    basic research, 91, 104, 110
    collaborative research, 95, 96
    contracts and grants, 102–106
    corporate participation, foreign, 99–111,
        122–124, 151
    disciplinary focus of foreign
        involvement, 94, 95, 99, 102, 103–
        104, 108, 109, 147
    expenditures for, 95–99, 128
    funding, foreign, 95–99, 129
    intellectual property rights, 104–106,
        137–138 n.61
    industrial liaison programs, 107–108, 134
        n.24
    industrial technology parks, 109–110

Japanese involvement in, 97, 99, 102–
    103, 104, 110–111, 129, 147
objectives of foreign participation in, 91,
    132 n.10
patent and technology licensing
    programs, 106–107
quid pro quo relationships, 102–103, 108,
    125, 156
standards of conduct, 155–156
students, researchers, and faculty, 8, 10,
    16, 92–95, 102–103, 118–122, 129
U.S. funding in foreign countries, 138
    n.64
volume of R&D, 91
University-industry research centers, 108–
    109, 119
University of
    Alabama, 100, 101
    Arizona, 98, 100, 103
    Arkansas, 101
    California at Berkeley, 98, 102–103, 104,
        107, 108, 109, 110, 132 n.9, 134
        n.25
    California at Davis, 98, 100
    California at Irvine, 104
    California at Los Angeles, 98, 103
    California at San Diego, 98, 103, 105,
        106
    California at San Francisco, 98, 105, 133
        n.17
    Illinois at Urbana, 98, 103, 132 n.9
    Maryland at College Park, 98
    Michigan, 97, 98, 103, 106, 108, 119,
        138 n.61
    Minnesota, 98, 103, 132 n.9
    Pennsylvania, 103
    Southern California, 103
    Stuttgart, 95
    Texas at Austin, 98, 101, 103, 131–132
        n.5
    Washington, 98, 100, 103, 108
    Wisconsin at Madison, 97–101, 103, 107,
        108, 147
U.S.-Canada Free Trade Agreement, 71, 88
    n.38
U.S. competitiveness
    access issues and, 73, 135 n.39, 155
    basic research and, 155
    changing character of, 22, 156–157
    integration of global economy and, 19–
        22, 36

manufacturing, 19, 22
monopolies and, 6–7
publicly funded research and, 90, 112–
    113, 115, 151
technology-policy-for-competitiveness
    initiatives, 28
and technology strategies, 24–25
weaknesses of U.S. innovation system,
    25–26
U.S. Department of Commerce. *See also*
    National Institute of Standards and
    Technology
Advanced Technology Program, 9, 18,
    25, 28, 84 n.5, 116, 117, 129, 147
Annual Survey of Foreign Direct
    Investment, 83 n.2
definition of foreign investment, 84 n.7
definition of high-technology industries,
    13–14 n.5, 27 n.7
Technology Administration, 28 n.9

U.S. Department of Defense, 74–78, 83, 117,
    144, 146
U.S. Department of Energy, 113, 115–116,
    119, 134 n.32, 135 n.38. *See also*
    Federal laboratories.
U.S. Display Consortium, 84 n.5, 116, 118,
    137 n.51
U.S.-Japan Manufacturing Fellowship
    Program, 138 n.65
U.S.-Japan Structural Impediments Initiative,
    73

W

Wiley, John, 107

Y

Yale University, 103